ROMAN VOTING ASSEMBLIES

From the Hannibalic War
to
the Dictatorship of Caesar

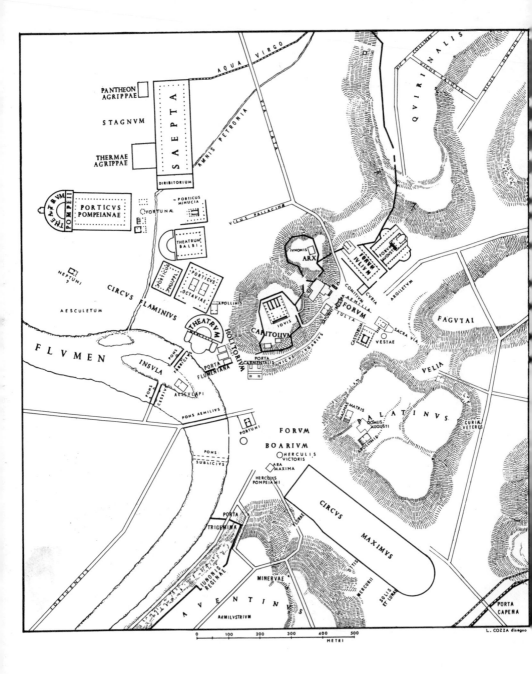

THE CENTER OF ROME
IN THE AUGUSTAN AGE

JEROME LECTURES

Eighth Series

ROMAN VOTING ASSEMBLIES

FROM THE HANNIBALIC WAR
TO
THE DICTATORSHIP OF CAESAR

BY

Lily Ross Taylor

Ann Arbor

THE UNIVERSITY OF MICHIGAN PRESS

25,655

To
T . R . S . B .
and
A . L . B .

Preface

This book on the assemblies in which Roman citizens of the Republic elected their annual magistrates, passed their laws, and gave their verdict on men accused of crimes against the state is limited both in the period considered and in the scope of the discussion. The period is from the Hannibalic War to the dictatorship of Caesar, that is, from 218 to 49 B.C. This is a time when, in contrast to the early Republic, for which the scanty and fragmentary sources are often unreliable, we have, in the histories of Polybius, Livy, and Sallust, and in the massive writing of Cicero, material that enables us to see in their political activity the senators, who always kept the initiative, and from time to time gives us a glimpse of the people. For the assemblies this period was one of decline, a time when Rome's possessions and alliances were steadily expanding overseas and when the institutions of the fifth-century city-state no longer served for the administration of Empire. The consuls and praetors who commanded Rome's citizen-soldiers were still elected by the people, but problems of imperial administration not in the province of magistrates were either left to the senate of ex-magistrates or were, toward the end of the period, submitted to the people, often under the influence of the great generals who were leading Rome down the road to monarchy.

As for the scope of the discussion, I shall put the main emphasis on procedure, which I shall try to place in its setting at Rome, where all the voting was held. I shall not in general attempt to analyze the conditions of candidacy or the campaigns for office or the character of the laws and accusations brought to the assemblies, subjects that I have, at least in part, considered elsewhere. My reason for the limitation is that new evidence for procedure, important for the nature of the assemblies, has recently come to light.

I mention first the discovery by Lawrence Richardson in 1954 in excavations of the American Academy in Rome, of the Comitium, the place of assembly, of the Latin colony Cosa on the Etruscan coast, ninety miles north of Rome, and the identification of the Curia (senate house), already partly excavated by Professor Frank E. Brown. These monuments, like the voting institutions of such colonies, are a reflection of Rome, and they help us to reconstruct Comitium and Curia there. Then there is the new identification of the site and the plan and the establishment of the general dimensions of the voting place used primarily for elections, the Saepta Julia in the Campus Martius. The identification, made through recent study of fragments most of which came to light four hundred years ago, is a new interpretation of the great Marble Plan of Rome which, shortly after 200 A.D. in the reign of Septimius Severus, was placed on the wall of a building in the Forum Pacis, close to the later Basilica of Maxentius. On this plan the real site of the Saepta, which had been incorrectly identified, was found by Guglielmo Gatti, and, although he published his discovery in 1937, it still seems to be unfamiliar to many Roman historians. A full statement of Gatti's results, supplemented by Lucos Cozza's identification of the Diribitorium where the votes were counted, is now available in the splendid publication brought out by the Comune di Roma in 1960, *La Pianta marmorea di Roma antica,* of which, with Gatti and Cozza, Gianfilippo Carettoni and Antonio Maria Colini are coauthors. Immediately after the publication Gatti made another remarkable combination of fragments which resulted in a new site for the Circus Flaminius, an important place for public meetings. For the understanding of the monuments, a study of Plinio Fraccaro, published in 1913–14 but until recently little known either to historians or to archaeologists, is of the greatest significance.

On procedure in the assemblies there is a new document, a bronze tablet found in 1947 at the site of the ancient Colonia Heba at Magliano in Tuscany, a much-discussed inscription generally known as the *Tabula Hebana.* It gives the text of a law of 19 A.D. with regulations for an assembly of senators and knights charged with the *destinatio,* a species of nomination of consuls and praetors. For voting procedure, particularly in the centuriate assembly which chose consuls and praetors, this tablet is not less revealing than the charters of two Spanish towns with Latin rights, found more than a century ago, and shown by Theodor Mommsen to reflect the procedure at Rome in elections held by the tribes.

Opportunities to visit excavations in Rome and in Italy, to discuss problems with the excavators of Rome and Cosa, with the discoverers of Saepta and Diribitorium, and with historians and epigraphists who have worked on the *Tabula Hebana* have been provided by a three-year tenure of a professorship at the American Academy in Rome (1952–55) and by the hospitality of the Academy on four subsequent visits, the last as Jerome Lecturer in 1964. Two grants from the research funds of the American Philosophical Society have contributed to my traveling expenses and have provided the necessary funds for the map, the plan of the Saepta, and the photographs in this volume. My visits to Rome and my preliminary investigations were also facilitated by a fellowship from the John Simon Guggenheim Memorial Foundation, awarded for 1960 on presentation of a plan for a general book, as yet uncompleted, on Roman politics in the Late Republic.

For the study of procedure in the assemblies there has also been an important experience in the United States—the close observance of political meetings, which are perhaps more like the Roman assemblies than anything else to be found in the world today: the great conventions held every four years to nominate by the vote of delegates the candidates of the Republican and Democratic parties for President and Vice-President. These conventions differ from the Roman assemblies in that they include many speeches, which were banned in Roman elections, and lay great stress on programs, which were avoided by candidates at Rome. But they are like the Roman elections in that all the voting is in one place and is carried out by units, the states. These similarities are significant, although the voters in the conventions, unlike the Romans in the *comitia,* are chosen as representatives, and the value of the state vote, in contrast to that of the Roman units, depends on the population of the states. Further points of similarity are to be found in the power of the presiding officer and in the use of successive voting (not always employed at Rome), by which the announcement of results for the units voting first has influence on later votes. Although I have tried always to keep the differences in mind, my two visits to the scene of the conventions and the hours I have spent listening to radio and television coverage of the conventions have contributed to my reconstruction of the Roman assemblies.

The arrangement of the material, which may seem illogical, results from the fact that the book is based on my Jerome Lectures, the first two of which, given originally in Italian in Rome, include in Chapters

II and III material on which I hoped, not in vain, to have criticism and comment from archaeologists in Rome. In spite of some inevitable repetitions, I decided to retain the arrangement, for the study of the places of preliminary meetings and assemblies contributed to the problems of procedure in the tribal and centuriate assemblies treated in Chapters IV and V. All dates in my discussion, unless specified as A.D., are B.C. The term "legislative" is often used to describe both legislative and judicial assemblies in which the procedure was similar.

My obligations are numerous both in Rome and in the United States. In Rome the director of the Academy, Mr. Richard A. Kimball, facilitated my work in every possible way, taking particular interest in helping me to make experiments with lot-casting, Roman fashion. Professor Frank E. Brown, now Mr. Kimball's successor as director of the Academy, gave me help and advice on problems of Cosa, and he and Dr. Ernest Nash, director of the Fototeca di Architettura e Topografia dell' Italia antica, put at my disposal their extensive knowledge of Roman topography. Among archaeologists who attended my lectures and made helpful comments I mention my friends Professors Pietro Romanelli and Attilio Degrassi, Professor Giuseppe Lugli, to whom I am grateful for a recent letter on Saepta and *pomerium*, quoted in the notes of Chapter I, Professors Ferdinando Castagnoli and Axel Boëthius, who have added to the debt I owe to their published work and their stimulating lectures on Roman topography, and Professor Gatti, with whom I had already had a fruitful discussion of his epoch-making discoveries. Three ancient historians, Professors Emilio Gabba, Giovanni Forni, and Ernst Badian, asked searching questions, some of which I have tried to answer in the book. My former colleague, Professor Berthe Marti, made clearer the Roman combination of voting and lot-casting by calling my attention to important medieval and Renaissance parallels.

Dr. Lucos Cozza has made tangible contributions to the book. He prepared with careful measurements the reconstruction of the Saepta (Pl. XI) on the basis of my interpretation of the monument. He also made the map of the center of Rome showing the Republican and the Augustan monuments on the map of Giuseppe Lugli and Italo Gismondi (*Forma Urbis Romae Imperatorum Aetate* 1949), with corrections and additions resulting from recent studies (Frontispiece). Of importance here are the sites of the Saepta, the Diribitorium, the Circus Flaminius, and Cozza's as yet unpublished identification of the location of the Porticus Minucia, which seems in the Empire to have been the headquarters of the tribes. Like the other new evidence, this discovery depends on the Marble Plan, into which Cozza has fitted a fragment inscribed MINI. On the map the combination of Augustan with Republican buildings is valuable because of Augustus' attempt to show that he had restored the Republic. Since other period maps of Ancient Rome show either the Republican or the Imperial city, I believe that this map will be of general value to the student of a great epoch of Roman civilization and Latin literature.

At The University of Michigan I record my gratitude first of all to the former dean of the Graduate School, Dr. Ralph A. Sawyer, an eminent physicist who, as chairman of the Committee on the Jerome Lectures, has shown his enthusiastic interest in humanistic studies. He returned to Ann Arbor from the activities of his so-called retirement to welcome the lecturer and make the graceful introduction to the series. I am grateful also for the hospitality of Dean Stephen H. Spurr, now chairman of the Committee, and of Dean William Haber. The chairman of the Department of Classical Studies, Professor Gerald F. Else, left no stone unturned to make my stay in Ann Arbor a delightful experience, and I express to him, to the other members of the Department, and to the historians and art historians who welcomed me my warmest thanks.

The manuscript of my lectures was read and criticized by colleagues and former colleagues at Bryn Mawr, Professor T. R. S. Broughton, who in frequent discussions helped me to clarify difficult problems, Professor Agnes Kirsopp Michels, who made constructive suggestions for presentation and enlightened me on intricate problems related to the Roman calendar, and Professor Louise Adams Holland, who guided me to the explanation I offer for the representation of the Rostra on a coin. Professors Richmond Lattimore and Mabel Lang aided me in the interpretation of Greek texts and in the understanding of the Greek use of the ballot and the lot. For help with numismatic material I had the advantage of consultation with Professor Andrew Alföldi, to whose generosity I owe most of the illustrations of Roman coins which he allowed me to select from his vast collection. Dr. Aline Abaecherli Boyce, formerly curator of Roman coins of the American Numismatic Society, called my attention to important bibliography that I had missed and helped me in various problems of interpretation. I also acknowledge the aid I have received from the questions on intricate matters asked by students in Rome and Ann Arbor and by the members of the Seminars on Roman Politics which I have given in the past five years at Bryn Mawr and the University of Wisconsin. Throughout the investigation I have had constant assistance from the staffs of various libraries, especially Bryn Mawr College and the American Academy in Rome, where I have profited particularly from the bibliographical knowledge and ingenuity of Mrs. Yildiz Van Hulsteyn at Bryn Mawr and Mrs. Inez Longobardi at Rome. And finally I add a word of appreciation for the care and accuracy with which Mrs. Dudley Child has typed a very difficult manuscript, and Miss Alice Martin Hawkins has read the proof, eliminating various errors which I had overlooked.

To The University of Michigan Press I am grateful for the interest shown in the production of the book. I thank the printer for the most accurate proof I have ever had. Responsibility for errors rests entirely with me.

For the illustrations, the majority of which I owe to Professor Alföldi and Dr. Nash, I have had the help of two photographers, Mr. Johannes Felbermeyer at Rome and Mr. Karl Dimler at Bryn Mawr. The revised map of the Forum from the 1962 guide, *Roma e dintorni,* is reproduced with the much appreciated permission of the Touring Club Italiano. The text of the appropriate sections of the *Tabula Hebana* in the appendix is reprinted with permission of the editor and the authors from the standard edition prepared by James H. Oliver and Robert E. A. Palmer in the *American Journal of Philology* 75 (1954), 225–49.

The book is inscribed with affection and appreciation of long association to my former colleagues, T. Robert S. Broughton, who in 1965 assumed the Paddison Professorship of Classics at the University of North Carolina, and his wife, Annie Leigh Broughton, a former student of great promise, who has had a distinguished career as Director of Admissions at Bryn Mawr College.

Bryn Mawr, Pennsylvania
May 1966

Contents

Illustrations

MAPS

Abbreviations

This list comprises collections, books, and articles (including a number of my earlier publications) which are cited repeatedly. Abbreviations of names and titles of works of classical authors follow in general the list in the *Oxford Classical Dictionary*; abbreviations of titles of journals are based, with expansion in some cases, on the list in the *Année Philologique*.

I. Encyclopedias and General Collections

ARS—A. C. Johnson, P. R. Coleman-Norton, F. C. Bourne. *Ancient Roman Statutes.* Austin, Texas, 1961.

CIL—*Corpus Inscriptionum Latinarum.* Berlin, 1863–.

CRRBM—H. A. Grueber. *Coins of the Roman Republic in the British Museum* 1–3. London, 1910.

DE—E. De Ruggiero. *Dizionario epigrafico di antichità romane.* Rome, 1895–. Now under the direction of A. Ferrabino.

DS—Daremberg and Saglio. *Dictionnaire des antiquités grecques et romaines.* Paris, 1877–1919.

FIRA—S. Riccobono. *Fontes iuris Romani antejustiniani.* 1, ed. 2; Florence, 1941.

ILS—H. Dessau. *Inscriptiones Latinae Selectae.* Berlin, 1892–1916.

MRR—T.R.S. Broughton. *The Magistrates of the Roman Republic.* 1–2; New York, 1951–52. *Supplement.* New York, 1960.

PDAR—E. Nash. *Pictorial Dictionary of Ancient Rome.* 2 vols. London, 1961–62.

PM—G. Carettoni, A. M. Colini, L. Cozza, G. Gatti. *La Pianta marmorea di Roma antica—Forma urbis Romae,* published by the Comune di Roma, 1960. One vol. of text and one of plates.

RE—Pauly-Wissowa. *Real-encyclopädie der classischen Altertumswissenschaft,* now edited by K. Ziegler. Stuttgart, 1894–.

Sydenham—E. A. Sydenham. *The Roman Republican Coinage.* London, 1952.

TLL—*Thesaurus Linguae Latinae.* Leipzig, 1900–.

II. Books and Articles by the Writer

ComCent—Taylor, L. R., "The Centuriate Assembly before and after the Reform," AJP 78 (1957) 337-54.

FG—Taylor, L. R., "Forerunners of the Gracchi," JRS 52 (1962) 19-27.

PP—Taylor, L. R., *Party Politics in the Age of Caesar*. Berkeley and Los Angeles, 1949.

TiGLA—Taylor, L. R., "Was Tiberius Gracchus' Last Assembly Electoral or Legislative?" *Athenaeum* 41 (1963) 51-69.

VD—Taylor, L. R., *The Voting Districts of the Roman Republic; The Thirty-five Urban and Rural Tribes, Papers and Monographs of the American Academy in Rome*. 20. 1960.

III. Books and Articles Cited under Authors' Names

Bleicken, J., *Volkstribunat—Das Volkstribunat der klassischen Republik, Zetemata*. Heft 13. Munich, 1955.

Botsford, G. W., *RA—The Roman Assemblies*. New York, 1909.

Cassola, F., *GPR—I Gruppi politici Romani nel III secolo a. C*. Triest, 1962.

Castagnoli, F., *CM*—"Il Campo Marzio nell'antichità." *Memorie, Acc. dei Lincei*, Ser. 8, fasc. 4 (1947) 93-193.

De Ruggiero, E., *FR—Il Foro Romano*. Rome, 1913.

De Sanctis, G., *StorRom—Storia dei Romani*. 1-2, Turin, 1907, cited from the reprint, Florence, 1956-60; 3, 1916-17.

Fraccaro, P., *PVCTR*—"La Procedura del voto nei comizi tributi romani," *Opuscula* 2 (Pavia, 1957) 235-54, reprinted from *Atti della R. Accademia delle Scienze di Torino* 49 (1913-14) 600 ff.

Hall, Ursula, *VPRA*—"Voting Procedure in Roman Assemblies," *Historia* 13 (1964) 267-306.

Herzog, E., *RSV—Geschichte und System der römischen Staatsverfassung*. 1. *Königszeit und Republik*. Leipzig, 1884.

Kunkel, W., *URKV—Untersuchungen zur Entwicklung des römischen Kriminalverfahrens in vorsullanischer Zeit, Abh. bayerisch. Akad. d. Wissensch.*, N. F. Heft 56. Munich, 1962.

Lange, L., *RAl—Römische Alterhümer*. 1, 2, 3d ed., 3, 2d ed., Berlin, 1876-79.

Meyer, Ernst, *RSSG—Römischer Staat und Staatsgedanke*. 1st ed.; Zürich, 1948. 2d ed., much enlarged and revised, 1961.

Mommsen, T., *StR—Römisches Staatsrecht*. 1-2, 3d ed., 3, 1st ed.; Leipzig, 1887-88.

———*Strafrecht—Römisches Strafrecht*. Leipzig, 1899.

Rosenberg, A., *URZV—Untersuchungen zur römischen Zenturienverfassung*. Berlin, 1911.

Tibiletti, G., *FCC*—"Il funzionamento dei comizi centuriati alla luce della Tavola Hebana," *Athenaeum* 27 (1949) 210–45.

Wissowa, G., *RK²*—*Religion und Kultus der Römer.* 2d ed.; Munich, 1912.

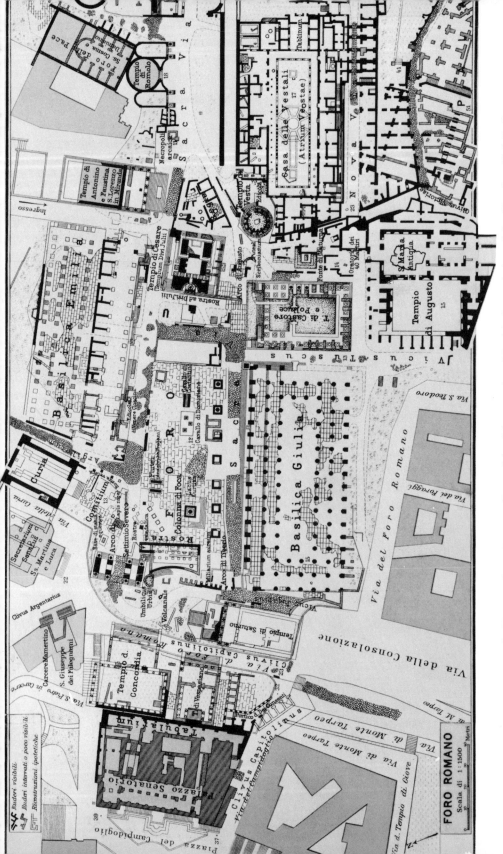

The Roman Forum in the Empire, from *Roma e dintorni* (1962), reproduced by kind permission of the Touring Club Italiano.

I

THE NATURE OF THE ASSEMBLIES:
ANCIENT SOURCES AND
MODERN INTERPRETATIONS

Voting was a major occupation of the citizens who lived in Republican Rome or were there when the assemblies met. Every year at a stated period they elected all the regular and the plebeian magistrates, amounting, after Sulla, to some seventy men; there were also special elections of commissioners of various types. Besides, the citizens voted on every law proposed and often, particularly before the gradual development of the public courts in the last century of the Republic, on the guilt or innocence of men accused of crimes against the state. There was hardly a season of the year when Rome was free both from voting assemblies and from the campaign in preparation for voting on choice of magistrates, on approval of laws, or on accusations.

Voting at Rome was, as in our national elections for President and Vice-President, entirely by units, but although the units might differ as much in their numbers of voters as our states do, there was no difference in the value of the unit votes such as we maintain in the electoral votes of the states. Nor was there in the voting any system of representation such as we have in the choice by each state of senators and congressmen. The names submitted to the voters might come from any of the units, and often included no one in certain tribes and centuries. Except for the report that not only all centuries but also all men voted to invest the elder Scipio with the command in Spain in 211 (Livy 26.18.9), there is no record of a total vote of individuals, but often all the centuries or tribes (that is the largest number of men in each) voted unanimously for a magistrate, a law, or a judgment. There are also, not infrequently, details on the number of units that voted for or against a certain measure.

Before the division of the voters into their units, there was always at Rome a preliminary public meeting in which the citizens appeared unsorted. Such a meeting, held often for other purposes besides voting, was known as a *conventio*, a "coming together"; except in certain early documents, the word appears regularly in the syncopated form *contio*.[1] When the *contio* was over, the citizens were ordered to go to vote (*ire in suffragium*) or simply to *discedere*, which, we are told, was a command not to go away but to go into their voting units. The word for voting assembly, *comitia*, preserves in its plural form a record of the divisions, for it means "goings together."

The distinction between the unsorted *contio* and the carefully sorted *comitia* had perhaps not always existed at Rome. The *contio* may be a survival of an early form of assembly, like that of the Homeric warriors or of the Spartans of later times in which men expressed their opinion by shouting. Here the origin of the word *suffragium* is significant, for it comes from the root of *frangere*, "to break," and means "to break into sound." There is perhaps a relic of an old gathering of warriors in the name *suffragia* given to the six ancient centuries of knights which voted separately in the major Roman assembly.[2]

But in the historical period a strict distinction was maintained in the functions of the *contio* and the *comitia*. The distinction, based on the writings of a learned colleague of Cicero in the augurate, is described by Aulus Gellius (13.16) in a passage in which *agere cum populo* ("to treat with the people") is used of the *comitia: Manifestum est aliud esse cum populo agere, aliud contionem habere. Nam cum populo agere est rogare quid populum quod suffragiis suis aut iubeat aut vetet; contionem autem habere est verba facere ad populum sine ulla rogatione.* ("It is clear that to treat with the people is one thing and to hold a *contio* is another. For to treat with the people is to ask the people something which by its votes it is either to order or to forbid; to hold a *contio* is to speak to the people without asking anything.") If any asking of the people was required, the unsorted *contio* had to be dissolved and the people had to reappear sorted into their units. The terminology of asking persisted in the *comitia*, for instance in the name of the *rogatores*, the men who, before the days of written ballots, asked individuals for their votes and in the word *rogatio*, the regular term for a bill for a law or judgment or for the formal request (*carmen rogationis*) that the citizens choose magistrates (Chap. V, n. 23).

With no such distinction in Greek lands between meetings for speaking and those for voting, Greek writers on Roman institutions have difficulty with the word *contio*. Polybius, with long residence in Rome in the mid-second century B.C., usually avoids the use of a word for assembly and refers to the people in both *contio* and *comitia* as the *demos*. The imperial constitutional specialist Dio Cassius often uses similar terms, but Plutarch and Appian, who may not have understood the difference, frequently render *contio* by *ekklesia*, the Greek word for the assembly that combined speaking and voting. *Contio* has also created trouble for modern translators unfamiliar with separate gatherings for speaking and voting. In English some translators, for instance of Livy, misleadingly render *contio* as "assembly," which, in a political sense, suggests a gathering at which action can be taken. The best solution is the one adopted by many translators of Cicero, rendering *contio* as "public meeting" and *comitia* as "assembly."

When the *contio* was dissolved by the word *discedite* or by the fuller command *ite in suffragium*, the nonvoters, including slaves and foreigners and women, if any were present, were removed, and the voters distributed themselves in the places appointed for their units. In the Roman Republic there were three types of units, *curiae*, based primarily on clans, *centuriae*, military units, and *tribus*, local tribes, representing divisions of Rome and its territory. The three types of assemblies were the *comitia curiata, centuriata,* and *tributa*.[3]

An attempt is made in the accompanying table to indicate in outline form the nature and functions of the three types of assembly. For centuries and tribes my brief statements here are to be supplemented by the discussions in later chapters. But for the *curiae* there will be only incidental comments later, for the ancient curiate assembly, though it persisted as an essential form, was no longer attended by the people.

The curiate assembly was an organization of thirty *curiae*, ten each from the three clan tribes, Tities, Ramnes, and Luceres, reportedly instituted by Romulus. It was said to have met in the Kingship to "create" (*creare*) successive kings and to have passed the *lex curiata* confirming the king's *imperium*, his right of civil and military command; it may have been simply a gathering which acted by acclamation. In the Republic it continued to pass each year the *lex curiata* establishing the *imperium* of the consuls and the power of the other magistrates. Until 471 it was credited with electing, under what was presumably an individual voting system, the tribunes of the plebs, instituted according to tradition in 494. The system (Chap. IV) seems to have had certain resemblances to the tribal assembly, which took over the election of tribunes, with every *curia* possessing a vote of equal value and one *curia* chosen as *principium*, presumably to cast the first vote. Just when the people ceased to take an active part in the assembly we do not know; for this period there is no evidence of popular participation. There were so many people who did not know to which *curia* they belonged that for the ancient festival of the ovens, celebrated by *curiae*, there was a special day, known as the *feriae stultorum*, the feast of fools, on which men who had not carried out the rites could perform them en masse.[4] The *lex curiata* confirming the *imperium* of the consuls and praetors and the power of other magistrates continued to be passed at the beginning of each year, but the people were not at the meetings. Perhaps as early as 218 the custom attested for the year 63 of having each *curia* represented by a lictor had developed (Cic. *Leg. agr.* 2.26–31). The meetings were conducted by consuls, praetors, or dictators and the vote, as far as we know, was always in the affirmative. The meetings were subject to veto by the tribunes of the plebs and to interference with the auspices. For that reason augurs, the priests concerned with the auspices, were in attendance or on call. We hear particularly of interference with special meetings of this assembly for grants of *imperium* to individuals, who sometimes went ahead with the functions of office, though lacking the confirmation of the *curiae*.

Besides the meetings of the *comitia curiata* under magistrates, the assembly could be called by the *pontifex maximus* for the inauguration of certain priests, and for the transference of patricians to the plebs, and for matters connected with wills, notably testamentary adoptions. The assembly was called by Caesar as *pontifex maximus* in 59 to transfer the patrician P. Clodius Pulcher to the plebs and in 44 to confirm Caesar's testamentary adoption of his grandnephew, the plebeian C. Octavius. At these meetings too the *curiae* were presumably represented by lictors.

The places of meeting are of some interest. The Comitium, an enclosed space to the northeast of the Forum, is specifically mentioned by Varro (*L.L.* 5.155) as the place of the *comitia curiata,* and the statement of Suetonius (*Aug.* 65) that Tiberius was adopted by a *lex curiata*

	Comitia Curiata	Comitia Centuriata, military organization
Voting units	30 curiae, 10 each from 3 ancient clan tribes, Tities, Ramnes, and Luceres	193 centuries: 18 of equites; 170 of pedites, classified after 241 within the 35 local tribes into centuries of 2 age groups and 5 classes based on property; 5 unarmed centuries
Citizens in attendance	People not present; in late Republic each curia represented by a lictor	Open to all citizens
Presiding officer	Consul or praetor or, for religious purposes, pontifex maximus (with auspices)	Consul or praetor or, before 201, dictator; if no consul was in office at the beginning of the year, an interrex for consular elections (with auspices)
Elections		Of consuls, praetors, censors
Rogationes (bills) a) Legislative	Passed lex curiata, confirming imperium of magistrates and power of lower officers; under pontifex maximus confirmed adoptions and certain wills	Once the chief law-making body of the state; rarely used after 218 except for declarations of war and confirmation of power of the censors. Passed law recalling Cicero from exile
b) Judicial (most functions transferred to public courts by late 2nd century)		On capital charges; limited after late second century (period of the Gracchi) mainly to charges of perduellio, ancient form of treason
Meeting place	Comitium (Capitol)	Outside pomerium, nearly always Campus Martius

Comitia Tributa	*Concilium plebis,* often called *Comitia Tributa*
Assemblies of the tribes, local divisions of Roman territory	
35 tribes, classified into 4 urban and 31 rural tribes	
Open to all citizens	Open to plebeians; patricians excluded
Consul or praetor; sometimes for jurisdiction curule aedile (with auspices)	Tribune of the plebs; aedile of the plebs (without auspices)
Of curule aediles, quaestors, lower officers, special commissioners	Of tribunes and aediles of the plebs and certain special commissioners
Legislation of any type except that restricted to the *Comitia Centuriata*	The majority of the laws were proposed by the tribunes of the plebs; their measures, properly called *plebiscita,* had the validity of *leges* after 287 B.C.
For crimes against the state punishable by a fine	Frequent judgments under tribunes, especially before institution of the public courts
For elections, at least in the late Republic, Campus Martius For legislation and judgments, the Forum (originally the Comitium?) or the Area Capitolina; in one case the Circus Flaminius	

in foro probably refers to the Comitium which, in imperial writers, is rarely distinguished from the Forum. But there is also some evidence for meetings on the Capitol. It was here that, when magistrates were lacking after the decemvirate, the *pontifex maximus* convened the *curiae* to choose tribunes of the plebs.[5] It was here that the *lex curiata* must have been passed for the dictatorship of Camillus at a time when the Comitium was occupied by the Gauls (Livy 5.46.10). On the Capitol was the *curia calabra,* in front of which the people gathered in *comitia curiata* to hear a *pontifex minor* announce the date of Nones and Ides.[6] Perhaps the Capitol was the scene of the *comitia curiata* held under the pontifical college to inaugurate certain priests, the *flamines* and the *rex sacrorum* (Gell. 15.27.1).

The units in which the people actually assembled for voting in our period were 193 centuries and thirty-five urban and rural tribes. The centuries (Chap. V) were a military organization traced back to King Servius Tullius; the first reported use for voting is the election of the first consuls in 509. As an *exercitus urbanus,* the centuries were made up of *equites* and *pedites,* with a small group of unarmed centuries. Since orders could not be given to an army within the sacred city limits, the *pomerium,* this army was always called together outside those limits, in our period regularly in the Campus Martius.[7] After the institution of the last two rural tribes in 241, the 170 centuries of *pedites,* who made up the major part of the assembly, became divisions of the tribes, separated according to age and property qualifications, with a great advantage in the vote to men of higher property. This assembly elected the two consuls and the praetors, from four to eight, officers who possessed *imperium,* the right of command over the citizen soldiers. It also chose every four or later every five years two censors who conducted the census which determined the citizen's classification according to property, and consequently the value of his vote (Chap. V). The centuriate assembly was the major law-making body of the state, but by 218 most legislative proposals had been transferred to the tribal assemblies. The centuries were still called for declarations of war and for confirmation of the census. They also had jurisdiction in capital cases of a political character, which, however, beginning in the mid-second century, were gradually transferred to permanent courts. By the end of that century criminal jurisdiction in the *comitia centuriata* had become limited to trials for *perduellio,* an ancient form of high treason. The voting procedure in the assembly seems to have been identical, whether the vote concerned an election of magistrates or the casting of a positive or negative vote for a law or a judgment.

The urban and rural tribes, local units (Chap. IV) on which, in our period, the organization of the *pedites* in the centuries was based, may not have been used for voting until the election of the plebeian officers was transferred from the *curiae* to the tribes, reportedly in 471. At that time there were only twenty-one tribes, but, with the growth of Roman territory, the number, consisting of four urban and thirty-one rural tribes, reached its final total of thirty-five in 241.

There were two assemblies of the thirty-five tribes, one presided over by a consul or praetor, the other by a plebeian officer, usually a tribune of the plebs. The former, the *comitia tributa* proper, could be attended by all citizens; the latter, known in strict terminology as the *concilium plebis,* was open only to plebeians, the few patricians in the state being excluded. Under consul or praetor, the tribes elected curule aediles, quaestors, military tribunes, and various special officers; under plebeian magistrates, usually tribunes, they chose the tribunes and the aediles of the plebs and also certain special officers. Either body could vote on legislation or judgments for crimes punishable by a fine. After the Lex Hortensia of 287 made acts of the plebs binding on the entire state, most legislation at Rome was proposed by tribunes and was passed in the *concilium plebis.* With the exception of the omission of the preliminary auspices when a plebeian officer was in charge, the procedure was practically identical in the two types of assembly. For the tribes differences in procedure and in places of meeting depended on the function of the gathering, with one system for elections and another for laws and judgments.

Under a consul or a praetor the tribes could meet anywhere, and once they were called by a consul to pass a law in the army camp at Sutrium in southern Etruria. But the tribunes, whose power was limited to the city and a mile beyond the *pomerium,* passed a measure forbidding such meetings in the future (Livy 7.16.7–8). That radius also limited the places where the tribunes could call meetings. In our period all assemblies of the tribes whose site is recorded were held in the Forum (with which I include the adjoining Comitium), on the Capitoline, in the Campus Martius, and (in one case) in the Circus Flaminius.

The major assembly of the centuries (*maximus comitiatus*) was, in our period, in nearly 90 percent of its voting units, a tribal organization. It differed, however, from the *comitia tributa* in that the voters within each tribe were subdivided according to property and age, with advantage for the vote of the richer men. The subdivisions, according to Cicero (*Leg.* 3.44), made the decisions of the centuries much wiser, but the procedure was more cumbersome, and that may have been one of the reasons why before 218 most legislation had been transferred to the tribes. A more important reason was that after 287 measures passed by the plebs were made binding on the whole state, and that after that time the tribunes were much more amenable to the wishes of the senate.

In procedure there was much in common between the centuriate and the tribal assemblies. Both were preceded by a *contio* attended by an audience not sorted into voting divisions. If the assembly was legislative or judicial, there were often earlier *contiones*, regularly at least three for judicial gatherings. The final *contio*, which occurred immediately before the citizens were ordered to divide into their voting units, had to be scheduled on a day marked *comitialis* in the Roman official calendar. In the Republic there were 195 such days, the majority of which were in the second half of the month, when they often came in immediate succession. The elective *comitia* usually took place in this period since, if the business was not completed before sunset, when the assembly had to be dismissed, voting could then be continued without interruptions that might last for days.

The *comitia tributa* under a regular magistrate also shared with the *comitia centuriata* dependence on the auspices, that is, on the signs from heaven that Jupiter was well-disposed toward the meeting of the assembly. The presiding officer went between midnight and dawn to the site of the assembly, carefully taking the auspices on the way if he had to cross the *amnis Petronia,* the brook separating the Campus from the city. He had with him an attendant who was directed to look for certain signs and who normally reported that he had seen them. These auspices could not be taken by the tribunes of the plebs, who held their assemblies without auspices (*inauspicato*). But there were other signs that colleagues of the presiding magistrates or tribunes could observe and announce (*obnuntiationes*) in order to prevent the assembly from convening. The most important of these signs was a flash of Jupiter's lightning which, if accepted, led to the postponement of the *comitia*. During the proceedings such signs could be announced even by private citizens. In these cases the magistrate, if he were not himself an augur, sought the advice of a member of this august priesthood chosen from the noblest families of the state. There was always an augur on hand for consultation, and if he replied *"alio die"* the assembly had to be postponed to another day (Cic. *Leg.* 2.31). Even the tribunes were eventually made subject to such signs in their legislative and judicial assemblies. The auspices clearly show that the *comitia* were under the protection of Jupiter, the god of light without which the assembly, which had to be dissolved at sundown, could not proceed. (*Dies* and Jupiter are related in origin.) The omnipresent augurs are described by Cicero (*Leg.* 2.20) as *interpretes Iovis optimi maximi.*[8]

All the assemblies except the elective assemblies of the plebs were subject to veto from tribunes of the plebs, who could thus forbid legislation of one of their colleagues. All the assemblies could be dissolved by the presiding magistrate because of violence. That was only one aspect of the power of this magistrate.

There was almost complete identity in methods of balloting in centuriate and tribal assemblies. The voting was oral until a series of laws was passed between 139 and 107 which instituted the written ballot, first in electoral assemblies of all types, then, with some limitation, in judicial assemblies, next in legislative assemblies, and finally in the treason trials of the centuriate assembly. In both centuries and tribes the votes were gathered and counted by men known first as *rogatores* and later, when ballots were written, as *custodes,* chosen in general from upper-class voters, eventually from the official jury lists. In both, the lot was used to select the tribe or the section of a tribe which was to have priority, either in voting or in the announcement of the vote (Chap. IV).

Ancient Sources on the Assemblies

The earliest Roman historian, Q. Fabius Pictor, was probably already a member of the Roman senate at the beginning of the Second Punic War, which opens the period under consideration here. His memory and the memories of people he knew well went back more than a generation before that time. For an earlier period the Romans themselves had only the bare outlines of official records and certain traditions and documents such as funeral orations from the leading families. Fabius, who wrote in Greek for the Greek world, and the Roman historians who succeeded him in the second and early first century are known to us only from the reflections of their work in later writings. But there is one very important direct source from the mid-second century, the universal history written by Polybius of Megalopolis. As a hostage he spent sixteen years (167–51) in Rome, in close contact with the conqueror of Macedon, L. Aemilius Paullus and with his son, who, after his adoption by a son of the elder Scipio Africanus, conquered Carthage in 146. Polybius' history, undertaken to show how in less than fifty-three years (220 to 167) the Romans had subjected almost the entire inhabited world to their rule, has, except in the first five books, come down to us in fragments, and most of the Roman sections contribute much more to a study of magistrates and senate than to the assemblies. Of the sixth book, which dealt in detail with the Roman constitution, comparing it with other constitutions, the portions preserved contain only four chapters relating to the assemblies,[9] and neither there nor elsewhere is there any discussion of the types of assemblies. A lost section on the organization and growth of the Roman state must have included valuable material on the early history of the assemblies. It is unfortunate that the only other account of the Roman constitution that we have, the *De Re Publica* of Cicero, is also fragmentary. The second book, on the development of the constitution, is, in the view of some scholars, based on the lost section of Polybius.[10] Whether or not it is (and I record myself among the doubters), it provides significant evidence, particularly for the centuriate assembly.

In general Cicero is our great source for the assemblies. On procedure far more important than his two political dialogues, the *Republic* and the *Laws,* are his orations and his remarkable collection of letters. There is also much of value in his philosophical and rhetorical essays. If at times we have a clear picture of the way the people functioned in their assemblies, our debt to Cicero is far greater than to any other writer.

Two contemporaries of Cicero, M. Terentius Varro and Q. Sallustius Crispus, both members of the senate also, provide significant evidence. The antiquarian Varro gives technical details of procedure in his essay on the Latin language and in other works known only from stray quotations; he made a great contribution to our knowledge by putting the dialogue of the third book of his *De Re Rustica* in the interval when the interlocutors were waiting in the Campus Martius for the announcement of election results. The historian Sallust, in his two monographs on the Jugurthan and Catilinarian wars, in the fragments of his *Historiae,* and in two letters to Caesar, which I accept as his work, is also a good source, particularly in his account of tribunicial legislation in the *Jugurtha.*

Fabius and the majority of the Republican historians whose work is lost, as well as Cicero, Varro, and Sallust, were themselves former magistrates, familiar with the controlling group in Roman politics. The Greek Polybius was in intimate relationship with the highest echelons of the nobility. Our great lack is in sources which give us a view of the ordinary man except as he is seen through the eyes of the upper political group. Catullus, who must have attended *contiones* and *comitia,* failed to leave any reflection of his experience to set beside the precious bit we have from him (*C.* 53) for the reaction of the populace at a public trial in the Forum. Plautus, whose plays pleased the people more than a century earlier, uses popular language and some political terms of his day, and occasionally refers to the assemblies,[11] providing in a scene in the *Casina* the best evidence we have for the method of casting lots at the *comitia.* And Cicero, who put a high value on the public's appreciation of oratory, shows, notably in a speech against a tribune's agrarian law, that he could discuss with his audience rather technical details of procedure.

For constitutional developments, next to Cicero, our greatest dependence is on the Augustan Livy, whose history is preserved for the Kingship and the Republic down to 167 B.C., with a gap for the years 293 to 219. Unlike his most important lost precursors, Livy was not a senator and could not speak from personal experience of procedure. Nor was he an analytical historian. But he had a vivid and controlled imagination, and he can make his readers see and hear the electoral and legislative contests of the past. Many details in his accounts of the early Republic, where he had no contemporary source, are unreliable, but the details of procedure are often revealing for later times.

For the origin of the centuriate assembly, Livy and Dionysius of Halicarnassus, who wrote in Greek after long residence in Rome under Augustus, give us, with slight variation, the canonical Roman version of Servius Tullius' institution of the census, the local tribes, and the centuriate organization. Dionysius' twenty books, fully preserved only to about the middle of the fifth century, are valuable because of all the books he had read (they did not include Livy) and because of an occasional comment on his own experience in Rome. His accounts of early *comitia,* with the interminable speeches of the tribunes, lack Livy's vividness and contain more anachronisms.[12] For instance, he represents the Romans of the beginning of the Republic making use of written ballots, and, as Fraccaro has shown, he misled modern scholars, even Theodor Mommsen, on the procedure in the tribal legislative assemblies.

Three other writers in Greek are of varying value on comitial procedure: the biographer Plutarch, who wrote at the end of the first and the beginning of the second century A.D., and the historians Appian, of the middle of the second century, and Dio Cassius, who wrote at the beginning of the third. Along with many revealing incidents and anecdotes, Plutarch, in his Roman biographies and in a few of his essays, has obviously unreliable details, such as references to elections of consuls in the Forum, which show his lack of understanding of Roman institutions.[13] Appian, who at times used a source employed by Plutarch, also has similar blunders along with much of value in his history of Roman civil wars from the Gracchi until the period of the second triumvirate.[14] Much more reliable is the history of Dio, preserved in fragments for events before 67, and after that continuously until late in the reign of Augustus. He had a deep interest in and understanding of constitutional problems, and his statements on what happened, though not on motives of men, are deserving of careful consideration.[15]

There is much besides in the imperial antiquarians, the most important of whom are Festus, whose work *De verborum significatu* is a summary of the Augustan Verrius Flaccus, and the Antonine Aulus Gellius, one significant example of whose treasures is the distinction between *contio* and *comitia* quoted above. The scholiasts who comment on ancient writers include one writer of great value, Asconius, whose discussions of Cicero's orations, belonging to the Age of Nero, emphasize historical and constitutional matters. Valerius Maximus' *Memorabilia* of the time of Tiberius and Macrobius' *Saturnalia* of the fourth century A.D. are often useful. And finally, in this list, which makes no claim to completeness, one should mention the jurists whose contribution is illuminated by Mommsen.

Inscriptions are another major source. For procedure in the assemblies the two most important, the pertinent passages of which are quoted in the Appendix, are the recently discovered *Tabula Hebana,* discussed in the Preface, and the Charter of the Spanish town Malaca (Malaga) which was given Latin rights by Vespasian. The latter document, usually known as the Lex Malacitana, was discovered in 1851 and was interpreted by Mommsen in an epoch-making paper of 1857. The voting units in the town were *curiae,* and the voting method corresponds in various details with that of the Roman tribal assemblies which took over some of the functions of the ancient Roman *curiae.* The charter is particularly revealing for tribal elections at Rome, especially for the procedure followed in the announcement of the votes.

More significant for legislative assemblies are the texts of ancient laws, preserved mainly from inscriptions, with new documents coming to light from time to time. Most of these laws belong to the Republic and were actually read aloud in the *contio* immediately before the citizens were ordered to separate into their voting units. The length and complexity of an extortion law and a land law of the late second century B.C. provide striking evidence for Roman endurance.[16]

Modern Interpretations of the Roman Assemblies

The student of the assemblies and of the Roman constitution in general is fortunate in having at his command the masterpiece of one of the greatest historians of all time, the *Römisches Staatsrecht* of Theodor Mommsen.[17] The first two volumes, which came out in 1871, appeared in a third edition in 1887–88 with the first and only edition of the third volume in which the assemblies are treated. In spite of new evidence and of important scholarly investigations, the *Staatsrecht* remains supreme.[18] In a preface Mommsen has left a moving statement of the impossibility of the task he had set himself and of his own inadequacy in carrying it out. "At least," he goes on, "I have the conviction that I have used all my power to labor and to think to gain possession of every usable building stone and to think through every thought to the end."[19] To appreciate the *Arbeits und Denkkraft,* one should read carefully the three thousand-odd pages of the *Staatsrecht,* a task that, after a half century of admiring consultation, I have accomplished only recently. The building stones available to him are all there and the great feature of the work is the way Mommsen's controlled thinking enabled him to fill the empty spaces, for some of which the building stones that he had imagined have now come to light. That is notably true of his analysis of the reformed centuriate assembly (Chap. V), but it is often true also of analysis of sources. Many a scholar must have had my experience of finding that a discovery he thought he had made had already been made by Mommsen, who had put it in its proper and often subordinate position. The book should be read in Mommsen's magnificent German, but even today, if a translator could be found like W. P. Dickson, to whom we owe the splendid English version of Mommsen's *History of Rome,* there is a place for an English translation, annotated with new evidence that often confirms and sometimes refutes Mommsen's interpretations.[20]

Two excellent German treatments of the Roman constitution which came out before the final edition of the *Staatsrecht* have much value in them, although they have been overshadowed by Mommsen—Ludwig Lange's *Römische Alterthümer,* in three volumes, the most recent editions of which appeared in 1876–79, and Ernst Herzog's *Geschichte und System der römischen Staatsverfassung,* of which the first volume, dealing with Kingship and Republic, was published in 1884. Useful handbooks in English are F. F. Abbott's *Roman Political Institutions* (3rd ed.; Boston, 1911), A. H. J. Greenidge's *Roman Public Life* (London, 1911), and Leon Homo's *Roman Political Institutions from City to State* (London, 1930, from the French text of 1929). Homo's book appeared in a new edition in 1962, with no changes except for extensive additions to the bibliography. Ernst Meyer's *Römischer Staat und Staatsgedanke,* first published in Zurich in 1948, came out in a much enlarged second edition in 1961, in which full account is taken of the *Tabula Hebana* and of many recent publications. The brief incisive discussions of the assemblies there have been very helpful to me. The first three volumes of Francesco De Martino's *Storia della costituzione romana* (Naples, 1959–61) deal with the Kingship and the Republic. The treatment is historical, with emphasis, from a Marxist point of view, on social questions.

George Botsford's volume, *The Roman Assemblies* (New York, 1909, pp. 521), is a penetrating discussion of the assemblies from the Kingship to the end of the Republic, based on thorough knowledge of sources and of available modern investigations. Particularly on origins, for which I have cited him several times in this chapter, and on the use of comparative material, which was deliberately avoided by Mommsen, he makes an important contribution. Even where new evidence has shown him to be wrong, he repays careful study. There has been a curious neglect of his work by German scholars, and by the Swiss Ernst Meyer, who knows Botsford only by reputation.

I make no attempt to discuss the treatment of the assemblies in the various histories of Rome (among which I cite particularly the books of Gaetano De Sanctis and Frank Burr Marsh). Specialized articles will be referred to in the notes of succeeding chapters. By far the most important of those published before the discovery of the *Tabula Hebana* is the collection in the second volume of Plinio Fraccaro's *Opuscula* (Pavia, 1957). An excellent review of investigations of the assemblies and the constitution in general since that discovery is published by E. S. Staveley, *Historia* 5 (1956) 74–122. As Staveley shows, the major interest has been in the Kingship and the early Republic, periods with which this investigation is only indirectly concerned.[21] My book, *The Voting Districts of the Roman Republic; the Thirty-five Urban and Rural Tribes,* published in 1960, is a new treatment of the tribes, including much evidence that has come to light since the work of Kubitschek was published in 1889, but, although the discussion of the centuriate assembly was detailed, slight attention, as Staveley noted, was given to the tribal assemblies.[22]

A recent paper deals specifically with the subject of this book, Ursula Hall's "Voting Procedure in Roman Assemblies," *Historia* 13 (1964) 267–306. Her careful collection of sources has brought to my attention evidence that I had overlooked. She is more concerned with the origin of voting systems than I am, but she agrees with me on the great importance of Fraccaro's study of procedure in the tribal assemblies, accepting his suggestions on the beginning of simultaneous voting which I reject (Chap. III). Neither she nor, as far as I know, anyone else has tried to reconstruct the setting of the assemblies in the light of Fraccaro's results and the new evidence for the Comitium and the Saepta.

II

PUBLIC MEETINGS IN THE FORUM,
ON THE CAPITOLINE,
AND IN THE CIRCUS FLAMINIUS

THE *contio*, the unsorted public meeting at which the magistrate in-
formed the people of questions to be asked in the *comitia* (Chap. I),
was summoned for many other purposes besides the voting assemblies
for which it was an essential preliminary. The magistrate alone had
the right to summon the people to a public platform and to select the
men who were to be associated with him in addressing the people.
The lower magistrates could call the people for affairs connected with
their offices, but only the consul (or dictator if there was one) or, in
the absence of both consuls, the urban praetor could summon them
to report on matters of general public interest and welfare. The tribunal most often used in our period was the speaker's platform close to
the Curia or senate house in the Comitium, known from its adornment with beaks of captured ships as the Rostra, the Beaks. There news
and reports on discussions in the Curia were conveyed to the waiting
throngs. There the people were warned of dangers and admonished
against practices not in conformity with the customs of their ancestors.
After the institution, reportedly in 494, of the office of tribune of the
plebs as a state within the Roman state, the tribunes gained the right
to use the public platform without interruption. There were penalties
for men who took an audience away from a tribune. On such a charge
a censor was brought to trial before the people and a praetor had his
curule chair smashed.[1]

The main feature of the *contio* in the Forum was speaking, and
the word *contio* had the derived meaning of a speech to the assembled

people. A famous example of a *contio,* a favorite of General MacArthur, President Franklin Roosevelt, and President Johnson, is the warning against armchair strategists at Rome delivered by the consul L. Aemilius Paullus just before he departed for the Third Macedonian War. Paullus' friend Polybius (29.1) suggests that Paullus made such a speech, but it could hardly have been as good as the version Livy (44.22) wrote for him a century and a half later.

The only speeches made in Roman *contiones* that have come down to us are seven orations of Cicero, two of which, the second and third against Catiline, are splendid examples of a consul's fulfillment of his duty to inform the people of present danger to the state. For tribunicial oratory the speeches of Sallust in the *Jugurtha* and the *Histories* are perhaps our best source, for Sallust, who had himself served as tribune, knew the traditions well.

As for *contiones* before *comitia,* they did not include prepared speeches if the business of the *comitia* was to elect magistrates. The Roman campaign for office was conducted by personal solicitation of voters (*PP,* Ch. III), not by oratory. For elections *contiones* consisted in the prayer for the favor of the gods with which every *contio* opened and in the necessary direction to the voters. But in the *contiones* which preceded legislative and judicial assemblies there were always speeches, often so many of them that they had to be delivered in a series of meetings. By custom and eventually by law, the bill (*rogatio*) embodying the proposed law or judgment had to be posted twenty-four days (an interval of three market days, known as *trinum nundinum*) before the voting *comitia.* The bills required explanation, for they were often long and complicated. Two of them, with a text preserved only in part, run to some fifteen printed pages each.[2] Couched in the difficult legal language that is part of our inheritance from the ancient Romans, they were no more intelligible to the literate citizens of the late Republic than most of our legislative bills are to us.

Before discussing the procedure in these *contiones,* we shall consider the tribunate of the plebs, for most of the officers proposing laws and prosecutions were tribunes. The tribunate was a revolutionary office, and its early history is a constant battle with the patricians who held the major offices and priesthoods, and, through senate and magistrates, directed Rome's relations with other peoples. But after the tribunes were successful in bringing plebeians into the consulship (367) and into the major priesthoods (300) and after the passage of the Lex

Hortensia (287), which made acts of the plebs binding on the state, the tribunes became more reasonable, more disposed to follow the authority of the senate of which they expected to become members. Except in the rebellion against the senate on the part of Gaius Flaminius and his followers, most laws from the beginning of the third century to the middle of the second seem to have been proposed by tribunes, usually with the authority, often at the direct request of the senate.

A change in the character of tribunicial legislation can be detected about the middle of the second century *(FG)*. After that time it reflected more and more the will of leaders, often great generals, who, in conflict with the senatorial majority, made use of tribunes to advance their own interests. At the same time the legislation made capital of the genuine wrongs of the citizens who, retained for years in military service outside Italy, fell into debt, lost their farms, and failed to produce the children needed for the Roman legions. In the tribunates of Tiberius and Gaius Gracchus (133, 123–22), opposition to the will of the senate developed into open revolution and both Gracchi met death by violence. Later, other tribunes rose, inspired by the memory of the martyred Gracchi, and the Forum resounded with their fiery eloquence. This eloquence was checked by Sulla, who removed the tribune's lawmaking power, and for a time, as Cicero tells us, the Rostra were deserted.[3] But the full powers of the tribunes were restored by Pompey, and in the last two decades of Republican institutions the demagogic eloquence of tribunes again echoed through the Forum.

Whether or not they were obedient to the will of the senatorial majority, tribunes were, then, the chief sponsors of legislation throughout our period. They were continually calling *contiones* not only for their legislation but also for prosecutions. Until the gradual development of the public courts (149–80) they frequently accused and tried in the tribal assembly citizens held guilty of minor public offenses, and they demanded the trial in the centuriate assembly of men charged with capital crimes, holding in the Forum the preliminary *contiones* for the prosecution. Except in the requirement that the regular magistrate could speak only on a tribunal inaugurated as a *templum,* a subject to be treated later, the *contiones* before *comitia* were very similar for the two types of magistrates. I emphasize the tribunes in my discussion because they provide most of the evidence.

The earlier *contiones* on a bill to be presented could take place on any day in the Roman calendar, but the final *contio* on the date appointed for the voting *comitia* had to be put on one of the 195 days in the Roman year that were marked *comitiales*—days when the *comitia* could meet. The days were actually more limited in number, for *comitia* could not meet on the *nundinae,* the market day of the eight-day Roman week.[4]

The *contio* consisted of speeches by the presiding magistrates and the men called to the tribunal, of which he had control. Sometimes the tribune adopted what we may call a press conference technique, asking questions in friendly or unfriendly fashion. Thus, an unfriendly trib-une, who was preparing legislation to avenge the death of Tiberius Gracchus, brought to a tribunal *ab ipsa paene porta* Tiberius' relative Scipio Aemilianus, who had just returned from the conquest of Numantia. The tribune asked Scipio's opinion on the murder of Tiberius and Scipio replied that he was *iure caesus,* justly slain. When the mob shouted in disapprobation, Scipio answered: "Be quiet, you who are not children but stepchildren of Italy," an allusion to the slaves and freedmen in the audience, many of whom, Scipio declared, he had brought to Rome in chains.[5] Pompey, waiting outside the *pomerium* in 61 for his triumph over Mithradates, got friendlier treatment when he was asked at a *contio* in the Circus Flaminius what he thought about the jury law favored by the senate for the approaching trial of Clodius. Pompey, Cicero ironically comments, answered in aristocratic fashion that the authority of the senate always had the greatest weight with him, *et id multis verbis (Att.* 1.14.2).

The choice of men called to the tribunal was determined by certain rules. They had to include other magistrates and men, usually from the senate, *privati,* who were not in office at the time. They were also expected to include men who opposed the measure, for the other tribunes had to hear them in order to determine whether to accept the bill or to exercise the veto that was the right of every tribune. The men called sometimes included well-known opponents, who otherwise might be given the chance to speak in a *contio* held by another tribune.[6] In that case the presiding tribune would not have had the chance to catechize the speaker. We have one speech by a magistrate in support of a bill, that of Cicero as praetor on the bill of the tribune Manilius to give Pompey the command against Mithradates—one of the most brilliant of Cicero's speeches. The oration ends with the assurance to Manilius of Cicero's full approval of the measure (*istam tuam et legem et voluntatem et sententiam laudo vehementissimeque comprobo*) and with the promise to use all his prestige and power to secure a favorable vote. Another speech of Cicero, the *De lege agraria,* delivered at a *contio* which he himself called, shows how a consul could oppose a tribunicial bill. The bill was a far-reaching agrarian measure which, when Cicero entered upon his consulship on January first, had already been proposed by a tribune whose office began on December tenth. The first *contio* of the consulship, when it was customary for the magistrate to thank the people for electing him, was used by Cicero to warn against the dangers of the bill, which, perhaps as a result of a threatened veto, was abandoned. There was a great expenditure of tribunicial oratory on bills that had to be given up when it proved impossible to prevent a veto. Sometimes there were repeated *contiones* over weeks and months. Throughout all the period the proposer of the bill remained in charge of the measure, making no changes in the text unless he was in agreement.

Before judicial assemblies, there was a specific requirement that the voting *comitia* should be preceded by three *contiones* prior to the final one on the day of the voting, a meeting spoken of as the *quarta accusatio.* In these cases the first three *contiones,* belonging to the *anquisitio,* the investigation, were held, probably on the Rostra, with intervening days, before the bill for the accusation could be promulgated. Then there had to be an interval of twenty-four days before the *quarta accusatio* at which the prosecutor and his associates and also the chief members of the defense spoke. These rules could be suspended if the accused wished the accusation to be made without delay.[7]

The Rostra and the other public platforms used by consuls and praetors were inaugurated as *templa,* that is as rectangular precincts, not in such cases walled in, from which the augurs had by established ceremony removed everything profane.[8] Tribunes could speak on these inaugurated tribunals but were probably not limited to them, for their office did not possess the direct relation with Jupiter implicit in augural discipline. Before discussing the Rostra and the other tribunals in the Forum, the chief site of *contiones,* I shall consider the places of *contiones* outside the Forum, leaving until the next chapter the tribunal in the Campus Martius whose position is determined by the evidence for the Saepta Julia and the earlier Republican structure for voting in that region. Most of the *comitia* held there were elections, in which the *contio* was used not for oratory but for directions to voters and the announcement of results.

The high *podia* of Roman temples, which were inaugurated, offered a good place for a public speech, always provided that there was enough space in the area in front of the temple to hold a crowd. I shall consider later the use of the Temple of Castor in the Forum for that purpose. The *podium* of the Temple of Bellona, which had a large area, was the scene of a consular *contio* of Cicero, who was trying to quiet a demonstration of the people in a neighboring temporary theater (Plutarch, *Cic.* 13.4). But the temple most often used was that of Jupiter Optimus Maximus on the Capitol, where the Area Capitolina was large, though not always large enough for the crowds. The only certain examples of *contiones* here are those immediately preceding *comitia;* earlier *contiones* on laws and accusations to be voted on were apparently held at the Rostra.[9] The Capitol is associated with the end of both Gracchi. After Tiberius' last voting assembly, which was held here, was dissolved, he is represented in a tendentious pro-Gracchan speech as calling a *contio* at the temple and opening with the accustomed prayer, when his enemy, the *pontifex maximus,* Scipio Nasica, "sweating, his eyes gleaming, his hair on end, his toga twisted" (*sudans, oculis ardentibus, erecto capillo, contorta toga*), darted from the temple of Jupiter and prepared the way for the final catastrophe.[10] The violence that led to the death of Gaius is said to have broken out on the Capitol when Gaius, no longer tribune, was attending a *contio,* a preliminary meeting before *comitia* called to revoke one of his laws.

For tribunes of the plebs there was a place for *contiones* which was probably not inaugurated, the Circus Flaminius, whose site beside the Tiber is now definitely established by the work of Professor Gatti.[11] The Circus, like the Via Flaminia, was built by the effective popular leader Gaius Flaminius; it was in a region perhaps already known as the *prata Flaminia,* where the plebeian tribal assembly had, according to tradition, met in 449 to end the tyranny of the decemvirate. The site thus had strong associations with the plebs. C. Flaminius took advantage of those associations and perhaps of the fact that the meadows, for some mysterious reason, were already known as Flaminian,[12] when in his censorship of 220 he chose the site for his great gift to the people. After his time the Circus Flaminius was used for *contiones,* but only by tribunes of the plebs. It was convenient for the tribunes, for they could call to the platform there generals who, like Pompey in 61, were awaiting a triumph, and were not permitted to cross the sacred limits of the city, the *pomerium,* until the day of triumph.[13] The only recorded voting assembly there in our period was held to vote on the revocation of the command of the great M. Claudius Marcellus in 209; the site was used to permit Marcellus to be present.[14]

The Comitium and Forum were the normal places for *contiones* and also often for votes of the tribes on legislation and judgments. The Comitium, an enclosed space, site of the *Curia* in which the senate met, is specifically mentioned as the place of meeting of the ancient *comitia curiata* which the people, now represented by lictors, no longer attended in our period.[15] The ancient speaker's platform, according to Dionysius of Halicarnassus, was at the shrine of Vulcan above the Comitium,[16] but perhaps what he found in his sources was simply the word *templum,* which indicated that the speaker's platform was inaugurated. It is referred to as a *templum* by Livy in two records of the fifth century.[17] The *templum* may have been an inaugurated platform in front of the Curia. Steps from the Curia, as we know from descriptions of the death of Servius Tullius, led down to the floor of the Comitium.[18]

Of great significance here, as the excavator L. Richardson has pointed out, are the Curia and the stepped Comitium below it found in the Latin colony Cosa, for such colonies were based on Roman models (Pl. I).[19] The remains of the curious theater attached to the senate house of another Latin colony, Paestum, founded in the same year, 273, as Cosa, have contributed to Richardson's interpretation of the Comitium at Cosa as a circular stepped area. A similar interpretation of the Comitium of Rome had already been proposed by Petersen, Pinza, and Sjöqvist, and they are followed by Richardson and by John Arthur Hanson, who shared in the excavation of the Comitium of Cosa.[20] I suggest that until 338 b.c. the speaker's platform was on the steps leading down from the Curia to the floor of the Comitium. But in that year, perhaps because the Comitium had proved to be too small for the audience, a new platform was built. There was reason for provision of extra space, for that year was the end of the great Latin War, when large numbers of Latins who had remained faithful to Rome were added to the citizen body. The new tribunal, inaugurated, Livy says, as a *templum,* was built and was adorned with the beaks of ships captured from the people of Antium, a decoration which gave to the platform the name Rostra.[21] The position of the Rostra close to the Curia is known from various descriptions and there can be no doubt that it was between the Comitium and the Forum, perhaps approximately in the position marked Rostra Vetera on the Map of the

PLATE I

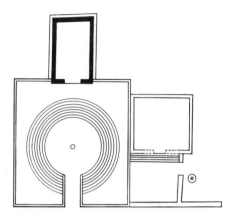

1. Cosa. Plan of the Comitium and of the Curia in its original form.

2. Cosa. Remains of steps of Comitium, looking northeast.

Forum.[22] I refrain from any effort to identify remains to be assigned to the Rostra.[23] The façade on which the beaks of ships were placed was, I believe, on the side of the Forum, and there the masses must have come to hear the speeches of magistrates on laws and public matters and the funeral laudations of the great nobles (Pl. II).

This view is not in accord with the description that Plutarch gives of an act that he attributes to Gaius Gracchus.[24] "While all popular speakers before him had turned toward the senate and the region called the Comitium, he was said to have been the first to make a public speech after having turned outward toward the Forum (and others are said to do so thereafter from his example), thereby, with a small deviation and alteration of posture, making a significant move and in a way changing the constitution from aristocracy to democracy, the implication being that it behooved the orators to set their aim not at the senate but at the masses."

This passage is full of errors. I begin with the character of the tribunate in which Plutarch sees a change at this time. It had always been the business of the tribunes to set their aim at the people, not at the senate. Polybius (6.16.5), writing some twenty-five years before the tribunate of Gaius, uses Plutrach's word στοχάζεσθαι of the tribune's aim at the populace. The tribunes might, and did for long periods, defer to the will of the senate, but even at those times they maintained the fiction that they belonged to the people. They kept their house doors open all the time and were constantly on hand at the tribunes' benches near the Comitium to hear appeals; they avoided magisterial insignia and identified themselves with the people by sitting not on a curule chair but on a low bench.[25] They could never have directed their public speaking at the senate.

For an understanding of what happened we must turn to Cicero and Varro, writers much nearer to the incident, men whose Latin terminology is based on experience in Roman public life. Both of them attribute the act not to Gaius Gracchus but to C. Licinius Crassus, tribune of 145 B.C., more than twenty years before Gaius Gracchus, and no one doubts that they are right. But almost no one (Ludwig Lange and Otto Gilbert are exceptions) follows Cicero and Varro in their account of what Crassus actually did.[26] Cicero's statement is that Crassus *primus instituit in forum versus agere cum populo*. As Aulus Gellius explains (13.16, quoted on p. 2), it was one thing to hold a *contio* at which there was speaking and quite another to *agere cum*

Modern reconstruction of Augustan Rostra on site of Caesar's Rostra.

populo, that is to ask the people a question to which they were to reply by their votes. That is the meaning of *agere cum populo,* of the magistrate's *ius agendi cum populo* of which we hear often in Republican literary sources.[27] Varro is not less clear, though, instead of turning, Crassus is represented as leading the people out of the Comitium into the Forum (*R.R.* I, 2, 9), *primus populum ad leges accipiendas in septem iugera forensia e comitio eduxit.* We need not pause on the baffling *septem iugera forensia,* which obviously refers to the center of the Forum.[28] The important element is the phrase *ad leges accipiendas,* a technical expression for turning a bill into law by giving a favorable vote on it.[29] Crassus did not turn on the Rostra (Pl. III) to address the people in the Forum, for from the time when the Rostra was built in 338 it had, I believe, been customary for the speakers in *contiones* to face the Forum where there was room for the masses. It was for another purpose that Crassus turned on the Rostra. Before that time the tribes, which, as Fraccaro has shown,[30] voted one by one in legislation, had been, I think, called into the Comitium one after another, and the magistrate in charge of the assembly then faced the Comitium. Crassus moved the vote to the Forum side and now faced the Forum for the *comitia* as well as for the *contio.*[31]

The encumbered state of the Forum in front of the Rostra and the difficulties of arranging for voting there, a subject to be considered in Chapter III, may explain why another tribunal for *comitia* and preliminary *contiones* in the Forum was established at the Temple of Castor. A separated speaker's platform, perhaps mainly used for the annual review and the census of the *equites,* already existed in front of the temple when L. Caecilius Metellus Delmaticus, consul of 119, rebuilt and enlarged the temple with the spoils of his Dalmatian campaign. Metellus' temple, as Tenney Frank has shown, making use of Richter's study of the later reconstruction carried out by Tiberius in 6 A.D., included a tribunal as an organic part of the temple. I shall try in Chapter III to show how this tribunal, which in Frank's view was wide enough to extend beyond the walls of the pronaos, was arranged for voting.[32] On the temple restored by Tiberius, Richter found evidence for a balustrade in front of a 19 m. wide platform; in his reconstruction (Pl. IV) he adorns the platform with beaks of ships, for which, as he states, he found no architectural evidence. There probably were beaks of ships in the spoils of Metellus' trumped-up Dalmatian campaign, for the region was infested by pirates who, working from

PLATE III

Augustan Rostra, rear view showing steps and curve.

PLATE IV

1. Temple of Castor, Richter's restoration.

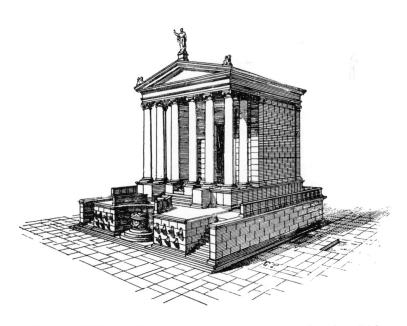

2. Temple of Divus Julius, restoration from a drawing based on Richter.

bases on the Dalmatian coast, menaced shipping in the Adriatic.[33] The only evidence that the platform here was called Rostra is to be found in the regionary catalogues of the fourth century A.D., which list in Regio VIII, Forum Romanum, Rostra III (*tria*).[34] Richter's view was that the three Rostra were the old Rostra, moved by Caesar and restored by Augustus, the Rostra constructed on the Temple of the Divine Julius and adorned with beaks of ships captured at Actium (Pl. IV), and the Rostra of the temple of Castor as restored by Tiberius in 6 A.D. (a platform on the temple, adorned already, in my opinion, with the beaks captured from Dalmatian pirates).[35]

The tribunal of the Temple of Castor became prominent as the scene of *contiones* and *comitia* at the end of the second century. In a law probably to be dated then, it is specified as the spot on which magistrates were to take the oath to abide by the law; they were to stand to swear in front of the Temple of Castor, in the light, *facing the Forum*—a significant detail in connection with the report on C. Crassus ([*pro ae*]*de Castorus* (sic) *palam luci in forum vorsus*).[36] Later, there are various records of speeches and voting here. The tribunal was the scene in 62 of a battle royal between Cato, then tribune, and his colleague Metellus Nepos, aided by Caesar, who was then praetor. Cato is described as bounding up the steps and forcing himself into a position between Caesar and Metellus, whom Cato prevented from reading the bills about to be presented to the voters.[37] Here Caesar seems to have put his first agrarian law to the vote in 59, and this was apparently the site of most of the legislation of Clodius in the following year.[38]

The meetings, according to Cicero, became steadily more disorderly, more like the public meetings of the frivolous *Graeculi*, referred to with a scornful diminutive. In describing them thus, Cicero discounts the shouts and acclamations that had always characterized the Roman *contiones*, which he elsewhere compares to the theater as a place for the expression of popular will. At the *contiones* there was undoubtedly participation on the part of the audience just as there was in the acting of Plautus' popular plays. But things went too far when demagogues like Clodius had hirelings to shout at the meetings [39] and introduced the Greek custom, which Cicero says was at variance with Roman tradition, of *asking* the gathering questions (that is, usurping the business of the *comitia*) and, when there was a response from the mob, of announcing that the shouts were an expression of the will of the people.[40] It is of interest that Milo, Clodius' opponent, in carrying out policies favored by Cicero, tried a similar method.

Of importance here is the fact that the Romans did not, like the Greeks, have the audience sit down at the meetings. There is an illuminating passage in the *Pro Flacco* of Cicero, the defense of a governor of Asia whose prosecution for extortion was supported by resolutions passed by cities of Phrygia and Mysia. The resolutions, Cicero says, were voted by men seated in a theater, men who simply raised their hands and passed resolutions: "Oh, if only we could keep the splendid tradition, the discipline that is our heritage from our ancestors; but somehow or other it is slipping out of our hands. It was the will of those men of the greatest wisdom and purity that there should be no potency in the *contio*. As for what the plebs might approve or the people might order, when the *contio* had been dispersed, when the people had been distributed in their divisions, when men had been divided by centuries and tribes into ranks, classes, and age groups, when the supporters of the measure had been heard, and the measure had been made public many days ahead and was understood, then it was their will for the people to give their orders and their prohibitions. But among the Greeks all public affairs are administered through the rash action of a seated public meeting. To pass over the Greece of today, long since overthrown and lying prostrate in its councils, the famous Greece of old, in the flower of its wealth and dominion and glory, fell because of this one evil, the unrestrained liberty and license of its public meetings. When inexperienced men, raw and ignorant of everything, had taken their seats in the theater, then they were wont to undertake harmful wars, to put revolutionary men in charge of public affairs, to drive from the state the men of the highest merit. But if things of this sort used to happen in Athens when her light shone not only over Greece but over almost all nations, what restraint do you think has existed in the public meetings of Mysia and Phrygia? Our public meetings are often thrown into confusion by men from these peoples. What do you think happens when they are by themselves?" The resolutions presented, Cicero goes on to say, were produced by such men raising their hands.[41]

The Greeks then, according to Cicero, sat down in a theater at their public meetings, and that somehow made them rash. They voted at once without time to deliberate, or to arrange the voters in divisions (which at least at Athens they never did). They were disorderly. With the coming of men from Greek lands to Rome, much of the disorder of the Greek assemblies was being introduced at Rome.

The Romans, as we know from abundant ancient evidence, always stood at their *contiones*. They also stood as they waited to vote at the *comitia,* though here the evidence is much less extensive. They had no permanent theater such as the Greek cities of Cicero's day had long used for their assemblies which, unlike the Roman gatherings, combined speaking and voting.[42] The passage in the *Pro Flacco* suggested to me that fear of the license associated with Greek assemblies might explain Roman objections to a stone theater, objections which, until Pompey's theater was completed in 52, prevented the city of Rome from possessing a stone structure such as existed in various Italian towns—Pompeii for instance. I looked in vain through the modern literature on the ancient theater for such a suggestion and then found it buried in a footnote of the third volume of Mommsen's *Römisches Staatsrecht.* The *Pro Flacco* was his starting point, and he had far more evidence for the standing *contio* of the Romans than I had found at the time.[43] The discussion that follows does not depend on Mommsen, who devotes only a couple of lines to the question.

The objection to a permanent theater did not prevent men from sitting down during spectacles, for the prologues of Plautus' plays show that the audience sat, presumably on temporary seats provided for the occasion. The prohibition of permanent seats took definite form when, through senatorial action, a stone theater begun by censors of 154 was destroyed. The moving spirit was the stern *consularis* P. Cornelius Scipio Nasica, the moralist who held, against the elder Cato, that Carthage must not be destroyed because its existence was needed to keep the Romans on their guard. Nasica's reasons for opposing a permanent theater, presented in a speech in the senate, were that the theater would injure public morals; that the seats, unsuitable for a warlike people, would bring in Greek luxury and *desidia* (literally, sitting down on the job). The suggestion in Appian that the seats might give rise to sedition and in Valerius Maximus that the inherent vigor of the Roman race would be exhibited by men on their feet may also come from Nasica's speech († *standi virilitas propria Romanae gentis nota esset*). According to the epitomator of Livy (48), the people for a time (*aliquamdiu*) stood to watch the games, but the time was not long, and it was again customary for magistrates to provide temporary stepped structures for seats long before Pompey completed his great stone theater in 52. Hence opposition to a seated audience at the games does not explain the failure of the Romans to construct a permanent theater in the succeeding century.[44]

The real explanation, I think, was the desire of the ruling classes to keep the people from following in their assemblies the custom of the frivolous "Greeklings" who debated and voted while seated. Although constitutional historians (I quote, besides Mommsen, Becker, Lange, Botsford, and recently Ernst Meyer) have realized that the Romans stood at their public meetings and assemblies, archaeologists, who have tried to figure how many people could have sat in the Comitium, have not been familiar with the evidence.[45] Lawrence Richardson, reporting on the stepped circular Comitium at Cosa, which he excavated, notes that steps of the height (ca. 33 cm.) and width (ca. 40 cm.) of those at Cosa were "not designed for comfortable seating" and concludes that "the Cosans must have stood in their assemblies."[46] He suggests that the Romans may also have stood. They certainly did, and the old Comitium seems to have been a stepped circular or semi-circular area for a standing audience.

Here I bring up a question submitted to me orally by John Arthur Hanson who, in his valuable book *Roman Theater Temples,* has discussed the relation to the theater of the Comitium at Rome and at Cosa. The question was whether Pompey meant to have *contiones* and *comitia* transferred to his splendid theater. If he did, Caesar countered his action by starting in 54, the year after Pompey's still uncompleted theater was dedicated, a permanent marble building in the Campus Martius for the elective assemblies of the tribes and for all meetings of the centuries. It had a new element unknown in the temporary structures for such assemblies in the Campus, a roof (*tecta*) or covering, another subject to be discussed in the next chapter. Servius states specifically that it was for the *stans populus Romanus.* Caesar was maintaining the old Roman custom of having the people stand, but giving the voters welcome shade in the broiling sun.

Yet, as Bekker noted long ago,[47] there was one place where the Romans may have sat down at their *contiones* and that was the Circus Flaminius, for it was provided with seats and the audience could hardly have been kept from making use of them. The Circus was, as I have noted, used for *contiones* of tribunes, especially when they wished to interview generals waiting for a triumph. The only known assembly held there after the Circus was built was that to vote on the command of Marcellus, who could not cross the *pomerium,* and that took place during the Second Punic War when many constitutional restrictions were disregarded. The tribunes may not at other times have wished to detract from the manliness of their audiences by holding *comitia* there.[48]

Cicero exaggerated when he credited the Greek elements in the *contiones* for the growing confusion and violence of his day. It is true that the great importation of slaves who, according to Scipio Aemilianus, had infiltrated the shouting mobs a century earlier, had, by the easy process of manumission at Rome, changed the composition of the citizen body by bringing in masses who were unfamiliar with Roman traditions. The number of freedmen was particularly large in the city; it had been increased by the state subsidized distribution of grain, inaugurated by Gaius Gracchus, for freedmen were eligible for the distribution, and we are told that many masters brought their slaves to Rome and set them free to have them fed by the state (*VD,* Chap. 10). On the free grain lists they joined the dispossessed farmers, the men in debt and want, to create the group described by Cicero (*Att.* 1.16.11) as *illa contionalis hirudo aerari, misera ac ieiuna plebecula* ("those meeting-going leeches of the treasury, the poor hungry little fellows"). A group of this sort, unemployed and plagued by poverty, offered a temptation to the demagogues of the late Republic, and Catiline and Clodius organized them into bands and armed them with sticks and stones and sometimes with daggers.

The mobs in the *contiones,* however much they may have been influenced by the "Greeklings" in their midst, were not responsible for later developments. The masses in the city were no longer important; the citizens who counted now were the professional soldiers bound in loyalty to the great generals. When Caesar appealed to his legions and won supremacy, Republican institutions were at an end. It is significant that the only famous *contio* under the dictatorship of Caesar is the one he called on the outskirts of Rome to speak to the soldiers of the tenth legion, the speech in which he quelled a mutiny by addressing the soldiers as civilians, *Quirites.*

But Republican forms still remained, and Caesar provided for future *contiones* by moving the Rostra to the spot it occupies today and making elaborate plans for its adornment. He established the ceremonial use of the Rostra that continued through the Empire; it was there that he or Antony staged the scene of the offering of a crown at the festival of the Lupercalia. It was there too, following Republican usage in this case, though Antony's elaborate stage setting was new, that Antony delivered his funeral oration over the dead Caesar. Augustus, who was more zealous than Caesar about Republican forms, not only completed in splendid fashion the reconstruction of the Rostra, he also built a new Rostra facing the old Rostra at the top of the platform of the temple in which Caesar was enshrined as a god. The speaker's platform on the temple of Castor was not forgotten. Although the advantages of its position were lessened by the building of Divus Julius, it was maintained in Tiberius' magnificent reconstruction of the temple in 6 A.D. and, I believe, went down in history as one of the three Rostra of Rome.

At the three Rostra in the Forum, with Castor's doubtless declining in use, *contiones* went on in the Empire, but in orderly fashion, for troops were at hand to check disorders. The obsequious crowds, who acclaimed the rulers and gave perfunctory support to the measures they proposed, retained one feature of the Republican *contio*. The men who attended did not sit down on the job; instead they stood on their feet, and let the world see the vigor inherent in the Roman race.

IIII

METHODS OF VOTING AND
PLACES OF ASSEMBLY OF
CENTURIES AND TRIBES

THE methods of casting and counting the votes, closely related to the choice of sites for the *comitia,* were essentially the same for the centuries and the tribes. As Professor J. A. O. Larsen has shown in his illuminating paper, "The Origin and Significance of the Counting of Votes" (*CP* 44 [1949] 164–81), the origin was Greek. But the Romans, when they began to record votes, went their own way, counting always in units, that is, in our period in centuries and tribes, and neglecting to record total numbers of individual voters. Nor did they adopt the best attested method of voting in Greece, *cheiritonia,* a show of hands. Instead, the Romans selected from men of prominence in the state a group of *rogatores,* "askers," who asked the citizens one by one to give the names of their favored candidates for office or their answer, positive or negative, on a bill for a law or judgment. The *rogatores* recorded the votes by putting dots, *puncta,* on tablets prepared in advance.[1] Under this system every man's vote was known and there was opportunity for intimidation and falsification. The oral vote was maintained until 139 when a radical tribune of the plebs secured the adoption, against the will of the senate, of a law introducing a secret written ballot for the elections. There followed in the second century three other tribunicial ballot laws, establishing written ballots in legislative and judicial assemblies both of the centuries and of the tribes.[2] Here the Romans were independent, selecting their own type of ballot, rejecting the pebbles, mussel shells, olive leaves, and beans used in various Greek cities.[3] The Roman ballots, known elsewhere only in local voting in Roman citizen communities, were small wooden tablets,

34

covered, as were the tablets for brief correspondence, with wax, *tabellae ceratae*.[4] For elections they were large enough to contain the names (the initials seem to have been sufficient) of the preferred candidates.[5] For laws or judgments the tablets would have been smaller, for all that was needed was space for one letter to indicate a positive or negative vote. The positive vote on a law was V for V(ti), *uti rogas*, "as you ask," and the negative was A for *antiquo*, "I maintain things as they are." In judicial assemblies the votes were L and D for *libero* and *damno*.[6] As Larsen has pointed out,[7] the ballot laws seem to have represented a more general popular movement than the radical legislation of the Gracchi. The citizen could now vote as he liked, and his patron knew nothing about it. The nobility, as we know from Cicero, was bitterly opposed to the secret ballot. Cicero himself, who preferred the oral vote, admits that the tablets, to guarantee liberty, *quasi vindex libertatis*, must be maintained, but he makes the curious suggestion that the ballots should be shown to the chief men of the state, that is, should be written but not secret.[8]

The institution of the written ballot, associated in some instances with the goddess Libertas,[9] is celebrated on the coinage of the two among the four families of the sponsors of ballot laws whose members served as officials of the mint. The families are the Coelii and the Cassii, the latter the house of Caesar's assassin, who, like his associate Brutus, descendant of tyrannicides, could thus claim that his house had championed the liberty of the people.[10] The coinage, with two additional series of coins of other moneyers, one of which also has on it a head of Libertas, will be considered in some detail, since it provides significant evidence for the tablets and for the voting process.

The reverse of a *denarius* of a Cassius Longinus, who is perhaps the brother of Caesar's assassin, shows a man clad in the toga who is putting into a receptacle a voting tablet on which is to be seen the letter V, initial of *Vti rogas*, a favorable vote on a law (Pl. V no. 1).[11] The receptacle is the wicker basket, *cista*, familiar in the sources and described collectively in the *Tabula Hebana* (18) as *cistae vimineae grandes*. On an almost contemporary coin of the Cassii there is a receptacle that in some examples seems to be a vase, not a basket, and a tablet with the letters A C for *absolvo, condemno*, terms not of the assemblies but of the public courts (Pl. V no. 2).[12] The two coins honor L. Cassius Longinus Ravilla, who sponsored the law of 137 providing for tablets in all judicial cases except for *perduellio*, and who after-

PLATE V

Roman *Denarii* showing voting symbols.

ward in 113 served as the judge of three Vestal Virgins charged with breaking their vows. It is possible that Ravilla included in his legislation of 137 provision for a secret ballot not only in the assemblies but also in the only public court that surely existed at that time, that for extortion. It is to be noted that while on the first coin the obverse shows only the head of Vesta, a head of Libertas appears, with the same reverse, instead of Vesta in another issue of the second moneyer (Pl. V no. 3). On the reverse of another coin of the Cassii (Pl. V no. 4) is a figure in a *quadriga,* usually interpreted as Libertas with a *pileus,* the cap of Libertas, in her hand. Association with the secret ballot laws is suggested by the receptacle behind the head of Roma on the obverse.[13]

The ballot used in judicial assemblies, different from that in the public courts, is represented on a coin issued by a grandson of C. Coelius Caldus, who in 107 sponsored the law introducing the secret ballot in trials for *perduellio* in the centuriate assembly (Pl. V no. 5). Beside the portrait of his grandfather on the reverse is the ballot marked, in this case, L, D, for L(ibero), D(amno), the regular form of the vote in the judicial assembly.[14]

The head of Libertas and voting symbols also appear on coins of a certain Palicanus from Caesar's dictatorship, and the meaning of the representations, although correctly interpreted by De Ruggiero, has not been generally appreciated (Pl. VI no. 1). Palicanus is usually identified as the son of the tribune of 71 B.C., M. Lollius Palicanus, and the association of his coinage with the rights of the tribunes proves the relationship. In the long struggle over the restoration of the tribune's law-making power, which was revoked by Sulla, the father played a decisive role, not only demonstrated by his energy in the office but also by the fact that he obtained from Pompey a promise that, if elected consul, he would restore the power of the tribunes. That promise, which Pompey, after his election, also made in a *contio* to the people, was fulfilled, and Palicanus naturally saw himself as the chief architect of the restoration.[15] With Libertas on *denarii* issued by his son when Caesar, as dictator, was putting an end to the goddess' regime, is a representation of the Rostra, whose curious curved form will be discussed later. On the Rostra is a *subsellium,* the bench which the presiding tribune, long absent from the Rostra, could now occupy in order to legislate.[16] A *quinarius* of Palicanus shows the voting urn and the voting tablet, once more available for tribunicial legislation (Pl. VI no. 3).[17]

PLATE VI

Roman coins showing Rostra with tribune's bench, a voting scene, and symbols of augurate.

A voting scene, the only one known,[18] is represented on *denarii* of another moneyer, P. (Licinius) Nerva of the late second century, a man of unknown identity (Pl. VI nos. 4, 5).[19] There is an elevation with planks at either end, evidently the *pons* which led to the voting basket. On it are two men, one of whom, probably to be identified as a *custos*, who took the place of the earlier *rogator,* is handing an object, surely a voting tablet, to a man at a lower level, who, presumably, has to mark the ballot before coming up to the *pons*. The other man to the right is a voter who is about to place a tablet in a *cista* at the end of the plank on the right. The *cista,* on a stand, has a cover with pointed ends. It is to be noted that the men wear the toga, not the ordinary dress of the common man in Rome, but evidently essential at the *comitia.* Behind are two parallel lines which Mommsen interpreted as divisions between voting units, and above is another line on which stands a tablet with traces of a letter identified by one observer as P.[20] Mommsen's suggestion was that the letter indicated the name of a tribe, for instance Papiria or Pupinia.

The *pontes* were an ancient feature of the *comitia,* designed perhaps to check abuses by keeping the voters in view. For elections we hear of a *pons* on which the presiding magistrate sat. The original plan of the conspirators was to throw Caesar down from his *pons* while he was conducting a tribal election.[21] In legislative assemblies there were *pontes* for the voting units, and their destruction was a favorite method of interfering with the voting.[22] We know that the *custodes,* as well as the earlier *rogatores,* sometimes, even in the days of written ballots, used the *pontes* to influence votes. C. Marius as tribune in 119 tried to remedy abuses by making the *pontes* narrower (Cic. *Leg.* 3.38), thus checking efforts of the *custodes* to win votes. It may be that the coin of Licinius Nerva, which belongs to the end of the century, was issued by a partisan who was glorifying Marius' tribunate.[23] For the *custos* on the Nerva coin handing a voting tablet to a man below the *pons* the *Tabula Hebana* (18–19) is of interest, with its provision that the *cistae* are to be placed in front of (*ante*) the tribunal of the magistrates and that along the front of the *cistae* are to be as many waxed tablets as necessary.

For divisions beween the various tribes waiting to vote, Dionysius, describing a judicial trial in the Forum, uses the word περισχοινίζειν, from σχοῖνος "rusk," meaning "to surround with a rope," a description that would fit the lines interpreted as tribal divisions on the coin.[24]

A more substantial division between voting units is suggested by the plural form of the name Saepta for the structure for *comitia* in the Campus Martius and by *consaepta* employed for electoral units in the *Tabula Hebana* (16) and the Charter of the Spanish colony (55) where all the units voted at once in a municipal election. Although derivatives of *saepire* could be used for any type of enclosure, they are commoner in descriptions of fences, such as were used on farms, particularly for animals.[25] As we shall see, another name for the Saepta in the Campus was *ovile* ("sheepfold").

This difference of terminology is made clearer by Plinio Fraccaro's important study of procedure in the tribal assemblies, a paper of 1913–14, which, until it was reprinted recently in his collected works, has been little known either to constitutional historians or to archaeologists. In opposition to Mommsen, who believed that in the tribal assembly all the tribes voted at once, Fraccaro (*PVCTR*), by an acute analysis of the sources, showed that, while the vote was simultaneous in tribal elections, the tribes in legislative and judicial assemblies were called to vote one by one.[26] With simultaneous voting, effective divisions, suggested by the word *consaepta,* would have been essential, but for successive voting ropes would have been sufficient to indicate the places where the tribes waited until they were called in (*introvocatae*) one by one to vote. The coin of Nerva would then show a tribal legislative vote. The tablet at the top of the coin would have on it the name of one of the tribes, members of which waited in various parts of the Forum or the Area Capitolina for the call to vote. Similarly, in the ancient festival of the ovens, where the divisions were *curiae,* there were, according to Ovid (*F.* 2. 529 f.), many tablets in the Forum showing the place of each *curia:*

> Inque foro multa circum pendente tabella
> signatur certa curia quaeque nota.

A single *pons* would have accommodated all the voters on the way to the baskets, but, as we shall see, there is reason to believe that they advanced in two lines with two *pontes.*

The difference in procedure between electoral and legislative assemblies is, as Fraccaro showed, closely related to the place of the assembly. For simultaneous voting in the tribal elections, for which thirty-five divisions were needed, much more space was required than for the vote of a single tribe in legislation. That explains why in the sources no tribal election is attested in the Forum, site of all legislative assemblies whose place is recorded before 218 and after 100 b.c. and frequently used in the intervening period, though often in that time the voting took place on the Capitol. For the Forum the adjoining Comitium appears to have been used until 145 [27] when C. Licinius Crassus led the voters from the Comitium out into the center of the Forum.[28] It is to be noted that the Rostra, whose original form seems to have been preserved after Caesar moved it to a central position, had steps at the rear (Pl. III) which could have been used by voters in the Comitium. But there were no steps on the Forum side of the Rostra, which Crassus adopted as the place of the vote. Before discussing the problem of the position of *pontes* and voting baskets at the Rostra, I shall consider another site often used in the late Republic for *comitia*, the temple of Castor. This is the spot to which De Ruggiero (*FR* 69) believed that Crassus led the voters, but it seems to me more likely that *comitia* were not held here until the tribunal became an organic part of the temple in Metellus' reconstruction after 117 (Chap. II, with notes 24–31).

Before the Temple of Divus Julius and the Arch of Augustus were built, there was probably more free space for *comitia* in front of the Temple of Castor than there was on the Forum side of the Rostra. There is, moreover, an architectural feature of this temple, going back to the temple rebuilt by Metellus after 117 and maintained in the reconstruction of Tiberius in 6 a.d., which I would associate with voting. The tribunal of Castor was approached not by central stairs (which existed above it) but by two lateral staircases, one on each side of the forecourt. The central stairs, represented as a feature of the temple on the Marble Plan (*PM,* Tav. XXI), and shown in a photograph of 1871 (Pl. VII), have been proved by excavations (Pl. VIII) to be later than the temple of Tiberius.[29] The side stairs were, I believe, built to accommodate voters, and that would explain why Clodius, in his opposition to a tribunicial bill to restore Cicero from exile, tore down the stairs of the temple.[30] Since *pons* occurs in the plural in descriptions of legislative assemblies,[31] I suggest that the voters from each tribe, called one by one into the precinct, marched to two *pontes* in two lines on either side of the temple, and that the *pontes* over which they walked to the voting basket were attached to the stairs on either side. In making this suggestion I am influenced by the staircases on either side of the façade of Divus Julius, a temple dedicated in 29 b.c. Here too there was a tribunal, surely in this case adorned with Rostra (Pl.

PLATE VII

Temple of Castor from photograph of 1871 showing central stairs.

Temple of Castor, 1895, after removal of central stairs.

IV). The use of Divus Julius as a place for voting is proved by the text of a law of 9 B.C. passed *in foro pro rostris aedis divi Iulii*.[32] It would, I suggest, be worthwhile to investigate other temples with two staircases leading to a tribunal.[33] An example is the Temple of Jupiter in the Forum of Pompeii, which may have been the site of voting in Pompeii.[34]

But how did the voters in the Forum leave the Rostra which they approached over the *pontes?* The steps in the rear led down to the Comitium. Here I note the curious phrase *pro rostris* which ought to mean "in front of the Rostra," but which, according to Festus (252, 257 L), was equivalent to *in rostris. Pro rostris* occurs in certain documents of the Republic but I have been unable to find an example of it in Cicero or in the Augustan Livy, both of whom frequently say *in rostris.* On the other hand, Valerius Maximus in the time of Tiberius constantly uses *pro rostris* for *in rostris,* and it is common in the Empire.[35] It occurred to me that the phrase might have originated from a temporary wooden structure set up for voting in front of the Rostra. This suggestion, like the explanation I had for the objection to a permanent theater at Rome, I found in a footnote of Mommsen, this one added, after the *Staatsrecht* was printed, to the table of contents. Mommsen's interest was not in voting but in the question whether there was a lower level on the Rostra, the *locus inferior* from which Caesar as praetor in 62 forced the august Q. Lutatius Catulus to speak (Cic. *Att.* 2.24.3). In answer to objections that the structure of the Rostra allowed for no such *inferior locus* and arguments that the phrase described the level of the Forum, Mommsen proposed in the footnote that there could have been a temporary wooden structure attached on occasion to the Rostra. A subsequent paper of Richter's analyzing the meaning of *inferior locus* and *pars inferior* in Livy 8.33.9 has met with general acceptance, and the view has been that men not admitted to the Rostra by the magistrate in charge sometimes spoke from the pavement below.[36]

But the puzzling representation of the Rostra on the coin of Palicanus seems to me to support the suggestion that there was a temporary attachment for the Rostra which may have provided a lower level. In the example on Pl. VI no. 1 there seem to be two levels at the top of the structure, with the tribune's bench on the higher level. The levels are less clear on another issue of the coin, no. 2, which also accentuates a curved front that is difficult to explain, since the Rostra, as an inaugurated *templum,* should have been rectangular. Beneath the outer line, the border of what I regard as the lower level, are five arcades, three of them complete, with supporting columns. In these three arcades, I believe behind them, one sees three curious objects, generally identified as Rostra, which the artist has represented not in a frontal view but in profile. I suggest that we have here a representation of a curved wooden structure attached to the Rostra when legislative or judicial assemblies were to be held there, and that the tribune's bench, on what I interpret as the upper level, was on the Rostra proper, whose adornment can be seen in the beaks of ships under the arcades. The openings in the arcades would have been designed to keep the beaks in view. The coin would then show the Rostra prepared for *comitia* and would thus emphasize the role of Palicanus' father in restoring the full powers of the tribunes.[37] The erection of such a structure would explain the original meaning of the phrase *pro rostris* as the place where a bill was passed, "in front of the Rostra."

As for the *pontes,* they would lead on either side to the attachment of the Rostra, and one would have to assume, for the descent of the voters, the existence of stairs to right and left, where the arcades are incompletely represented on the coin. The height of the Rostra, almost identical with that of the tribunals of Castor and Divus Julius, about twelve Roman feet (three and a half meters), seems excessive for the *pontes,* too high, even allowing for compression in the representation, for the scene on the Nerva coin where a ballot is being handed down to a voter who is on the ground level. The lower level of the attachment that was, I believe, used for the Rostra, would diminish the height, and it is possible that at the temples of Castor and Divus Julius the *cistae* were on a lower step on which the *pontes* rested. In that case the voter would have descended the steps immediately without going to the tribunal.

For the voting arrangements in the Circus Flaminius and at the temple of Jupiter Optimus Maximus in the Area Capitolina, we have no evidence either from the sources or from such excavations as have been made on the sites. The Flaminian meadows, in which the Circus Flaminius was said to have been constructed, were reportedly the scene of the assembly held by tribunes to restore the consulship and the right of appeal in 450. The Circus Flaminius became a favorite place for tribunicial *contiones,* to which generals, forced to remain outside the *pomerium,* were called, and it was apparently the site of the unsuccessful vote on a tribunicial bill in 209 to revoke the command of M. Claudius Marcellus (Chap. II, with notes 11–14). For the Area Capitolina all the legislative and judicial assemblies recorded were also presided over by tribunes of the plebs. The space was too small to accommodate the crowds, and one may ask why it was preferred to the Forum. Perhaps the tribunes, who had no auspices, were asserting in choosing this site that they were under the protection of Jupiter from whom the auspices came. Or perhaps, not requiring senatorial authority for their measures, they were seeking to separate themselves from the vicinity of the Curia. There was probably a tribunal for speakers and also equipment for voting on the broad steps of the temple, perhaps with *pontes* rising from the area to the height of several steps. The legislative and judicial assemblies recorded on the Capitol all took place between 211 and 121.[38] Soon after the latter date the Metellan tribunal of the Temple of Castor was made available, and was frequently used by tribunes as well as by the consul Caesar for legislation.

In view of the limited area, full of shrines, statues, and honorary monuments, it is surprising to find two records of elections on the Capitol in the second century.[39] The area could hardly have had room for thirty-five columns of voters. Fraccaro, followed by Mrs. Hall, suggested that in the days of oral balloting the tribes cast their votes in succession in elections as well as in legislation, and then changed to simultaneous voting because the other method was too slow with written ballots. But Fraccaro concedes that there is no proof of his view. I believe that the Romans would have learned how to save time by simultaneous voting long before there was a written ballot. I have examined the sources of the two elections on the Capitol, and I do not believe either case provides valid evidence. The earlier one, the choice of colonial commissioners in 194, was, I suggest, a token vote in the old curiate assembly, for the commissioners were given *imperium,* which had to be confirmed by that body.[40] The other case, which I have discussed in detail elsewhere, was the last assembly of Tiberius Gracchus which, in the account of Appian, was held for the reelection of Tiberius as tribune.[41] No other source describes the assembly as an election, though the point constantly made is that he wished to be tribune again. The voting, as described by Appian and Plutarch, appears to have been successive, and I have argued that the assembly was legislative and that the vote was on a bill, such as was passed three years later, to permit the reelection of tribunes.

The only other evidence for the site of tribal elections before the first century is provided by Plutarch's statement that Gaius Gracchus was elected to the tribunate in the Campus.[42] That is the regular site for all tribal elections in the period of Cicero, when the evidence is abundant. In my opinion the wide spaces of the Campus, needed for thirty-five columns of voters, had long been in use for elections in the tribes as well as in the centuries. The marble building in the Campus planned by Caesar and dedicated by Marcus Agrippa was known as the Saepta Iulia, the Julian Enclosures. Saepta, in the plural, like *comitia,* to indicate the voting units, is a description of enclosed spaces resembling the folds of flocks, and therefore also known collectively as *ovile*. Indication that there was a perhaps temporary Republican structure which served the same purpose is found in Servius' comment on Vergil's use (*Buc.* 1.33) of *saepta* for fold: *Saepta proprie sunt loca in Campo Martio inclusa tabulatis in quibus stans populus Romanus suffragia ferre consueverat.* ("The Saepta are spaces in the Campus Martius with wooden enclosures in which it had been customary for the Roman people on foot to cast their ballots.") [43] Of interest is the word *tabulatis,* referring to wooden boards, a description of the structure before Caesar, and the use of *stans* (in all the manuscripts except one) to show that the people were on foot.[44] To prevent voters from returning to cast their ballots a second time, the Saepta were enclosed and also guarded.[45]

The Saepta, though associated by Cicero (*Att.* 4.16.8) and Dio (53.23.2) with the tribal assembly, were also employed for the centuriate assembly, a fact that is clear from Livy's use of *ovile* (26.22.11) for that assembly and from Caesar's sudden decision on one occasion, after the citizens had gathered for a tribal assembly, to elect a consul in the centuriate assembly (Cic. *Fam.* 7.30.1). In the centuries, where the vote was successive by classes and apparently simultaneous within the classes, there were, as we shall see in Chapter Five, eighty-two divisions in the first class, composed of the higher propertied citizens, with thirty-five centuries of *iuniores* and thirty-five of *seniores* in the thirty-five tribes and twelve of the centuries of *equites*. If these three groups were called one after the other, the thirty-five divisions already prepared for the tribal assembly would have been sufficient. It is to be noted that in the assembly of senators and knights of the *Tabula Hebana* the senators were called first and then the knights.

The Republican Saepta were, we know, near the imperial Iseum and the Villa Publica, where the census was taken, and not far from the ancient altar of Mars from which the Campus took its name. Castagnoli is probably right in holding that the Republican site was approximately that of the Saepta Julia, now fixed by Guglielmo Gatti's important work on the Marble Plan of Rome.[46] It appears that there was no cover over the Republican Saepta and that particularly when, from the time of Sulla, the elections were scheduled in July, the voters must have suffered from the summer sun of Rome.

It is not strange then that Caesar, wishing to build from his Gallic booty a monument to rival Pompey's splendid theater, which might have offered to the citizens the temptation of sitting down in their meetings and assemblies, should have thought of a building which would protect the waiting throngs of voters from the broiling sun. Caesar's plans, in which Cicero had a share, are known from a letter to Atticus, written in 54, the year after the still unfinished theater of Pompey was dedicated (*Att.* 4.16.8): *Efficiemus rem gloriosissimam; nam in campo Martio saepta tributis comitiis marmorea sumus et tecta facturi, eaque cingemus excelsa porticu ut mille passuum conficiatur; simul adiungetur huic operi villa etiam publica.* ("We shall produce something truly glorious, for in the Campus Martius we are to construct marble Saepta, with a covering, and we shall surround the building with a lofty portico, so that it will be a mile in circumference. To this structure at the same time the Villa Publica will be adjoined.") [46a]

The Saepta and the portico were constructed after the death of Caesar by the triumvir M. Aemilius Lepidus, and the building was completed and adorned as a sort of museum by Augustus' associate Marcus Agrippa, who dedicated it in 26 B.C., when the *comitia* were only a pale shadow of the Republican institutions.

As a result of earlier studies of the Marble Plan, the Saepta were located along the Corso Umberto, the ancient Via Lata, and various remains in the region were attributed to them. But from Gatti's investigation in the mid-1930's, still unknown to most constitutional historians, the plan once attributed to the Saepta is now proved to belong to the *porticus Aemilia* on the Tiber beyond the Aventine. Instead, Gatti showed that the Saepta were to the west of the location previously accepted, and that the front was on the Via del Seminario, which leads from the façade of the Pantheon to the Corso Umberto; remains of a wall in existence on the east side of the Pantheon belonged, Gatti showed, to the west Porticus of the Saepta [47] (Pl. X;

for map of the region see Frontispiece). In subsequent study of the Marble Plan, Cozza has found the site of the Diribitorium, a building begun by Agrippa, who was responsible for the Pantheon in its original form and for the completion of the Saepta.[48] Saepta and Diribitorium are shown on Pl. IX from the Marble Plan. A confirmation of the site of the Saepta is provided by Frontinus, who says that the arches of the Aqua Virgo, another work of Agrippa, ended along the front of the Saepta.[49] Remains of its arches have been found in the Via del Seminario. Since the Saepta are known to have been a *locus auspicatus,* a *templum,*[50] it is significant that the structure was perfectly oriented with its façade on the north. The walls of the Saepta, according to the estimate that Dr. Cozza has made for me on the basis of the plan and the available space, enclosed an area about 94 m. wide and 286 m. long. A construction of this size cannot have been completely roofed. The *tecta* of Cicero's description must, then, have been provided at least in part by the use of awnings, first used in Rome for coverings of theaters in 69 B.C.; as we know from Lucretius, awnings were familiar in the period of Cicero's letter.[51]

Since, with the exception of the wall of the western portico (Pl. X), there are no remains on the site which help us to reconstruct the Saepta, we must turn to the scant indication on the Marble Plan, disregarding all discussions published before 1937, when the Saepta were thought to be located along the Via Lata, and when various remains there were identified with the divisions for voting units.[52] We must, with the evidence of Frontinus and of the plan, place the entrance not on a long side but on the northern short side. On this side a lost fragment, known only from a drawing, shows a series of dashes which Cozza identifies as openings. At the southern end of the west wall there was at least one exit, with probably a similar one on the other side. There are no indications of other openings on the sides either on the fragments of the plan or in the wall of the portico preserved from the west side. In the interior there is, not far from the east end of the south side, an "element" that Cozza finds difficult to interpret,[53] which he suggests may be a base or platform, and there is a trace of a similar element on the other side. This is perhaps a long tribunal extending across the southern end of the interior, of greater extent in front than in the rear.

The Saepta, built by Lepidus and completed by Agrippa, probably followed the designs made by Caesar when the *comitia,* whose power

PLATE IX

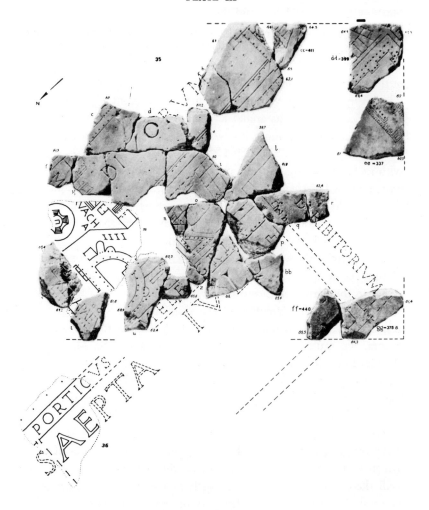

Saepta Julia and Diribitorium from Marble Plan. The top of the map is at
the southeast.

PLATE X

Outer wall of west porticus of Saepta.

he did much to diminish, were still a vital force in Roman politics; they were presumably adapted to the *comitia* of the late Republic. But the plan we have dates more than two centuries later, when such voting as existed seems to have been carried out simply by acclamation and when the building, used for senatorial meetings, *contiones*,[54] and gladiatorial games, had been reconstructed at least twice, once after the disastrous fire of 80 A.D. Yet the size, the exact orientation and the relation of the structure to the extensive building activity of Agrippa may well be relics of the original plan. The absence of permanent divisions for the voting units probably was a feature of the building Agrippa dedicated, for it was used nine years later for a meeting of the senate (*CIL* 6.32,323, line 50). It seems not unlikely that the divisions were temporary in the Republican wooden Saepta. The numerous entrances from the portico would have been useful for effective distribution of the voters. Fewer exits would have been needed, since the men would have left one by one. The enclosed sides would have made it possible to guard against the entrance of unauthorized persons. The curious platform at the southern end may represent the original tribunal, with provisions in the rear for the magistrates, perhaps on a slightly higher level than the front part where the voters, after reaching the voting baskets over *pontes* for each unit, might cross to descend steps leading to the side exits at either end.[55] To interpret my theory that the plan followed that of the original Saepta, Dr. Cozza has made the drawing on Plate XI, showing entrances and exits and the temporary divisions for the most important units, the thirty-five tribes. I shall try in Chapter V to show how the tribal divisions could have been used for the centuriate assembly. There are, of course, uncertainties in the interpretation, but we can, I think, be sure that the divisions put in for the units at the *comitia* ran from north to south, and not, as usually believed, from east to west.

Since we have no figures on the number of men who voted in the assemblies and none for individual tribes, it is worthwhile to try to estimate the number of citizens who could have been accommodated in the Saepta in tribal elections when all citizens voted at once. Each division, allowing space for the major and the minor *pontes,* would, according to Cozza's estimate, be about 260 m. long and two and a half m. wide. The voters were expected to be orderly and not to jostle their neighbors (Cic. *Cael.* 19). I have found no reliable figures for numbers of men in queues, but I would estimate that in a moving line of men

PLATE XI

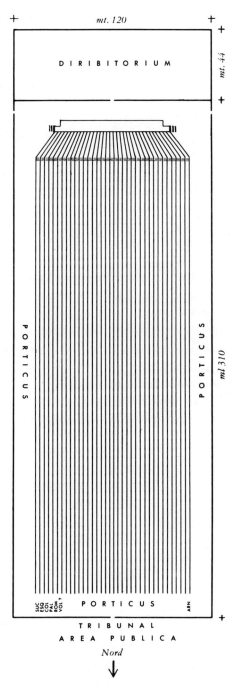

Saepta, proposed reconstruction of interior for voting.
Drawing by Lucos Cozza.

there could hardly have been more than two men to the meter and
that four men could have stood abreast in each tribal division, with
room for the tribal officers and the *custodes* to pass back and forth for
their examination of the voters. Under these conditions there could have
been about two thousand men in each division, with a possible total,
if all tribes were filled, of some seventy thousand voters. The number
should perhaps be smaller, for if, as on the coin of Nerva, the ballots
were handed down to the voters to be marked below, some provision
for the writing of names or initials of, for instance, ten candidates for
the tribunate of the plebs would have had to be made. And space would
also have been required to line the men up to go over the *pontes,* one
by one.

The available voters, in any case, were not equal in numbers in
all the tribes. Small tribes of the late Republic, the Lemonia and the
Romilia for instance (*VD* 99, 157), could hardly have mustered two
thousand men, and there were big tribes from which much larger numbers might have been on hand. I cite for instance the masses from the
Teretina and neighboring tribes who, according to Cicero (*Planc.* 21–
23), came to Rome to vote for their fellow tribesman or neighbor Cn.
Plancius when he was a candidate for the curule aedileship. If the story
is not unduly exaggerated, we can imagine that, as at the first election
of Gaius Gracchus to the tribunate, there was not adequate room at
the *comitia* for all the men who came from the country, and that after
benefitting in the campaign from his throngs of supporters, the candidate had to see some shut out. We are told by Plutarch (*C. Gracch.* 3.1)
that Gaius' voters who could not get in expressed their support by
shouting from neighboring rooftops.

The largest number available at all the *comitia* were from the men
always on hand in the four urban tribes, which included the lower
population of the city and all the freedmen, numbers of whom, after
the time of Gaius Gracchus, were brought to Rome by their patrons
to be fed by the grain dole. Perhaps the illiterates and the men who
had no toga or no clean one would have stayed at home. There was
probably coercion exercised to check the entrance of undesirable voters.
That is perhaps why Clodius, on one occasion, failed to carry his tribe,
the urban Palatina, for his candidate for the curule aedileship.[56]

After all the citizens had voted, man by man in one block in the
tribes, and class by class in the centuries, the Saepta were empty and
the voters were outside in the Campus waiting for the votes to be

counted and the announcements to be made. The task of counting was long and arduous, particularly for the elections after written ballots were instituted. The counting was done by the *custodes,* who watched each other. The ballots were sorted out, tribe by tribe, and placed in containers called *loci* or *loculi,* and there were sometimes altercations over the count.[57] The process must have taken a good deal of time in the Republic, especially for the election of ten tribunes of the plebs and of the twenty quaestors chosen after Sulla. No special building for the counting is known, but there must have been a temporary place with protection from the sun. Agrippa's Diribitorium, named from the word for counting, *diribere* (*dis* + *habere*), was conveniently placed directly behind the Saepta. It was not completed until 7 B.C., five years after Agrippa's death, a time when even the shadow of liberty in the elections had almost disappeared. But in its large size and in its roof of such span that when it was destroyed in 80 A.D. no one could restore it, the Diribitorium must have reflected the need of space and shade felt in Republican vote-counting.

For the period of waiting for the announcement of results we have evidence in the dialogue on birds, bees, and fish that makes up the third book of Varro's *De Re Rustica.*[58] A group of seven men, at least three of whom, including Varro, are senators, have cast their ballots for their candidates for the two places in the curule aedileship, and, while waiting for the results, seek the shade of the Villa Publica, which adjoined the Saepta Julia and was the center of the census on which the classification of the centuries depended. The exact site of the Villa is unknown now that Gatti has shown that the sections of the Marble Plan formerly assigned to it belong to another building.[59] Varro's interlocutors included an augur who left the group when he was summoned for consultation by the consul in charge of vote-counting. A supporter of one of the candidates rushed away when he heard that the *custos* of his candidate had been caught stuffing a storage box for ballots. The dialogue, to judge from its length, would have required about two hours before it was broken off by the news that the herald was singing out the names of the tribes in the announcement. The time required to count the vote on ten tribunes of the plebs would have been much longer, and sometimes was not completed in one day. The long wait for the announcement in such cases explains why Cicero chose the tribunicial *comitia* of the year before his election to the consulship to begin his electioneering. I think of him wandering about, during the vote-counting, among the citizens in the Campus, and seiz-ing the hands of men whose names the nomenclator supplied to him, and imploring them to vote for him for the consulship.[60]

Electioneering would have been interrupted by the news that an-nouncements of results were being made, and many men in the Campus, with more zeal than Varro's speakers showed, would have flocked to hear the report. The place of announcement could not have been the enclosed and divided Saepta which were now empty. Here it is significant that the Charter of Malaga (59) provides that the candi-date's oath to observe the law had to be taken *in contionem palam,* openly in a *contio,* before the final declaration of election could be made. The place would have been the same used for the unsorted open-ing *contio* which preceded the voting. Discussion of its location, post-poned from Chapter II until the site and the plan of the Saepta had been considered, is now called for.

The place was surely the north end of the Saepta, the site in the Via del Seminario, where, according to Frontinus' indications (n. 48) the front of the Saepta was. In the consular *commentarii* quoted by Varro (*L.L.* 6.88) the consul directs his attendant (*accensus*): *voca in licium omnes Quirites huc ad me,* and *in licium vocare* according to Festus (100 L) means to call to a *contio.* That meaning is clear from the order actually given by the attendant in Varro's account: *Omnes Quirites, ite ad conventionem huc ad iudices,* where the consuls are named *iudices* and *contio* appears in its old unsyncopated form. *In licium* must mean "into the belt," suggesting a roped-in space for the *contio.*[61]

This site was used not only for the opening *contio* but for sub-sequent *contiones,* employed for announcements, only one for the tribal assembly where all votes were announced at once, but one for each successive class in the centuriate assembly. The use becomes clearer from a reexamination of the sources in the light of what we know now of the plan of the Saepta.[62] Here would have been a tribunal auspicated as a *templum* for the presiding magistrate and his colleague or col-leagues. There is some reason to believe that if a consul was in charge, the praetors were present and also the ubiquitous tribunes of the plebs, always on hand to help or hinder candidates.[63] Here too would have been the candidates who stood in sight of the voters in a conspicuous place. There is a significant account of a candidate for the praetorship who, when he saw, after partial announcement of votes in the centuriate assembly, that he was being preferred to the son of the elder Scipio Africanus, descended from the platform described as a *templum,* threw off the whitened toga (*toga candida*), the sign of candidacy, and began to electioneer for the young Scipio.[64] It is likely that the candidates stayed outside during the voting, but the presiding magistrate, perhaps with his colleagues, would have made his way to the major *pons* in the Saepta.

A word may be added on the character of the *contiones* here. For elections they consisted simply of a prayer, directions to voters, given in the *comitia centuriata* as orders to an army, and a regular formula (*carmen rogationis*) of asking the voters to choose the magistrates for whom the assembly was called (Chap. V, n. 23). If the meeting dealt with a law or a judgment (which occurred only for the *comitia centuriata*) there seem usually to have been speeches. Thus, Livy reports a speech made by the consul of 200 urging the citizens to cast their ballots for the war with Macedon. After the speech, evidently delivered outside the Saepta, the citizens were sent in to vote and gave their approval.[65] The only law of the years 70–50 known to have been proposed in the centuriate assembly, that to recall Cicero from exile, was preceded by *contiones,* most of which were probably in the Forum. But certainly Cicero's enemy Clodius, and probably the consul Lentulus, Pompey, and other supporters of Cicero spoke in the Campus Martius, presumably on the day of the *comitia.*[66] Again, the speeches would have been made outside the Saepta.

In a judicial assembly of the centuries where, as in the tribes, three earlier *contiones* were required, and then a fourth one just before the *comitia,* the final speech, known as the *quarta accusatio,* would have been made in the Campus outside the Saepta.[67] The censor of 169, C. Claudius Pulcher, who dispensed with the preliminary *accusationes,* must have been accused here by two tribunes who had asked the urban praetor to set the day for a meeting of the centuries (Livy 43.16). He pled his own case and, besides his accusers, his friends must have spoken. At the announcement of the unfavorable vote of the first class, evidently made outside the Saepta, the leading men of the state (*principes civitatis*) laid aside their gold rings, changed their garments, and went about among the people to beg for his acquittal. (One wonders whether they had had their slaves bring dark garments for such an eventuality.) Then the other censor, the elder Ti. Sempronius Gracchus, as the people shouted that he was not in peril, took a formal oath that he would share the fate of his colleague, and the condemnation of Claudius was averted by a close vote.

The reconstruction of the assemblies in their Roman setting which I have tried to present in these two chapters depends largely on the building activity of Augustus and of his associates in power, Agrippa and Tiberius, who cooperated with Augustus in seeking to maintain the fiction that the Republic still existed. There was the splendid restoration of the Rostra on the site to which Caesar had moved it, a spot far less encumbered by obstructions than the old Rostra had been. The restoration preserved the steps in the rear, once used when the Comitium was the voting place. There was a new voting spot in the Forum, the Rostra of the temple of Divus Julius, decorated with the beaks of ships captured at Actium, approached by stairs on each side for entrance and exit of voters. There was a restored place for voting, also with two stairways, on Tiberius' reconstruction of the Temple of Castor. In the Campus Martius for the centuriate assembly and for elections in the tribes there was the splendid marble structure, the Saepta Julia, completed by Lepidus and Agrippa on Caesar's plans, a building with a covering that Caesar may have designed to keep the Romans from adopting the iniquitous Greek custom of sitting down while they voted. There was, finally, attached to the Saepta, the Diribitorium, a spacious structure, undoubtedy much needed in the Republic to facilitate the task of the counting of votes. These buildings reflect the needs of Republican political life, and although they were not completed until laws had almost ceased to be presented to the people and choice of magistrates depended primarily on the commendation of the emperor, they help us to reconstruct the scene in the days when the Roman people, at least in theory, were free to pass their own laws and choose their own magistrates.

IV

THE THIRTY-FIVE TRIBES AND
THE PROCEDURE IN THE TRIBAL
ASSEMBLIES

ALTHOUGH the tribal assemblies were later in origin than the centuriate assembly and less important in elections because they chose only the lower magistrates, they will be considered first since they are simpler in form and since the centuriate assembly had been reorganized not long before 218 on the basis of the thirty-five tribes. The essential difference in voting between the assemblies of tribes and centuries was that in the former all citizens within each tribe had a vote of equal value, while in the centuries the upper income groups within the tribe voted separately and had a favored vote—and thus, according to Cicero (*Leg.* 3.44), voted more wisely.

The thirty-five urban and rural tribes, unlike the ancient clan tribes which they largely displaced, were purely local groupings of citizens, depending on place of residence or property holding. Every full citizen was a member of one of these local tribes, and a man's tribe was an essential feature of his citizenship. An abbreviation consisting of the first three letters of his tribe was a part of his official nomenclature. Thus, Cicero, who came from Arpinum in the Cornelia tribe, would have written his name M. Tullius M. f. Cor. Cicero. The tribes were reportedly instituted by Servius Tullius not for voting but for purposes of the census taken locally and of the levy of troops and the collection of the citizen tax.

The origin and development of the tribes as a voting body are inadequately reported in the sources. One may question early accounts of tribal votes, for instance in the legendary trial of Coriolanus, at-

tributed to 492, two years after the tribunate of the plebs was believed
to have been instituted. But the transfer of the election of plebeian
officers from the *curiae* to the tribes in 471 is, in my view, to be accepted, and their use in legislation, with which I include jurisdiction,
seems to have followed very soon. From 471 to 387 there were, according to the tradition which I accept, twenty-one tribes,[1] and the uneven
number was convenient since the results depended on carrying the
majority not of the citizens but of the tribes. The uneven number was
maintained by the formation of new tribes, once four at a time and
five times two at a time. The importance of voting as a function of
the tribes is shown by the institution, perhaps soon after the Gallic
catastrophe, of an inferior class of citizens without the vote, *cives sine
suffragio,* men not assigned to a tribe.

The use of the tribes under the presidency of a consul probably
began by 447 when the quaestorship was made an elective office; there
followed election by the tribes of curule aediles, of various minor
officers, and special commissioners; some of the commissioners were
elected under a tribune of the plebs.

The voters in the tribes under the presidency of a tribune were
known as *plebs,*[2] and the assembly was properly called the *concilium
plebis;* the measures passed were *plebiscita.* Under the presidency of a
consul or praetor the voters were the *populus,* the assembly the *comitia
tributa,* and the measures passed were laws, *leges.* After the Lex Hortensia of 287 finally established the claim of the plebs that their *plebiscita* were binding on the whole body of citizens, the old terminology
became blurred. The great bulk of the legislation after 287 consisted
of *plebiscita* proposed, often at the request of the senate, by tribunes,
and the measures are constantly described as *leges.*[3] The voters under
a tribune, though properly called the *plebs,* are often loosely described
as *populus.* The word *comitia* becomes the common term for elections
voted on either by *populus* or by *plebs,* with plebeian elections often
called *comitia tribunicia* or *aedilicia.*[4] We can see the development in
Cicero, in whose works I find no example of *concilium* for plebeian
elective assemblies. But *concilium,* usually with the omission of *plebis,*
is Cicero's regular term for the plebeian legislative assemblies,[5] and in
certain comments on legislation he distinguished carefully between
populus and *plebs,* a distinction which is maintained in the prescript
of two laws of the first century.[6]

Although the method of calling the tribes to vote was practically identical for *populus* and *plebs*—differences of procedure depending primarily on whether the assembly was electoral or legislative—there were, and there continued to be, more differences in the tribal assemblies of *populus* and *plebs* than various modern writers (including myself, *PP* 206, n. 57) have been disposed to admit. My study of the setting in the assemblies has convinced me that Botsford went much too far in opposing Mommsen's view that there were lasting distinctions between the assemblies of *populus* and *plebs*.

The most important distinction was the exclusion of the patricians from the assemblies of the plebs. The exclusion is clearly attested for the period before the Lex Hortensia of 287 made plebiscites binding on the *universus populus*,[7] and, according to Mommsen and most modern historians of ancient Rome, the exclusion persisted throughout the Republic. But Botsford argued that patricians were shut out only for a brief period before the Lex Hortensia and not afterward. Since Botsford's work appeared in 1909 several scholars have maintained that in the late Republic patricians, although debarred from plebeian offices, took part in plebeian gatherings.[8] Their chief reason, like Botsford's, is the lack of evidence at that time for assemblies limited to plebeians. But they have overlooked the accounts of Clodius' efforts in 60, the year before Caesar superintended his adoption into a plebeian family, to acquire plebeian status. A tribune, who could not himself call the entire people, tried by a bill to force a regular magistrate to submit the question of Clodius' transfer to the plebs to the *universus populus* in the centuriate assembly, and the consul Metellus, though opposed to the action, promulgated a bill, on which no vote seems to have been taken. According to Dio, Clodius, having failed in his attempt to have the tribunate of the plebs opened to patricians, forswore his patrician status and, entering the plebeian assembly, laid claim to plebeian rights. Of importance is Dio's emphasis on Clodius' appearance at a plebeian assembly when the validity of his transfer to the plebs was in question. Besides this evidence, which suggests that a patrician would not have attended a plebeian assembly, there are in our period allusions in Livy and Cicero to the removal of nonvoters from the *contiones* that reflect in their language the stories of the removal of patricians from early Roman plebeian assemblies.[9]

The presence of patricians at plebeian gatherings is a major point in Botsford's argument against the exclusion of patricians from the plebeian assembly, but, with one exception, all the examples cited both

before and after the Lex Hortensia refer not to *comitia* but to *contiones,*
which patricians could attend and at which they could speak. When the
patrician Caesar, as praetor, appeared on the tribunal with the tribune
Metellus who was trying to carry a bill, the meeting was the final
contio before the voters had been ordered to divide into their tribes.[10]
The only occasion in Livy's records of the fifth-fourth century when
we find patricians actually present in the voting assembly is the session
on the tribunicial bill of 393 to move some of the Roman population
to Veii. The patricians, young and old, marched in a body to the
Forum and, scattering through the tribes, each pled with his own
tribesmen not to desert their native city (Livy 5.30.4–7). The result
was that the bill was defeated by a majority of one tribe. The scene,
as I see it, shows the tribes in separated groups in the Forum waiting
their turn to vote, and the patricians, presumably outside the ropes
that surrounded each unit, trying to persuade their *tribules* to vote
against the bill. These scenes are illuminated by Fraccaro's demonstration of voting methods in tribal legislative assemblies and by our
knowledge of the setting in the Forum.

There is then no reason for assuming that patricians who could
not hold plebeian offices could vote in an assembly of the plebs. The
exclusion of patricians had little effect on the numbers of voters, for
there had been a steady decline in patrician *gentes* after the Licinian-
Sextian laws of 367 led to the requirement that one consul in each
year should be a plebeian. Only fourteen patrician *gentes* were left at
the end of the Republic. But the exclusion resulted in the removal of
men of great prestige from the voters. The patricians could still try to
influence the vote of their fellow tribesmen. There is a story that
Camillus had his *tribules* at his house to persuade them to vote against
his condemnation in a tribunicial trial (Livy 5.32.8). But patricians
could also go down into the Forum and urge their *tribules* in the
enclosed spaces to cast votes favorable to their interests, and they may
well have been present in some numbers outside the Saepta to electioneer for their candidates for the tribunate in elective *comitia* which
they could not attend.

Besides the exclusion of the patricians from plebeian assemblies,
another lasting difference in the two types of assembly concerned the
taking of auspices, required of the regular magistrates but not of the
plebeian officers. The consul (or praetor) had to go between midnight
and dawn on the appointed day to the site of the assembly and ask,

under a carefully prescribed ritual, for the *auspicia* (Chap. I, with n. 8), which determined whether it was the will of Jupiter that the assembly should be held. He could be interfered with in the process and was subject later to charges of having neglected the proper forms. Before the assembly began and while it was in progress, he had also to take account of reports of adverse omens, usually thunder, which, even with the advice of the augur who was always on call, he neglected at his peril. Under two laws passed in the middle of the second century, the tribunes became subject to preliminary announcements of omens, *obnuntiationes,* in their legislative assemblies. This feature of the two laws was repealed by Clodius in 58. It seems not to have applied to elective assemblies of the plebs, which in recorded cases were not postponed except because of strife among the tribunes. In the period of anarchy after 57 B.C. the years often opened with no magistrates in office except the tribunes and aediles of the plebs.[11]

The plebeian elections were on a different schedule from that used for regular magistrates who had to be chosen in descending order of rank, consuls and praetors first in the centuriate assembly, followed by curule aediles, quaestors, and minor officers elected by the tribes. The lower officers could not be chosen until the election of higher magistrates was completed. But the choice of tribunes and aediles of the plebs, though in the late Republic assigned normally to the same month, July, were on an independent schedule.[12] A law of Clodius of 58 provided for legislation (I believe for the tribunes of the plebs, *FG* 23) on *dies fasti* (days available for any business except *comitia*) as well as *comitiales,* and it is not unlikely that the tribunes had had a similar privilege before the passage of the Aelian and Fufian laws.

Finally, I would mention the differences in the setting of the two types of assemblies, described in Chapters II and III, differences which would have made clear to every citizen whether the whole people or only the plebeians were included. The presiding consul or praetor appeared dressed in the purple-bordered toga and was preceded by lictors with their *fasces* and rods. The seat prepared for him on Rostra or tribunal was the curule chair that belonged only to the regular magistrates of higher rank. He seems to have been accompanied by colleagues and by tribunes of the plebs [13] to whom appeals could be made; there was also regularly an augur in attendance, on whom the presiding officer could call for the interpretation of the lot and the evaluation of *obnuntiationes.* In the plebeian assemblies the tribune appeared in the undecorated toga of the ordinary citizen, and the seat prepared for him on Rostra or tribunal was the tribune's bench, the long low *subsellium* to be seen on the coin of Palicanus (Pl. VI no. 1). Instead of lictors, his attendants were *viatores,* with no symbols of power in their hands (Livy 2.56.13). He was accompanied by his colleagues in the tribunate, but probably not by other magistrates,[14] and he also had an augur on call, a priest whose services would be needed to advise both on the attention to be paid to *obnuntiationes* and, I believe, to the lot.

In spite of the blurring of terminology, the difference between tribal meetings of *populus* and of *plebs* remained clear to the Roman citizen of the late Republic. The procedure in voting was, however, similar in the two types of assembly, with successive voting in legislative and judicial assemblies and simultaneous voting (at least in the late Republic) in elections.

The Thirty-five Urban and Rural Tribes

To understand the procedure we must consider the character of the tribes, a majority of which had to be carried for the passage of a bill or the election of a magistrate. The brief discussion here can be supplemented by the detailed treatment in my book *The Voting Districts of the Roman Republic.*

The institution of the tribes went back to a period when Rome was a small city state with a territory of perhaps 300 square miles, and a body of citizens who, if not resident in the city, could usually walk in to vote (*VD,* Chap. 4). The citizens were divided into four urban tribes, containing the industrial population of the city, and rural tribes, made up primarily of landholders, including many small farmers. In these rural tribes, which increased from fifteen to thirty-one (*VD,* Chap. 5), were also registered almost all the landholders who lived in Rome, that is, practically all the richer men in the city population. Thus, the organization had from the beginning subordinated the urban industrial elements to the agricultural population, and that characteristic of the division was intensified as time went on. The large urban tribes became the place of registration of the freedmen, who were prominent in industry, and of illegitimate sons and men under a stigma. The advantageous position of landholders, even small landholders, in the electorate has existed in many other peoples. We are

familiar with it in our state legislatures, now in the difficult process
of reapportionment, the result of a series of Supreme Court decisions,
the latest the famous "one man, one vote" decision of June 1964. But,
as far as I know, there was no attempt to change the situation at Rome,
partly at least because agriculture remained the most honorable method
of earning a living.

Members of the urban tribes were then always second-class citizens
at Rome (*VD,* Chap. 10). The fact was recognized and there were
persistent efforts to register the growing body of freedmen in the rural
tribes, efforts that had temporary success for some groups of freedmen
and permanent success after 188 for the sons of freedmen who had
once been limited with their fathers to the urban tribes. After that the
freedmen had some hope for their children, and that may have been
an important factor in preventing the freedmen themselves from
making a concerted attempt to better their status.

As Roman territory grew, old citizens were sent out as colonists
and new tribes were formed for them and for enfranchised men in the
regions (*VD,* Chap. 5). Four new tribes were instituted in 387 from
the territory of Veii, and ten more, two at a time, in the years 358–241.
The total number of tribes was always kept unequal, thus preventing
a tie vote in the assemblies where the number of units carried determined the result. Under the unit voting system the citizens in new
tribes far away from Rome had influence in the assemblies that lessened
the disadvantages of their distance from the polling place. But that
did not mean that these new tribes were free from the guidance of
the leading men, who were always ready to show their fellow tribesmen
how to vote. The leaders also got a share in the new land, and many
of them, while maintaining residence in Rome, were registered in
the new units. It is significant that more than half of the patricians
whose tribes we know were in the new tribes, established long after
their families had made a mark in politics (*VD,* Chap. 15).

After two tribes were created in 241 and the centuries of foot
soldiers became divisions of the thirty-five tribes, with advantages for
the propertied men, no new tribe was ever created and the term *Tribus
XXXV* became a synonym of *populus Romanus.* From that time on,
new citizen communities were put into old tribes, often through en-
largement of their territory. But some tribes were hemmed in by
other tribes or by the allied peoples of Italy and in many instances a
separated area was assigned to such tribes (*VD,* Chap. 7). That method

had, before 241, already been tried for a few communities of central Italy, along with tribal enlargements, and it became standard procedure after that date. Thus, Gaius Flaminius' extensive land settlements of 232 were put in an extension of the Velina on the Adriatic coast and into a new division of the old Pollia tribe, which, through subsequent extension in the Po Valley, became by far the largest of all the tribes.

It is sometimes hard to see the reason for tribal assignments. There must have been a great deal of jockeying, as there is in any political system over the establishment of voting districts (*VD,* Chap. 16). The question could not be settled in Rome as it often has been in the United States and elsewhere, by "gerrymandering," a name suggested after the painter Gilbert Stuart said that a district of Massachusetts created under Governor Gerry looked like a salamander. Roman land once put into a tribe could not be taken away; the tribe could be increased but not diminished. The problem for the censors responsible for the assignments was whether to make a tribe bigger or to keep it small, and that would depend on whether the censors or their friends were trying to gain control of a tribe in which they were weak or to keep control of one in which they were strong.

Before the outbreak of the Social War in 91 the majority of the tribes already had divided districts, and when all the allies south of the Po were added to the citizen body, a great many new divisions of tribes were created (*VD,* Chap. 8). Only about three of the thirty-one rural tribes were continuous areas when the distribution was completed in 86–85, and some of the others were now composed of as many as five or six separated areas. Thus, Cicero's tribe, the Cornelia, had the old territory of Nomentum, then, like most of Latium, largely denuded of voters, Cicero's own district of Arpinum, and other communities in Umbria, Apulia, and Bruttium. A tremendous problem was created for the politicians who had to carry the tribes. Even the task which Cicero's brother says must be mastered,[15] the memorizing of the tribal assignments of Italy, was, as I can testify from trying to do it, very difficult. Then one had to reach the voters who were widely scattered, with few common interests. We shall come back to the problem after considering the voters in the population of the city.

All the senators and many of the knights and men of smaller wealth had residences in Rome, and, except for a small group of them in two of the urban tribes, the Palatina and the Collina, they were distributed in all thirty-one rural tribes. The rural tribesmen in Rome were mainly richer men, a fact that is obvious from Tiberius Gracchus' efforts to bring men in from the country to vote for his measures.[16] The masses in the city were undoubtedly his supporters, but most of them were in the four urban tribes where their vote counted little.

The statement frequently made by modern historians that the votes in the assemblies were in the hands of the urban mob has no real support in ancient sources. Instead, we hear repeatedly of summonses sent to people of the countryside urging them to come in to vote. The first Roman law on malpractice, including bribery in elections, passed in 358 (Livy 7.15.12–13), was designed to curb the activities of candidates who went about settlements of citizens outside Rome to win support in their elections. In 218 there were still enough farmers living in the vicinity of Rome to provide a reasonable attendance at the *comitia,* but the situation changed in the next century or more, as most of the land in the Roman Campagna and neighboring territory was swallowed up by large estates, worked by slaves who had no vote. By that time people had to come from distant places, with plans made in advance. But they had good roads and easy communications, and they seem to have come in droves for the elections in July in the late Republic. Some of the candidates at that time went about Italy drumming up voters and arranging to bring them to Rome (*PP,* Chap. III). Thus, Cicero and others after him went to the Po region, and Caesar in 50 journeyed about in that section of his provincial government to ask men to go to Rome to vote for his friend Mark Antony. The leading men had connections all over Italy with communities which their ancestors had perhaps helped found and which their families had fostered for generations. If, like Cicero, they had no such ancestral connections, they could try to make up for the lack by establishing villas in various regions and by doing favors for men from whom they expected as payment a vote cast in Rome for them and for their relatives and friends. Cicero's villas were in six different tribes.

For the consular and praetorian elections in the centuriate assembly the men who needed to be brought in to vote were the wealthier citizens of Italian towns, especially the knights (there were 500 of them in Patavium in the Augustan Age) and the local magisterial class, with some men of smaller substance. These men had particularly close relations with Roman leaders and helped the nobility pass the consulship "from hand to hand" over long periods (*PP,* Chap. II). They were in Rome to vote for the lower magistrates immediately after the more important elections, but the results in these cases were much less certain, for prominent knights like M. Caelius Rufus and Cn. Plancius could import a fresh supply of voters from the lower population of the towns and carry the majority of the tribes even against candidates from the nobility. I quote from Cicero's words addressed to a defeated candidate for the aedileship (*Planc.* 18): "Your name on both sides of your house is consular. Do you doubt that all who favor the nobility...who are influenced by ancestral images and by the names in your house voted to make you aedile? I certainly do not doubt it. But if there are too few who love the nobility, is that our fault?"[17]

There was another point of importance for voting in the late Republic. By no means all the Italians had been registered after the Social War, and there was only one census, that of 70–69, completed between 85 and 49. Men could not vote in the centuriate assembly unless their position in the classes had been inherited from their fathers or established by the census, but they probably could in the tribes. Hence many men, particularly in the newly enfranchised communities, did not have the vote in the centuriate assembly, but could exercise their influence in the tribal bodies (*VD,* Chap. 9).

The regular scheduling of the elections (July after Sulla) and the provision of games and of special entertainment, gladiatorial shows for instance, contributed to the importation of many outside voters at this period. But that was not true of the votes on legislation which could come at any season according to the will of the consuls, praetors, or more often the tribunes who proposed the measures. Hence legislation depended much more on the votes of the people who resided in the city. To prevent legislation when many people were in Rome for the electoral assemblies, the Aelian and Fufian laws of the mid-second century actually forbade voting on legislation in the period immediately before elections (*FG* 22–24).

With tribes scattered in segments all over Italy, the organization of the tribal vote was extremely difficult. The center of organization was the tribal headquarters at Rome, to which candidates constantly went to ask for votes (*circumire tribus*). The Roman centers must have become increasingly important as the tribes became separated areas, and local connections among many of the *tribules* proved to be impossible. That was already true of many tribes before the Social War, and of all except three (the Teretina, the Falerna, and the Quirina) after the war (*VD,* Chaps. 11 and 14). The local connections loom large in Cicero's defense of Plancius, who came from Atina in the Teretina and had such associations not only in his own tribe but also in several neighboring tribes. But for many tribesmen there was no similar common ground (*VD*, 156 ff.). In the Horatia the men from Aricia in Latium, from Venusia in Apulia, and from Spoletium in Umbria would have known each other only in Rome. The Arpinates in Cicero's tribe, the Cornelia, had no local contacts with citizens from Samnium, Apulia, Bruttium, and Umbria in the same tribe. The result was a great increase of the power of the organizers who had their centers in Rome and maintained close connections with the noble and the senatorial families in the tribes.

Where the Roman headquarters of the tribes were is uncertain, though for one tribe, the Pollia, a common burial place on the old Via Salaria was discovered when the Via Po was opened at the beginning of this century (*VD,* 39 f.). But tribal headquarters must have been close together, and I suspect that they may have been near the Circus Flaminius, for it was there that on one occasion money, supposedly to be distributed to all the tribes, was said to have been discovered (Cic. *Planc.* 55). The Circus was built in his censorship by a great hero of the plebs, and it was, as we have pointed out, a favorite place for the *contiones* of tribunes. Perhaps the headquarters were the Porticus Minucia frumentaria, the center of the chief use of the tribes in the Empire, the distribution of free grain made to the citizens carefully classified by tribes (*VD* 15, n. 36). The site of this porticus, as I stated in the Preface, has now been established by Lucos Cozza, and is indicated on his map of the center of Rome.

The tribes had officers, the major ones known as *curatores,* who were called for the taking of the census by tribes, and were presumably present in the assemblies to see that the voters were properly divided. There were other officers known as *divisores* whose proper function was the distribution to the tribesmen of gifts made by their leading members. In the late Republic, when there was widespread corruption in politics, the *divisores* often gathered funds to be handed out as bribes to all the tribes (*PP* 63,67). The tribes probably elected their own officials and, under various laws, chose jurymen in the courts, where the juries were carefully divided by tribes. There is a report that the tribes elected the 300 knights whom Sulla added to the senate, his purpose being to provide an adequate supply of jurors in the public courts, which he transferred from the knights to the senate. In the jury law of 70 the jurors were equally divided among senators, knights, and *tribuni aerarii,* the last named being a special class in the state, representing the old paymasters of the army. As such, they seem once to have been officials of the tribes, but now were a special group with a census of a little less than that of the knights. They were probably divided equally among the tribes.

The division of tribes in the juries appears to have produced a trace of a representative system which, as Larsen's important book has shown, was, in general, lacking in Rome.[18] But in the election of magistrates there was, as far as I have been able to find out, no representation of tribes. The candidate had an advantage in his own tribe and those of the families into which his house had married; he counted too on the vote of the tribes of close political associates.

The Use of the Lot for the Selection of Tribes

An important feature of procedure in the Roman assemblies was the taking of lots. The combination of ballots and lots was familiar in Greek cities and was revived in medieval and Renaissance Italy, where the complicated method of electing the doges of Venice provides an interesting example.[19] In the Roman assemblies the most significant use of the lot was for the choice in the centuriate assembly of the *centuria praerogativa,* composed of members of the first class of one of the thirty-five tribes. This century, described as the *omen comitiorum* (Cic. *Div.* 1.103; 2.83), cast the first and often the decisive vote. In the tribal assemblies the tribe in which all the Latins were to vote was selected by lot. The lot also determined the order, often influential in the tribal vote, of calling the tribes in legislative assemblies and of announcing results in elective assemblies. For the use of the lot the evidence supplied by the Charter of Malaga is now supplemented by the *Tabula Hebana.*

Characteristic of the Roman emphasis on voting units is the fact that in the assemblies the lot was used primarily for the choice of tribes, rather than, as at Athens, for instance, for the selection of individuals for a magistracy.[20] After the elections, the lot was employed for the distribution of provinces and functions among colleagues, but not, as in Greece and in various European cities of the Middle Ages and Renaissance, for the selection of the holders of office among a group chosen by earlier vote. Completely foreign to Rome was the custom that prevailed under Athenian democracy of selecting entirely by lot from the members of each tribe the nonmilitary officers, the ten archons, and also the members of the council who prepared legislation, and the jurors.

Since for the assemblies the number of lots did not exceed the thirty-five for the tribes, there was no need of the elaborate Athenian lot machine, a model of which, based on the investigation of Professor Sterling Dow,[21] can be seen in the Agora Museum in Athens. At Rome the only equipment specifically mentioned in the assemblies is the lots and the receptacle, brought in at the end of the final *contio* to determine the tribe in which the Latins were to vote, and the order of voting on legislation. The receptacle was a *sitella,* diminutive of *situlus,* or an *urna,* terms which, like Plutarch's rendering *hydria* (*Ti. Gracch.* 11.1), describe water-carriers. The Roman water-carrier was of varying shapes, with or without spout.[22] The use of a water-carrier, employed in the scene showing lot-casting in the *Casina* of Plautus, suggests that the vessel was filled with water, and *effundere* in one source indicates that the water was poured out.[23] Consistent with the idea of pouring is the common use of *exire* for the appearance of the lot, with occurrences of *evenire, emergere, effugere;* not inconsistent is the employment of *ducere* and *educere* which may be used in the primary sense "to lead out" rather than in the secondary meaning "to draw out," suggested by an isolated occurrence of *extrahere*.[24] Instead of pouring, whirling the urn is indicated by the description of it in the *Tabula Hebana* (23) as an *urna versatilis,* a revolving urn. Here it is noteworthy that the verb *versare* is used of the urn by Horace in his familiar *omnium versatur urna serius ocius sors exitura* (*C.* 2.3.25–27) and by Lucan in a description of an assembly held by Caesar, *decantatque tribus et vana versat in urna*.[25] The method would have had some resemblance to the shaking of lots from a helmet familiar to every reader of the seventh book of the *Iliad*.

The lots are usually referred to simply as *sortes,* but here again the *Tabula Hebana* (23) is specific, calling for *pilae quam maxime aequatae,* balls made as equal as possible. The word *pila,* ball, is also employed for the lots for selection of jurors from the official lists.[26] In the assemblies the equalization of the lots (*aequatio*) was required before the lots were taken. Each lot would have been inscribed, probably in the regular three-letter abbreviation, with the name of a tribe. The lots, to judge from the *Casina,* were of wood, light enough to make them float on the water and thus to be easily poured or shaken out.

There is some Greek evidence for lots placed in a hydria. At Syracuse the annual choice of the priest of Jupiter was settled by the emergence of lots from a hydria.[27] Water in the hydria, not mentioned for Syracuse, is specified in the story of the lot taken by the Heraclids to determine the division of the Peloponnesus. The lots there were stones (or pieces of oven-baked brick) and a clod of earth which melted in the water. How the stones emerged from the water is not clear; one source indicates drawing by hand.[28] Further Greek evidence is suggested by the second act of the *Casina* of Plautus (295–428), where two slaves have recourse to the lot to decide who is to gain possession of the slave-girl Casina. The play, as the post-Plautine prologue states, is a version of the *Kleroumenoi* of Diphilus, described in Latin as *Sortientes*, The Lot-takers. That may have been the original name of Plautus' play. The allusions in the scene to the lot for the division of the Peloponnesus (*Casina* 307,398 f.), which, as the *Ajax* of Sophocles shows, was familiar to Athenians, provide reason for believing that the form of the lot came from Plautus' original. If so, the use of a hydria of water for the lot may have survived in Greek private rather than public life. It is not attested in the abundant sources for the Athenian lot in politics.

There is clearly a parody of the Roman assembly in Plautus' rendering of the scene, one of the many examples of his adaptation of his original to Roman customs. A pitcher, *sitella,* filled with water and two lots are brought from one of the houses to the street scene (341–63), and one can imagine that the placing of the *sitella* was carried out with the ceremony familiar at the assemblies. Each slave receives a numbered lot, and the pitcher is examined to see if a lot lurks beneath the water (380). The lots are evidently of wood, for one of the slaves expresses the fear that the other's lot may be of poplar or fir and may swim on the top of the water (384 f.). One slave utters in metrical form the customary prayer to the gods for success, *Quod bonum atque fortunatum sit mihi* (382). The wife of the master is put in charge of the lot and is ordered to see that they are equal (*aequa,* 387). The lots are placed in the *sitella,* and the wife is told to *sortire,* presumably to bring the lots out by pouring from the pitcher. She cries out "I've got a lot" (*teneo sortem*), perhaps at the spout, and the master tells her to bring it out (*ecfer foras*) (415). The *sitella,* the *aequatio,* the prayer, constantly used in Roman ritual, though not actually attested for the lot, and particularly the word *suffragatores* (299) used by one of the slaves for the supporters of his opponent, all belong to the assembly.

An experiment carried out with the aid of the director of the American Academy in Rome and of Sig. Giuseppe di Curzio was of interest for pouring versus whirling the receptacle. The proprietors of the Italian carpenter shop, Ricci and Pietrantoni, had fashioned on the lathe (with whose use the Greeks and Romans were familiar), a number of wooden balls two centimeters in diameter. The balls were of types of wood much used by the Romans, ash (*fraxinus*), Italian maple (*acer*), and the poplar (*populus*) mentioned for its lightness in the *Casina*. I was assured that the fir (*abies*), also mentioned in the *Casina,* was too coarse-grained for the lathe. I tried pouring the balls out of a pitcher and concluded that that method would have been effective when, as in the *Casina,* there were only two lots. But even with as many as nine, the balls tended to come out in bunches, and the order of emergence was hard to determine. Then I tried whirling them around in a small kettle filled with water, and the poplar balls, obviously lighter, for they rode higher in the water, usually came out ahead of the ash and the maple. The equalizing of the lots in the assembly would probably have resulted in the rejection of balls of lighter wood. The results of the lot indicate that sometimes the equalizing was not thorough. For instance when Caesar took the lot for the first tribe to vote on his law of 59 revising the contract of the publicans, the tribe that came out was that of the leading man of the publicans, the elder Cn. Plancius, who was promptly chosen to cast the first vote. Cicero's question suggests the suspicion that Caesar had a hand in the result: *utrum id sortis esse vis an eius qui illam legem ferebat?* ("Do you think this depends on the lot or on the man who was sponsoring that law?") [29]

As part of a much-needed investigation of the use of the lot in Roman politics, the types of receptacles employed and the possible use of a wheel or revolving table should be considered. Another subject that needs further study is the relation of the lot to religion, a relation that is clear in the *Casina* and in Cicero's comments on the *centuria praerogativa*.[30] The god of the *comitia* was Jupiter, and it is significant that on one occasion, for the choice of commands, not for an election, a priest once described as *interpres Iovis,* an augur, is called in to settle a dispute over a lot taken under auspices.[31] The augur decided that the lot was invalid because the tokens were placed in the urn before it was carried into the *templum,* the inaugurated spot. I suggest that for the *comitia* held with auspices by regular magistrates the augur, who was always on call, could be summoned if there was question of the fairness of the lot. Such a function of the augur may explain the symbol of the augurate frequently found on coins, the pitcher, combined with the *lituus,* the hooked staff which belongs to the priesthood (Pl. VI no. 6).[32] In every example the pitcher has a small opening usually with a spout, which may mean that it represents not the *urna versatilis* of the *comitia* but a pitcher that could be used to decide, with a smaller number of lots, the division of command for consuls and praetors.

Procedure in Tribal Legislative Assemblies [33]

The legislative and judicial assemblies, whose opening was signalized by the bringing of the urn and the lots, could take place at any season when comitial days were available. Presided over either by a regular magistrate, consul, praetor, or dictator, who had taken the auspices beforehand, or by a tribune of the plebs without benefit of auspices, these assemblies passed almost all the legislation of Rome and, until the institution of the permanent courts, begun in 149 and completed by Sulla in his dictatorship (82–79), frequently voted on judgments for crimes punishable by a fine.[34] The bill for a law or for judicial action had normally been posted at least twenty-four days before the final *contio* and the *comitia* were called by a herald.[35] In the intervening time, which might be prolonged, there had often been a number of *contiones* (at least three for a judgment), addressed by various magistrates and by private individuals. At the final *contio* there was sometimes an effort to take up time in order to prevent a vote before sundown when the *comitia* had to be dismissed.

The *comitia,* with its opening *contio,* could be postponed on the appointed comitial day by the announcement that an opposing magistrate was watching the heavens, in which case he would be expected to see and report unfavorable omens (*obnuntiationes*) which would interfere with proceedings. But if nothing of the sort had occurred, the *contio* met soon after dawn. The scene of the *contio* was the tribunal to be used by the magistrate in guiding the voting. The *pontes* would have been in place, probably attached to the side steps of the temple of Castor if that was the voting place. If the Rostra were to be used, I believe that after the voting ceased, in 145, to take place in the Comitium, where stairs led to the Rostra, a special wooden structure with stairs was attached to the front of the Rostra. That is my interpretation of the coin of Palicanus (Pl. 6 no. 1), which shows the *subsellium* in place for the tribune in charge; for the other tribunes (see n. 14) there were presumably other benches on the sides. If the presiding officer was a consul or a praetor, a curule chair in the center would have been provided for him, with others on the side for his colleagues.

After the final speech of the president and of the men he had called to the tribunal, the entire law was read. Then the urn for the lot was brought in and the order *discedite, Quirites*[36] was given, with the resultant removal of nonvoters and the distribution of the voters into their tribes. The last opportunity for acceptance of a veto from an opposing tribune was while the law was being read and during the period of the division up to the completion of the lot.[37] Interference with the reading of a bill is mentioned more than once in the late Republic, the most famous case being that of the younger Cato who, as tribune, snatched a bill from the herald's hand, and when the tribune proceeded to recite the bill from memory, had a colleague put his hand over the tribune's mouth.[38] But such vigorous action, characteristic rather of the time of anarchy than of more orderly days, was not necessary. It was enough for the tribune to say *intercedo,* and the veto stopped proceedings unless the opposer could be persuaded to give up. There was generally some knowledge of prospective vetoes in advance, and a great deal of persuasion went on behind the scenes, persuasion which often led either to the abandonment of the threat of veto or to the proposer's abandonment of the bill.

Another method of stopping the voting was interference with the procedure, for instance by theft of the *sitella* (Plut. *Ti. Gracch.* 11.1) or by removing the *pontes* or the voting baskets which were in place for the voters (Auctor ad Heren. 1.12.21).

The lot signified by the bringing of the pitcher[39] served two purposes. The first was the choice of the tribe in which were to vote the citizens of Latin colonies who were in Rome at the time of the *comitia*. Men from these towns, colonized in part by allies but mainly by Roman citizens, thus moved into a favored allied status and were given an advantage not possessed by other allies in Rome; their vote was, however, limited to the tribal assemblies, since they were not included in the census which classified the men in the centuriate assembly. But the advantage was not great since all these Latins were put into a single tribe, whose identity was not known until the assembly met.

The other purpose of the lot was to select the order of the tribes which, as we have seen, voted one by one in legislation. For legislation the name of the first tribe selected, known as the *principium,* was recorded with the name of the first voter in the official text of the law. There was a certain resemblance between the *principium* and the *centuria praerogativa* which cast the first vote in the centuriate assembly, but in legislation, when all tribes voted one by one, the influence was less great, and there is more stress in the sources on the way several of the first tribes voted than there is on the *principium.*[40] Like the announced votes of our states in our great nominating conventions, the early votes influenced later ones, producing a kind of bandwagon psychology.

With the choice of the *principium,* the tribesmen would go to the places, presumably roped around, that were appointed for each of them in the Forum or the Capitoline area. It was the business of the magistrate to see that no tribe was empty, and if, as sometimes happened, there were no voters or fewer than five present in some of them, he appointed men from another tribe to vote in the empty unit. Cicero speaks of laws that were passed with only five men each in certain tribes and says that these men belonged to a different tribe. The statement, often questioned, is now confirmed by the *Tabula Hebana.*[41]

The tribe selected for the *principium* was called into the voting place first, and the men made their way one by one, apparently in two lines (Chap. III with n. 31), to the *pontes.* On the *pontes* before the days of written ballots stood the *rogatores* to ask and record on their tablets each man's positive or negative response to the question on a law or judgment. After the secret ballot was introduced, the *custos* who replaced the *rogator,* if we can judge from the coin of Licinius Nerva, handed the ballot down from the bridge to be marked by a voter on the ground level. Cicero, listing measures designed to insure the secrecy of the ballot, says that a law of Marius provided for narrower *pontes.* That may mean that before his tribunate in 119 it had been customary to have ballots marked on the *pontes,* under the eyes of the *custodes.* Perhaps, as has been suggested, Nerva was an adherent of Marius and was, years later, recalling by the representation a famous act of Marius as tribune.[42] There is a report that the followers of Gaius Gracchus came to *comitia* held to revoke one of his laws, having deliberately provided themselves with *stili* of great size, and that one of them was used to kill a man (Plut. *C. Gracch.* 13.4). From this story it would appear that the voters brought their own writing implements and marked their own ballots. The single letter for a positive or negative vote on a law or a judgment was a far less severe test of literacy than was the writing in of names or initials of candidates, sometimes for a college of magistrates numbering as many as twenty. The general view that positive and negative votes were handed out already marked is based on Cicero's account of a bill proposed by a consul of 61 providing for the jury to try Clodius for sacrilege. The consul, who proposed it on the authority of the senate, was himself against it. Clodius' henchmen, perhaps as *custodes* appointed by the consul, occupied the *pontes* and served up the ballots (the word used is *ministrare,* often employed of serving food) in such a way that no affirmative votes were available. The younger Cato dashed to the Rostra, and, aided by various optimates, made a vigorous protest which led to the dismissal of the *comitia.* It is to be noted that Cato, who was a watchdog for comitial procedure, made a protest later against marked ballots in an election. The ballots, like those provided for in an extortion court, may have been marked with two letters, one representing a positive and one a negative vote, one of which the voter was to obliterate with the blunt end of the *stilus.* In this instance the positive vote will have been omitted. Two coins (Pl. V, 2 and 5) show *tabellae* with two symbols on each, one for a law court, the other for an assembly.[43]

Besides quarrels over the vote count, other types of interference, accompanied often in the late Republic by violence, might lead to the dismissal of the assembly at any time up to the final announcement of the results. The interferences included reports of omens, especially of thunder, which, if accepted, always led to the dismissal of the assembly. An augur was always on hand to give his view of the validity of the omens and could cause the dissolution of *comitia* or *concilia* by the words *alio die* (Cic. *Leg.* 2.31; Mommsen, *StR* 1.110).

If there was no such interruption, the counting of the individual votes, whether oral or written, would have taken little time, and the results of the vote would have been announced as soon as each tribe's vote was counted. Then the next tribe was called. If the method known from the *Tabula Hebana* was followed, the lot for the order of voting was taken not all at once, but after the completion of each tribe's vote. The matter was settled if there was a unanimous vote of the first eighteen tribes, a majority of the thirty-five, but the voting went on through the whole series. That fact is clear from specific evidence in various cases of total numbers of positive and negative votes of tribes.[44]

Sometimes the presiding magistrate tried to influence a vote which was going contrary to his wishes. Thus, Tiberius Gracchus tried to persuade his colleague Octavius to give up his veto of the first agrarian law. When he was unsuccessful, he presented a bill calling for the removal of Octavius from office. After seventeen tribes had voted for this bill, Tiberius stopped proceedings and again tried his persuasive powers on Octavius, who remained obdurate. With the vote of the eighteenth tribe, Octavius' dismissal was settled (Appian, *B.C.* 1.12.52–54; Plut. *Ti. Gracch.* 12). There was a similar case with a different outcome in the year 67, when the tribune Gabinius offered a bill to give Pompey the extraordinary command against the pirates. A fellow tribune vetoed, and Gabinius, following Tiberius' example, presented a bill to remove the tribune from office. In that case, after the vote of the seventeenth tribe, the tribune gave up the veto (Ascon. 72 C; Dio 36.30). That instance shows the willingness to yield, without which the Roman Republican constitution could not have endured so long.

Procedure in the Tribal Elective Assemblies

The tribal elections, according to my view (Chap. III), always took place in the Campus Martius, where an unroofed wooden structure known as the Saepta probably existed approximately on the site of the marble Saepta Julia. The differences in the setting between the regular *comitia* and the plebeian assemblies in the seats and attire of magistrates and in the provisions for auspices and for *obnuntiationes* (apparently not permitted for plebeian elections) have already been pointed out. For the reconstruction of procedure here the directions given for the election of local magistrates in the Charter of Malaga are of great importance, for they accord in various particulars with what we know of the tribal electoral assemblies.

On election day the opening *contio*, as was pointed out in the preceding chapter, consisted only of a prayer and of directions to the voters. The presiding magistrate, usually a consul or a tribune,[45] would be on a high platform outside the Saepta. On the same platform, in my opinion (Chap. III with n. 64), were the candidates, in a position where they could be seen by the voters. Occasionally, there was a demonstration for or against a certain candidate, sometimes with interposition from tribunes of the plebs, to whom candidates made appeals. Such intervention was said to have taken place when Scipio Africanus appeared as candidate for the curule aedileship of 213, and the tribunes pointed out that he was too young. Scipio was said to have replied, "If all the Quirites wish me to become curule aedile, I am old enough," and in these exceptional times the people were not deterred from electing him (Livy 25.2.6–8, see Chap. III, n. 64).

In the tribal elections as in legislation the determination of the tribe in which the Latins were to vote was presumably settled by lot.[46] After it was fixed, the presiding officer gave the order, *ite in suffragium, Quirites*.[47] He then proceeded to the major *pons,* seating himself, if he were a consul or a praetor, on a curule chair, if he were a tribune on a low bench.[48] The voters would march into the thirty-five divisions already prepared and designated for the tribes, probably arranged in their official order, with the urban tribes first.[49] The Roman feeling for rank may well have resulted in the yielding of places at the head of the line to senators. The story that the conspirators against Caesar planned first to throw him down from the *pons* as he was calling for votes in a tribal election (Suet. *Iul.* 80.4) suggests that the senators who formed the conspiracy would have been close together. In the space for each tribe besides officers of the tribes, there were at least three *custodes* (or *rogatores* before the secret ballot was introduced) appointed by the presiding officer, probably as in the Lex Malacitana (55), with at least one additional *custos* for each candidate. These *custodes* were men of prominence; they were chosen in the late Republic from the nine hundred senators, knights, and *tribuni aerarii* on the official jury lists; they were *custodes* of tribes to which they did not belong, and they voted in the tribe they were guarding. They also had the duty of counting the votes, and they were under oath to perform their duties faithfully.

In voting the men would go up single file and receive their ballots and mark them before ascending the *pons* to put their votes in the basket. It is probable that, as the *Tabula Hebana* (20) provides, the names of all candidates were posted in readable form on a large tablet. The candidate was expected to write in the names himself, and Cato succeeded in throwing out the votes and having the assembly dissolved when he discovered many written in the same hand (Plut. *Cato Min.* 46.2). There could also be write-in votes, as we know from a story from consular elections of the introduction of the names of the two tribunes who had opposed Caesar (Suet. *Iul.* 80.3), but it is unlikely that at any time names not accepted in advance by the president of the assembly would be considered.

The writing in of names, even if, as appears from one passage,[50] initials were sufficient, would have taken a great deal of time, particularly in the vote on ten tribunes of the plebs and twenty quaestors. It would also have been a severe test of literacy, which probably prevented a good many men from voting. There would also have been some delay over the choice of candidates, who, however, do not seem to have been much more numerous than the number of places to be filled. In the contest for the two places in the curule aedileship to which Cn. Plancius was elected for 55 there appear in the end to have been only four candidates.[51]

The delay in the Campus while the votes were being counted was discussed in Chapter III. It was in this period that Cato, serving apparently as *custos* for his friend Favonius and helping with the counting of votes, made the discovery of ballots written in the same hand. It will be recalled that one man in Varro's dialogue left the group when he learned that the *custos* of his candidate had been caught stuffing a ballot storage box.

When disputes, which might come up again in the law courts, had been temporarily settled, a report for each tribe was prepared, listing the candidates in the order of the number of votes received. The victors in the individual tribes would be the men with the largest vote, to the number of the places to be filled, two for the aedileships, ten for the tribunate. Although it was necessary for the victors in the election to carry a majority of the tribes, there was no requirement of a majority vote within the tribes. Tie votes were decided by lot, and it was perhaps to pass on such a lot that the augur was summoned from Varro's group in the *De Re Rustica*. Each tribe's vote would be taken to the presiding magistrate, to be read out by a herald [52] when, in an order determined by lot, each tribe was called. The view of Mommsen that there was a preliminary announcement of the vote of individual tribes has been made unlikely, in my opinion, by the explanation which Rosenberg and De Sanctis have presented for the directions given in the Charter of Malaga.[53]

When all the tribes had presented their reports, the presiding magistrate summoned the people to hear the results. Since the Saepta were now empty, the people were, I believe, summoned to the place of the original *contio,* the front of the Saepta. Here the Charter of Malaga is significant, for in it there is a provision (59) that before the final *renuntiatio* the candidates with majorities should take oaths *in contionem palam.* Again, the pitcher with water and the lots would be brought, and the herald would announce (or, according to Varro, *recinere*) the results showing who was the choice of each tribe. The herald apparently gave the numbers of votes in each tribe. As soon as a candidate had a majority of the tribes and had taken oath to observe the laws, he was declared elected. The calling of the tribes went on until all the places in the magistracy had been filled by men who had won a majority of the tribes. Then the assembly was dismissed without announcement of the votes of remaining tribes. If the full number of magistrates did not receive a majority, the voting had to be completed on another day, usually the next comitial day. For the tribunate of the plebs there are several records of failure to *explere tribus.*

A curious feature of the announcement of the votes by order of the lot was that the magistracies might go to men who did not carry the largest number of tribes. Here again we have the excellent commentaries of Rosenberg and particularly of De Sanctis, with his remarkable ability to make complicated matters intelligible. My illustration is based on his. Let us suppose that for the two places in the curule aedileship there were three favored candidates. That might well happen at Rome, where men who were not meeting with popular support often withdrew from the race. The two winners had to get first or second place in eighteen of the thirty-five tribes, and there were seventy such places in the tribes. Candidate A might have been first or second in the first twenty tribes called, and Candidate B in the first twenty-six. The announcements would then be discontinued, and the election was over. But if announcements had gone on through thirty-five tribes, A might have had twenty-nine tribes, B twenty, and C twenty-one. In that case C's victory over B would not be recorded. In a college of ten members, like the tribunes, it would have been possible (though very unlikely) for eighteen or nineteen men (Hall, *VPRA* 295, n. 118) to be listed in the first ten places in eighteen tribes. The condition for winning an election was to carry a majority of the tribes, and the size of the majority, except when it was unanimous, is rarely mentioned. There is one example, noted by Mrs. Hall, when the claim was made that a defeated candidate carried a majority of the tribes, the case of Gaius Gracchus when he sought a third tribunate and was, according to Plutarch, defeated by fraudulent announcement of the results on the part of his tribunicial colleagues.[54] But in general the Romans let Jupiter decide through the lot which winners of the majority of the tribes were to take office.

Throughout the *comitia,* and until the announcements were completed, it was possible for the presiding officer to dissolve the assembly because of violence or because of the advice of the augur at hand. But if nothing of the sort occurred, the candidates whose majorities were announced would, unless they were tribunes, don the purple-bordered toga and, surrounded by admiring friends, would be accompanied first, if we can trust Varro, to the Capitol,[55] presumably to give thanks to Jupiter, and then to their homes.

Before leaving the elections, we should consider the curious *comitia* created by employment of the lot to elect the *pontifex maximus.* This powerful semimagisterial priest had originally been chosen by the college of *pontifices,* but at some time between 287 and 218 a species of popular election from candidates in the college was instituted. Out of the thirty-five tribes, seventeen were chosen by lot, apparently just before the vote, and these seventeen tribes decided the choice among the candidates. The theory was that, though the majority of the people could not choose religious officers, *minor pars populi,* less than half, could do so, and seventeen tribes were just less than half. The election was then ratified by the *pontifices.* The choice of the *pontifex maximus* became one of the most hotly contested elections at Rome; the most famous example is, of course, the election of Caesar against two candidates of much greater seniority; his victory was a landmark in his advance to primacy in the state. These elections were infrequent, for the man chosen held his post of primacy for life. When the death of Lepidus finally freed the office for Augustus, a crowd from all Italy, such as had never been known before, attended his *comitia* of the year 12 B.C. One can imagine the throngs in front of the Saepta, the excitement over the lot to choose the seventeen tribes, and the impossibility of accommodating all members of the successful tribes in the Saepta.

The functions of this curious assembly of seventeen tribes were widened in 104 B.C., when the election of members of the major priesthoods, previously chosen by co-optation, was assigned to it. The system of co-optation was restored by Sulla, but the election by the seventeen tribes was reestablished in 63 under Caesar's influence.[56]

The discussion of the lot in this chapter and various details of procedure concern not only the tribal but also the centuriate assembly, which by this time was actually a tribal organization, with votes in subdivisions based on property. The unclassified vote in the *comitia tributa* was more democratic, and the officers selected came from a wider group than did the consuls and praetors chosen by the centuries. But even in the tribes there was a second-class vote for the urban masses without property, for the freedmen, and for the men under a stigma in the four urban tribes. The ideal of "one man, one vote" simply did not exist at Rome. Common to the two types of assemblies was the power of the presiding magistrate who could report omens and dissolve the assembly when he did not like the way things were going, could refuse to accept candidates for office (a power better attested for the centuries than for the tribes), could put men of his choice in empty tribes, and could influence the vote through the *custodes* he appointed. In elections this last power was limited by the privilege the candidate had to select a *custos* for every tribe, but in legislation the magistrate would have selected all the *custodes,* the men who, I have suggested, gave out marked ballots in the vote on the jury to try Clodius. Common also to the centuries and the tribes is the fact that the ordinary citizen emerges mainly as supporter or opponent of men in the magisterial class.

I. "Servian" Assembly   *No. of*
    Order of vote   *votes*

A. *Equites equo publico,* 18 centuries (6 ancient centuries from the clan tribes, Tities, Ramnes, and Luceres, and 12 centuries reportedly added by Servius Tullius).

B. *Pedites,* 170 centuries, divided into 2 age groups, *iuniores* (17–46) and *seniores* (46–60) and into 5 classes according to property.

Classes	No. of centuries	
I	80, 40 *iun.,* 40 *sen.*	80
II	20, 10 *iun.,* 10 *sen.*	20
III	20, 10 *iun.,* 10 *sen.*	20
IV	20, 10 *iun.,* 10 *sen.*	20
V	30, 15 *iun.,* 15 *sen.*	30

In addition, 5 unarmed centuries: artisans, musicians, *accensi, proletarii,* who voted with various classes.   5
                                                             193

The combined vote of 18 centuries of *equites* and the first class of *pedites,* 80, created a majority and, if they were unanimous, the assembly was dissolved without calling the other centuries.

II. "Reformed" assembly, in which *pedites* became divisions of the 35 local tribes: established between 241 and 220. The first class included 1 century of *iuniores* and 1 of *seniores* for each tribe (70).

    Order of vote   *No. of*

A. *Centuria praerogativa,* 1 century chosen by lot from   *votes*
    iuniores of first class.   1

B. First class, 34 centuries of *iuniores,* 35 of *seniores,* 12 of *equites,* 1 of artisans.   82

C. 6 centuries of Tities, Ramnes, Luceres (*sex suffragia*).   6

D. Classes II–V consisting of 100 voting centuries; divisions within classes unknown. 4 unarmed centuries (musicians 2, *accensi, proletarii,* voting probably with fifth class).   104
                                                             193

For a majority, the vote had to include the second class.

V

THE CENTURIATE ASSEMBLY IN THE LIGHT OF NEW DISCOVERIES

THE centuriate assembly, whose major function in the period under discussion was the election of consuls and praetors—the officers possessed of the right to command troops—was a military organization whose cumbersome procedure was literally loaded with anachronisms. Although as an *exercitus urbanus* the voters appeared unarmed in the toga (*StR* 3.386 ff.; 387, n. 5), they were viewed as soldiers under the orders of the presiding officer, and they could not meet inside the *pomerium* where no command could be given to troops. They had been called to the assembly first by an announcement from the tribunal, and on the day of the meeting were summoned by a trumpeter from the walls to appear at the voting place in the Campus Martius. While the assembly was in session a red flag flew on the Janiculum as a sign that the citadel was occupied by a garrison intended to protect Rome against foreign foes. The choice of the Janiculum suggests that the foe was Etruscan, somebody like "Lars Porsena of Clusium." The assembly of 193 centuries, organized, it was believed, by King Servius Tullius,[1] represented the forces that were once available for the annual military service which was an essential feature of the Roman state. The forces were made up of three groups, *equites, pedites,* and unarmed adjuncts of the army. The *equites,* men of higher rank who did their military service on horseback, consisted of eighteen centuries, of which six, composed originally of patricians, were formed, two each, from the ancient centuries of the clan tribes, Tities, Ramnes, and Luceres, attributed to Romulus. They were known as the *sex suffragia,* and they suggest the derivation of suffrage from the assembly of warriors who expressed their sentiments, as the Homeric soldiers once did and as the Spartans continued to do, by breaking into sound (Chap. I, with n. 2). The other twelve centuries of knights were said to have been added by Servius Tullius. The horses for these 1800 men—perhaps the only units in the assembly that maintained the exact hundreds implicit in *centuria*—were supplied by the state; the number was never increased although by 225, when we have records (Polyb. 2.24) of the number of *equites* available among citizens and Campanians, many more citizens were on call for service in the army on horseback.

The major section of the organization was the 170 centuries of *pedites,* the foot soldiers of the phalanx army; they were equally divided into centuries of *iuniores,* men liable to active service, aged seventeen to forty-six years, and of *seniores* from forty-six to sixty, much smaller units of men once expected to be on call to guard the city. The *pedites* were divided in the census into five classes according to property. The theory was that only men who had something to defend would make good soldiers. Their armor was heavy for the first class and successively lighter for the lower classes, the fifth class having nothing but slings and stones. The supply of small farmers proved inadequate for the legions in the second century, a situation that Tiberius Gracchus' agrarian law was designed to correct. Some of the armor described for each class by Livy and Dionysius had long been out of date, and little of it had relevance for the legionaries of the late second and the first century. As we shall shall see, the infrequency of the census in the first century resulted in inadequate representation in the classes of infantry.

The five unarmed centuries consisted of artisans, musicians (trumpeters and hornblowers), *accensi,* who were body servants of the centurions, to be called on for replacements, and finally a single century of the proletariate, men with no property or so little that it was not worth counting in the census.[2] This group in one enormous century actually provided the majority of the legionaries after the time of Marius, when the small farmers in numbers had lost their land and the policy was developed of filling the legions with men who served in the hope of a bonus that would put them in the propertied classes.

Originally, the eighteen centuries of *equites,* representing the officer class, were called on to vote in advance as *praerogativae,* those who were asked first, and were supposed by their vote, which was announced first, to show the other men how to cast their ballots (Festus 290 L). Then the first class was called, and it had a weighted vote, possessing eighty of the 170 centuries of *pedites,* and including in it all the men who supplied their own horses in the army, and also many men of smaller means, landed property of perhaps twenty *iugera* (about thirteen acres). These centuries were surely smaller than those in the lower classes.[3] The joint vote of the *equites* and the first class, ninety-eight centuries, produced a majority; if they voted unanimously the matter was settled and the assembly was dissolved without calling the other ninety-five centuries, consisting of twenty centuries each in classes two, three, and four, and thirty in Class five, with five unarmed centuries.

The centuriate organization, on which the enrollment of troops and the collection of the citizen tax were based, is said to have been designed by Servius Tullius for voting, and, after the expulsion of the kings, his notes (*commentarii, Livy* 1.60.3) are reported to have provided instructions for the election of the first consuls. Servius' object in the arrangement, Cicero states (*R.P.* 2.39), was to prevent the great masses from having the greatest power (*ne plurimum valeant plurimi*), and Livy's explanation (1.43.10) is similar: "Gradations were established so that no one would seem to be excluded from the vote and yet all the strength would rest with the leading men of the state" (*gradus facti ut neque exclusus quisquam suffragio videretur et vis omnis penes primores civitatis esset*). In spite of changes in organization, the stress on the richer and more important citizens remained a feature of the assembly, with the result that to the end of the Republic the choice of consuls and praetors was far more under the control of the aristocrats than was the election of lower officers.

The assembly was reorganized perhaps in response to pressure from the wealthier men who were excluded from the eighteen centuries of *equites* who had the first vote. The change was one that Dionysius of Halicarnassus describes as εἰς τὸ δημοτικώτερον, to a more democratic form.[4] It took place shortly after the last two of the thirty-five local tribes were organized in 241, and it made the centuries of the *pedites* into divisions of the local tribes in which the census for the classes was taken. Now the *centuria* became a part of a tribe (*unius tribus pars,* Cic. *Planc.* 49), and Livy's description of the change as a doubling of the number of the tribes in centuries of juniors and seniors is certainly true of the first class which was henceforth made up of thirty-five voting centuries of juniors and thirty-five of seniors, with a total in this class now reduced from eighty to seventy centuries for the *pedites.*[5]

Although the number of votes in each class is exactly known in Servius' assembly, we have no details after the reform on the numbers of centuries in each of the four lower classes. But it is clear that the first class and the *equites* no longer constituted a majority, and that the voting in the assembly had to go down further. Just how far it had to go depended on the number of centuries assigned to the lower classes. The subject became a numbers game, and gallons of ink have been spilled on it. A learned monk of the sixteenth century, Ottavio Pantagato of Brescia, interpreting Livy to mean that there were thirty-five centuries of juniors and thirty-five of seniors in each of the five classes, proposed a scheme of seventy centuries for each of the classes, and a total vote of 350 centuries of *pedites* in addition to the *equites* and the unarmed centuries, and his view obtained wide acceptance.[6] Pantagato's plan would have required the vote to go down through the third class to reach a majority, and it was in conflict with Cicero's account (*Phil.* 2.82–83) of an election of 44 B.C. which was settled as soon as the second class had voted. New evidence was provided in 1822 by the publication of the Vatican palimpsest of Cicero's *De re publica*. The assembly whose vote is described there (2.39–40) and apparently attributed to Servius, had seventy centuries in the first class and the total vote was still 193, which, as in the account of the election of 44, would have permitted a majority to be reached with the second class. In spite of this evidence, the majority of scholars preferred until recently to accept a modification of Pantagato's scheme, with a total in the reformed assembly of 373 centuries. This total was accepted by the high authority of Gaetano De Sanctis in Italy, by Ernst Herzog and Elmar Klebs in Germany, and by George Botsford and Tenney Frank in the United States.[7]

But Theodor Mommsen, who in his earlier work had accepted 373 centuries, changed his mind and in 1887 in the third volume of the *Staatsrecht* (275 ff.) argued on the evidence of Cicero that the full number of voting centuries after, as well as before the reform, was 193. He imagined the voters of the four lower classes meeting in 280 units, seventy for each class, but held that 280 units could be reduced in voting power to 100 by combining the units in groups of twos and threes. The voting centuries would thus have had no existence except that of the combinations in the voting baskets, and the combination would have varied from one assembly to another. Mommsen's plan met with a storm of criticism. De Sanctis called it the most *infelice* of all ex-

planations of the assembly and Rosenberg said it was *ein Monstrum*.
But the view supported by Cicero that the old number of 193 centuries
was retained in the reformed assemblies was accepted by Rosenberg in
Germany, Cavaignac in France, and Niccolini, Fraccaro, and Arangio
Ruiz in Italy.[8] One Italian scholar, Arnaldo Momigliano, went further
and accepted Mommsen's view of combinations of two and three tribes,
suggesting that to avoid the unfairness attributed to the scheme, the lot
might have been used.[9]

And now in the *Tabula Hebana* there has come to light an amazing confirmation of the method of counting favored by Mommsen and
Momigliano. The tablet provides for an assembly consisting of fifteen
centuries of senators and knights who voted, as the *centuria praerogativa* formerly had, on the *destinatio,* a species of nomination, of consuls
and praetors. The significance of the inscription as a parallel to Mommsen's idea of the voting in the *comitia centuriata* was pointed out by
Gianfranco Tibiletti in an epoch-making paper (*FCC*) published in
Athenaeum in 1949. I imagine that a number of scholars, when that
article appeared, did what I did and consigned to the waste-basket
work that was in progress on the inscription. There were still problems,
and there has been extensive discussion, but Tibiletti had brought out
the most essential material.[10]

Mommsen's plan for the reformed assembly, I repeat, called for a
gathering of voters in the 373 units in the scheme of Pantagato, but a
reduction of 280 of the units to a total of 100, the reduction being made
by having tribes in classes two to five vote in combinations of twos and
threes. Now let us look at the voting centuries of senators and knights
in the *Tabula Hebana.*

There were fifteen of them, ten named for Gaius and Lucius
Caesar, established by a law of 5 A.D. and five more added in 19 in
honor of Germanicus. The senators and knights who voted were arranged by tribes, thirty-three of them, two of the urban tribes, the
Suburana and the Esquilina, being excluded (a matter to which I shall
return later). The text shows exactly how thirty-three units are to be
reduced to fifteen voting centuries. The magistrate in charge in the
presence of praetors and tribunes and of the prospective voters from
senators and knights (lines 23 to 31) "shall order balls, made as nearly
equal as possible, for thirty-three tribes (omitting the Suburana and
the Esquilina) to be thrown into a revolving urn and shall announce
a lot and carry it out to determine which senators and which knights

are to vote in each basket; the assignment of lots shall be carried out in such a way that for the centuries named for Gaius and Lucius Caesar ⟨they were ten⟩ two tribes each shall be allotted for the first, second, third and fourth basket, three for the fifth, two each for the sixth, seventh, eighth and ninth, three for the tenth; that for the centuries for Germanicus Caesar ⟨five of these⟩ the lot shall be carried out in such a way that two tribes shall be allotted to baskets eleven, twelve, thirteen, fourteen, three to fifteen; that, when ⟨the magistrate⟩ has summoned a tribe whose lot has come out, he shall call from that tribe the senators and the men who have the right to express their opinion in the senate and order them to go to the first basket and cast their ballots, and when they have voted and returned to their benches, shall call the *equites* from the same tribe." A similar procedure is suggested for the other tribes as their names come out by lot.

The fifteen centuries which cast the preliminary vote in the perfunctory elections of the early Empire thus resembled the centuries in the four lower classes that Mommsen had imagined at the *comitia centuriata* in that they had no existence except that represented by labeled voting baskets, whose composition would vary from one election to another. The curious and complicated combination of the men in the various tribes was made in the imperial assembly by twos and threes just as Mommsen suggested that it could be in the centuriate assembly. The system he worked out, scorned by many scholars, demonstrates what Mommsen himself in another connection called "die divinatorische Sicherheit des Urteils die den eminenten Historiker bezeichnet," that is, the intuitive sureness of judgment that is the mark of the eminent historian.[11]

Most scholars today accept 193 as the number of voting centuries before and after the reform, and only a few have rejected Mommsen's view that the method of counting was similar to that in the meaningless assembly of the *Tabula Hebana*.[12] It would be interesting to know whether such methods of counting were known in the Greek world and whether some specialist like Caesar's adviser on the calendar, the astronomer Sosigenes, was imported to assist the censors in the reform.

As to the exact method of counting the voting centuries, there is wide disagreement. I have suggested that for classes two to four the number twenty was retained and that for the fifth class, whose census rating seems to have been lowered in this period, the vote was raised from thirty to forty.[13]

The procedure, in any case, was complicated, and the men who held the *comitia* had to know the rules exactly. The language of the *Tabula Hebana* may give us some idea of the type of instruction found in the consular *commentarii* (Varro, *L.L.* 6.88). The complications explain why, after an expert juggler in figures had worked out the scheme, the Romans never interfered with it by creating additional tribes. Henceforth all newly enfranchised regions were put in the old tribes, which became more and more broken up.

It remains to consider other elements in the assembly, for several of which, as we shall see later, the *Tabula Hebana* provides illumination. The really important change in the assembly, which also seems to have taken place soon after 241, was the substitution of a century composed of members of a tribe in the first class, selected by lot, for the centuries of knights which once made known to the people the way the upper classes wished them to vote.[14] The new custom of selecting by lot, after the voters had gathered for the *comitia,* a single century which, though containing men of wealth, would have in it many small farmers with twenty to twenty-five *iugera* of land, meant that the senatorial groups had less chance of influencing the outcome of the election.[15] It not only suggested, as our advance vote of the state of Maine once did, and as our polls sometimes indicate now, how the election would come out, but it also influenced later votes because of the Roman's feeling that the lot indicated the will of heaven. Cicero calls the *praerogativa* the omen of the election and tells us that the man put in first place by the *praerogativa* practically always got the consulship.[16] In the perilous times of the Second Punic War there were attempts to discredit or to change the vote of the first century. Other signs of the importance of the *praerogativa*'s vote are the stories of a fabulous bribe offered in 54 B.C. to any tribe successful in the lot (Cic. *Qfr.* 2.14.4) and of Pompey's dismissal of the assembly because he "heard thunder" after the *praerogativa* had voted for his enemy Cato (Plut. *Cato min.* 42). Of all the uses of the lot in the assemblies, the choice of the powerful *centuria praerogativa* was the most important.

The bestowal of the *praerogativa* on the first class far outweighed the loss in the reform of ten centuries in that class. I suspect that the richer men in the juniors of the first class, who were serving in the cavalry and outnumbered many times the eighteen hundred men listed as *equites equo publico,* knights with public horse, were the moving spirit in the change. They were important in military service, and in the twenty-four years of the First Punic War they may have expressed resentment over the influence exercised in the assemblies by the more aristocratic (though not necessarily richer) *equites* with public horse. Since senators were not forced to give up their public horses until the time of the Gracchi (Cic. *R.P.* 4.2), many of the members in the equestrian centuries must have been senators and older knights. Here it is significant that in all three cases in which we know the identity of the century selected for the *praerogativa* it was a century of *iuniores* from one of the thirty-one rural tribes, whose name in each instance is given. This fact has led to the question whether it was always chosen from the *iuniores* and whether the urban tribes were excluded from the lot.

Some support for the belief that the *praerogativa* was always limited to *iuniores* is to be found in one of the explanations of the Roman proverbial expression, *sexagenarios de ponte deicere* ("to hurl the sixty-year-olds from the bridge"). The Romans had various explanations of the proverb, of which the most common was that the bridge crossed the Tiber and that the old and infirm (or images representing them) were thrown down from it.[17] But another explanation, accepted by antiquarians of the Ciceronian-Augustan Age and by some modern historians, is that the *pons* was the one which led to the voting basket, and that *iuniores* at the *comitia* made a vociferous claim to the right to choose their commanders and demanded that the old men who performed no public function should be hurled down from the bridge, that is should be deprived of their vote.[18] I am inclined to accept this meaning of *sexagenarii de ponte,* for we can imagine such a claim from *iuniores* worn out from long service in war, and we can see how, for reasons of the annual levy of legionaries, they could have won the right to the *praerogativa*.

As for the share of the urban tribes in the lot for the *praerogativa,* there is significant evidence in the *Tabula Hebana* (23,32 f.), where, in the centuries of senators and knights which voted as *praerogativae* on the choice of consuls and praetors, two of the urban tribes, the Suburana and Esquilina, are excluded. These two tribes, it has been generally recognized, were inferior in the Empire to the other two, the Collina and the Palatina. Contrary to the general view, the inferiority went back to the Republic, when senators are known from the Palatina and Collina and practically no men of any rank from the other two tribes. There must have been few men in the first class of any urban tribe, and practically none in the Suburana and Esquilina, and the presiding officer's privilege of filling empty units by men of his choice would have contributed to the manipulation of the assembly.[19] Hence, either when the assembly was reformed after 241 or later, the Suburana and the Collina were, I believe, eliminated from the lot for the *praerogativa*.

In the assembly this lot was taken before the voters entered the Saepta, and the tribe on which the lot fell was called in first, while the others remained outside. The vote of this first tribe was formally announced before the rest of the first class voted. The stories in Livy of quarrels over the votes of the *praerogativa* during the Second Punic War deserve detailed consideration. In the election of consuls for the year 214 (Livy 24.7.10 to 9.3), the lot fell on the Aniensis iuniorum, that is on the century of juniors in the first class of the Aniensis tribe. This century voted for two consuls whom the consul holding the *comitia*, Q. Fabius Maximus, did not consider suitable commanders against Hannibal. The announcement of the vote of the *praerogativa* was evidently made outside the Saepta, and Fabius spoke there to the assembled citizens. He condemned the choice and ordered the herald to call back the Aniensis iuniorum to vote again. One of the men for whom the century had voted complained bitterly and declared that Fabius wanted to be consul himself (which was true). Fabius sent lictors to bring the complainer to order, and the Aniensis iuniorum voted again and chose Fabius and his friend, the great M. Claudius Marcellus, as consuls. All the rest of the centuries without variation voted for these two men. Four years later one of the consuls was holding the *comitia* and the *praerogativa,* Voturia iuniorum, cast its ballot for an aged man of distinction, T. Manlius Torquatus. As throngs surrounded him to congratulate him (evidently outside the Saepta where the announcement was made) he came to the tribunal, asked the privilege of speaking, and said that the condition of his eyes made it impossible for him to command (Livy 26.22). He urged that the Voturia iuniorum be called back to vote again, bearing in mind the fact that war was being waged in Italy against the Carthaginians and that their general was Hannibal. The spokesmen of the Voturia iuniorum said that they wished advice from their *seniores* in the same tribe, and asked for a place for a private conference. The place assigned was the *ovile,* another name for the Saepta. The advice of the elders was to choose among three men who were already tried commanders, Fabius and Marcellus and M. Valerius Laevinus. The older men were sent out of the Saepta (*senioribus dimissis*) and the juniors voted for Marcellus and Laevinus. Again all the other centuries followed the example of the *praerogativa*.[20]

The third example in the following year (Livy 27.6) was somewhat different. Another distinguished general, Q. Fulvius Flaccus, as dictator, was holding the *comitia,* and the *praerogativa,* Galeria iuniorum, voted for him and the aged Q. Fabius Maximus. The other centuries would have followed the example of the *praerogativa* if tribunes of the plebs had not intervened, evidently outside the Saepta. They protested against repeated consulships for the same individual and against the hideous precedent, *foedum exemplum,* of having the man holding the *comitia* make himself consul. The assembly was broken up and the tribunes were finally persuaded to follow the advice of the senate, which had already sponsored a law permitting repeated election of the same man during the period when the war was going on in Italy. Hence at a second assembly Fabius was elected to his fifth consulship and Fulvius to his fourth.

These were exceptional times, when, with the co-operation or connivance of men who appreciated their own merits, experienced generals were, by suspension of the laws, constantly reelected to the consulship. Evidently it took some persuasion of the *praerogativa* (or of the tribunes) to guide the assembly along these lines. Although there were later suspensions of the laws for emergencies, there is no later record of similar interruptions in the procedure of the assembly.[21]

These accounts are valuable not only for the names given to the *centuria praerogativa,* in each case the juniors of a rural tribe, but also for the evidence they provide for setting and procedure. In the election for 209 the juniors of the Voturia, after having voted, were sent to confer with their seniors into the *ovile,* that is the Saepta, and then, after the seniors were dismissed, the juniors voted again. Clearly the announcement of the vote was outside the Saepta. Inside there would have been a special enclosure for each tribe, such as is provided for the *curiae* in the Charter of Malaga (55). The incident helps us to see how the same site, eventually the Saepta Julia, could have been used for centuriate and tribal assemblies. Cicero (*Att.* 4.16.8) and Dio (53.23.2) both describe the Saepta Julia as a building for the tribal assembly, but in our period the centuriate assembly was a tribal body. The building was the site of the elections of consuls and praetors which followed the "nominating" convention of the *Tabula Hebana.*[22] The use of the same structure for centuries and tribes is indicated by Cicero's story (*Fam.* 7.30.1) of an election of a substitute consul on the last day of the year 45. Caesar had taken the auspices for an election of quaestors in the *comitia tributa.* At the second hour when a chair had been put in place for the *consul suffectus,* Q. Fabius Maximus, word came that he had died. Caesar, exhibiting the scorn he felt for Republican institutions, suddenly changed plans and called the centuriate assembly to elect a consul for the rest of a single day. He could disregard the auspices (he had shown in his first consulship how little he cared for them) and the omission of proper notification through a trumpeter from the walls and preparation of an armed guard on the Janiculum, but he could not have gone ahead with the assembly unless the voting place could have been accommodated to 193 centuries as well as to thirty-five tribes. The adjustment was easier because the centuries were now divisions of the tribes.

The seat for the *consul suffectus* was probably on the tribunal in front of the Saepta, the scene of the opening *contio,* of the announcement of votes, and of interruptions like those on the vote of the *praerogativa* or the protests of tribunes of the plebs against proceedings. It is likely that besides his colleague the consul had with him praetors and perhaps tribunes of the plebs, and that the candidates were on the same tribunal or certainly nearby where they could be seen (Chap. III, notes 61, 62).

The preliminary *contio* opened with a prayer, and was followed by speeches only if the centuries were called to pass on a bill for a law or judgment; for an election there was a regular formula (*carmen rogationis*) for asking the people to choose two consuls or the required number of praetors.[23] There were specific directions given as orders to the voters.[24] The presiding officer had already, one may assume, appointed men to vote in empty units, which always, I believe, existed in the urban tribes,[25] and in the late Republic, as I shall point out later, would probably have been common in the lower classes of foot-soldiers.

The urn would then be brought for the lot to determine the all-important choice from the first class of thirty-five or perhaps thirty-three tribes for the *centuria praerogativa.* The irregularities attested for the lot on other occasions probably affected the choice of this tribe less often, for the candidates would have had their *custodes* on guard. There is, in fact, reason to believe that for the *praerogativa* the candidate had more than one *custos* to look out for his interests.[26] The men in the first class of the tribe chosen by the lot would then be sent into the section assigned to their tribe in the Saepta, and the voting and counting of votes would be carried through while the crowd waited outside for the announcement. It was undoubtedly greeted always with manifestations of pleasure and disappointment, but, as far as we know, without protests from the voters such as had led during the Second Punic War to the recall of the *praerogativa* for a second vote. On one occasion, however, the presiding officer, Pompey, when the *praerogativa* voted for his enemy Cato for the praetorship, dissolved the assembly because he said he had heard thunder, a sign that always led to the dissolution of *comitia*.[27]

The procedure for a consular election in the year 44 is given by Cicero as follows: *sortitio praerogativae ... renuntiatur ... prima classis vocatur, renuntiatur, deinde, ita ut adsolet, suffragia, tum secunda classis*.[28] The lot for the *praerogativa* was followed by the vote and the announcement of the result for this century; then came the vote and announcement of the first class, then that of the six centuries of knights known as the *suffragia*, and then the second class, which in that case settled the issue, since there was a majority for the one candidate for office at this managed election. This passage indicates that the voting in the centuriate assembly was successive by classes. It is reasonably assumed from the passage that voting was simultaneous within the classes; this assumption is supported by the fact that Caesar, without much delay, could use for the centuriate assembly a building already prepared, presumably with the divisions for the thirty-five tribes already in place (Cic. *Fam.* 7.30.1).

The first class of *pedites*, from which one century of juniors had already voted as the *praerogativa*, could have been accommodated by taking the thirty-four centuries of juniors first, perhaps putting with them in the place of the *praerogativa* the century of artisans which Cicero lists with the first class; then would come the thirty-five centuries of seniors. A separate count of their vote is suggested by Horace in the *Ars Poetica* (341 ff.), who imagines the seniors exercising suffrage on the merits of poetry. It is to be noted that similarly senators and *equites* voted successively within each tribe in the *Tabula Hebana* (27–32).[29]

But there were other centuries in the first class. According to

Livy's account of a trial in the centuriate assembly, the twelve later
centuries of knights voted with the first class, making a total of eighty-
two centuries in this class.[30] The vote of the knights would presumably
have been called after that of the juniors and seniors. These centuries
were already established and they would not have had to be rearranged.

The whole count of *iuniores, seniores,* and *equites* would have to
be made before the vote of the first class was announced, and that
must have been a lengthy business, though the juniors could have
been counted while the seniors voted and the seniors while the knights
voted. The announcement of the entire first class, as we know from
Cicero, was then made, evidently outside the Saepta, and in the announcement the herald asked for the votes of each century individ-
ually.[31] It was apparently after the announcement of the vote of the
first class that a candidate for the praetorship of 174, not wishing to
be preferred to a member of the Scipionic house, pulled off his
whitened toga (*toga candida*), the sign of candidacy, and descended
from the tribunal, described as a *templum,* and began to electioneer
for the scion of the Scipios.[32] The story is valuable for the picture it
gives of continuous electioneering when votes were reported by classes.

Next would come the six most aristocratic centuries of knights,
known as the *sex suffragia,* divided not into the thirty-five urban and
rural tribes but in the ancient tribes of Romulus. It is striking that
Horace, imagining an assembly voting its estimate of poetry, lists as
voters not only the centuries of *seniores* but also the *celsi Ramnes,* one
of the centuries of Romulus. The count here would have been rapid,
and would also have been announced outside the Saepta. Since the
second class would often bring the decisive vote, Staveley's suggestion
that these *sex suffragia* served as *praerogativae* for the second class is
attractive.[33] These centuries were the voting place of the young men
of the nobility whose support (Q. Cicero, *Comm. pet.* 6) added greatly
to the dignity of the candidate for the consulship.

Probably before the second class was called into the Saepta, the
urn for the lot would be brought to the tribunal outside, and the
names of the tribes would be shaken from it to determine successively
which tribes of juniors and which of seniors should vote in each basket.
Let us assume that my figures are right and that the vote here had to
be reduced to twenty, ten for juniors and ten for seniors. One could
imagine two sets of baskets numbered from one to ten on either side

of the tribunal inside the Saepta. The members of the tribes which had been assigned to the numbered baskets would enter twenty of the thirty-five divisions of the Saepta, and proceed at once to vote.[34]

The total vote announced at this point would have amounted to at least 109, and if the required majority of 97 was reached for a law or judgment, the assembly would be dissolved.[35] When one candidate in an election obtained a majority, he was declared elected and presumably took the oath at once. Great stress was put on priority of announcement which brought with it certain advantages in the consulship, including the first place in the listing. Repeatedly we hear in the sources of elections by all the centuries, which means all until a majority was reached.

If only one candidate was chosen at this point, the balloting would go on to chose his colleague, the centuries voting now, it would seem, for only one man. Cicero as a candidate in 63 was evidently declared elected after the second class had voted, for he tells us that all the centuries voted for him. The voting was continued apparently to the end, and Antonius, who won, got only a few more centuries than Catiline.[36] The voting could not go on after sunset, and sometimes it was not completed at that time, or no second candidate had an absolute majority of the centuries.[37] Then the voting would have to be continued on the next comitial day in the calendar.

That must have occurred very frequently for the eight places of the late Republic in the praetorship, when both the voting and the counting of votes must have been slow. Sometimes there were disturbances or religious omens which required a complete repetition of proceedings. That was true of Cicero's election to the praetorship, which was carried out three times, in each of which, he tells us, he was put in the first place by all the centuries (De imp. Cn. Pomp. 2).

The lower classes had ceased before the beginning of our period to have real meaning for distinctions in types of armor once needed for the phalanx army. A temporary second century registration in the rural tribes of freedmen who had a census at least of the second class would have added to the enrollment in the first two classes,[38] but it is likely that the registration of the three lower classes declined in that century as the land of small farmers was steadily being swallowed up into large estates, and the supply of men for the legions and the vote was vanishing. The solution, already attempted from time to time, of drawing recruits mainly from the proletariate was definitely established by Marius at the end of the second century, and after that the registration in the classes, which had no meaning except for the vote, must have been more and more perfunctory and incomplete. Then came the great influx of new citizens after the Social War, when the Romans were far more statesmanlike in granting citizenship than they were in registering the citizens (*VD,* Chap. 9). Only a few were enrolled in the census of 86, and in the next recorded census, that of 70–69, the practical doubling of the citizen rolls certainly did not include all the new citizens, who were much more numerous than the old citizens. The richer men who could travel, many of them with enough property to be listed as *equites,* even though there was no place for them in the centuries of knights, were surely registered in the first class in much larger numbers than the poor men were in the four lower classes. The failure of five other sets of censors in the years 65–50 to complete the enrollment kept many eligible men off the lists. Cicero refers to the situation when in an oration of 56 he notes among other signs of decline in the state that *suffragia discripta tenentur a paucis,*[39] which means, I think, that there were few voters in the classes. Very likely there were empty units at the elections, and the consul in charge filled them as he liked, thus increasing the already extensive power of the presiding magistrate.

The old divisions of voters into classes were recognized as obsolete and there were efforts to discard them. Gaius Gracchus is said to have planned a law on the abolition of the classes, and a candidate for the consulship, who failed to be elected for 62, had a similar program which, according to Cicero, made people turn against him because they (or Cicero's friends among them) objected, he says (*Mur.* 47), to having all grades of dignity removed (*PP* 57). In the letter to Caesar just before his dictatorship, of which I think Sallust was the author, Caesar was urged to do away with the classes (Sall. *R.P.* 2.8.1), but they still existed in 44. They may have been removed in the sham assembly of the Empire, for we never hear of them after Caesar. It is significant that the *praerogativa centuria* chosen by lot from the *iuniores* of the first class no longer functioned in the centuriate gatherings of Augustus and Tiberius. The fifteen centuries of senators and knights of the *Tabula Hebana* took its place for a time and made known to the populace, as the eighteen centuries of knights with public horse had once done, the names of the men for whom they expected to vote.

The cumbersome procedure of the *comitia* was time-consuming. The voting and counting of votes in Caesar's assembly to elect one consul at the end of 45 took five hours, and, since there was only one candidate, the assembly must have been dissolved after the second class voted. The length of time required for the vote was undoubtedly one factor in the decreasing use of the *comitia centuriata* in the late Republic for any purpose except the election of consuls, praetors, and censors. It was used for the confirmation of the census (Cic. *Leg. agr.* 2.26), probably, as Botsford holds (*RA* 237), a perfunctory vote, and for declarations of war (*RA* 230), which seem to have been rare in the latter part of the period under study. For the Second Macedonian War the centuries voted adversely on the consul's first proposal of a bill for a declaration of war, but were persuaded by his speech at the *contio*, an effective oration in Livy's version (31.6–8), to change their vote on a second submission of the bill. Although a law passed by Sulla as consul in 88, later revoked by Cinna, restored the centuries to their old organization, he seems as dictator to have preferred the tribes for his legislation. The only attested legislative use of the centuries is for his restoration of the citizenship he had taken from the people of Arretium and Volaterrae (Cic. *Dom.* 79). In the year 60 a bill to be presented to the centuries was promulgated by the consul Metellus Celer, but was not voted on since Metellus himself was opposed to it (see Chap. IV, n. 9). The only bill of the years 70–50 known to have been voted on by the centuries was the one to recall Cicero from exile, a bill which, since it was connected with a capital charge, was not unrelated to the chief nonelective function of the centuries in our period, the judicial vote on *perduellio*, high treason, the most serious of all capital charges.[40]

The prosecutor for *perduellio* was regularly a tribune of the plebs whose motive was political, and the accused was an ex-magistrate (or occasionally a magistrate) who was charged with hostile action against the state, including action that lowered the dignity of the Roman people or of the tribunes who represented the people.

Although charges for minor political offenses punishable by a fine could be brought by aedile or tribune directly to the *comitia tributa* or the *concilium plebis*, a capital charge, to be punished by death or exile, was required, by provision of the Twelve Tables, to be submitted to the centuriate assembly. Such a charge, made by a quaestor, is reported in a corrupt passage of Varro's *De Lingua Latina* (6.90). Here the quaestor is ordered to send a message to a consul or praetor to ask for the auspices. The general view is that the major auspices and *imperium* essential for summons of the centuries were loaned to the quaestor by the higher magistrate. The capital charge for the prosecutions in the period we are considering was regularly *perduellio,* and in all cases except the incident in Varro the prosecutor was a tribune of the plebs. He is repeatedly represented as asking a praetor to fix the day (*diem dicere*) for the comitial trial. The usual view is that he received the auspices as a loan from the praetor and that he then called and conducted the centuriate assembly. The loaning of auspices and *imperium* to a quaestor is not too hard to imagine, for he was a minor magistrate with minor auspices, and he often assisted the consul or praetor. But for a tribune who was an officer not of the *populus* but of the *plebs* and had no auspices, the loan is startling. Could orders be given to the *exercitus urbanus* by a man clad in the undecorated toga of the ordinary citizen, seated on a low bench instead of on the curule chair, unattended by lictors bearing the axe and rods that symbolized power? Mommsen was troubled by the problem, but noted that the tribune of the plebs who abandoned the prosecution of the elder Tiberius Gracchus, censor of 169 (Livy 43.16), appears to have been in charge of proceedings (*StR* 1.195 f.; *Strafrecht* 168, n. 5).

But in my view the tribune and the quaestor of Varro were in charge not of the *comitia* but of the preliminary *contio*. Varro's citation comes from a *commentarius anquisitionis,* and the *anquisitio,* the investigation which preceded a comitial trial, consisted of four *contiones,* the last held immediately before the *comitia*. For cases tried in the tribal assembly the first three *contiones* were held with intervening days on the Rostra, and at the third *contio* the charge was fixed. The presiding officer, tribune or aedile, set the time, at least twenty-four days later, for the final *contio* (*quarta accusatio*) and the *concilium plebis* which he would conduct. For a capital charge the preliminary *contiones* followed the same system and, after the third, the tribune asked a praetor to set the day for a meeting of the *comitia centuriata*. That, in my view, was what the quaestor was ordered to do in Varro's quotation from the commentary. The whole emphasis, both in the document and in Varro's discussion, is on summoning the people. Neither in Varro nor in the sources for tribunicial trials for *perduellio* is there a word to show that the prosecutor was in charge of the voting.[41]

The right secured by the tribunes of the plebs who were debarred from trying capital cases in the *concilium plebis* was, I believe, not the right to preside with borrowed auspices over the *comitia centuriata* but the right to ask for (*petere*) or to demand (*poscere*) a meeting of the centuries, and to hold a *contio* for the final accusation in front of the Saepta before the praetor submitted the tribune's charge to the assembly. This right, perhaps already possessed by the quaestors, was acquired by the tribunes before the mid-third century. When the *contio,* with accusation and defense, was completed, the tribune would dissolve it and the praetor would call another *contio* and present to the assembled citizens the charge on which they were to give a negative or positive vote (*libero, damno*). Then he would give the command, *ite in suffragium, Quirites,* and the voters would file into the Saepta. The praetor would also preside at the announcement, class by class, of the vote and would dissolve the assembly as soon as a majority was reached. It is to be noted that at the trial of Rabirius for *perduellio* in 63 a praetor called off the assembly before the voting began. The idea of loaning the auspices to a tribune is based on a confusion in the sources between the preliminary *contio* and the *comitia.*[42]

Various charges of *perduellio,* others of which were dropped before the voting, are recorded in our period and are listed by Lange (*RAl* 2.557–65). The most fully attested trial of the second century is that of the censor P. Claudius Pulcher in 169 (Livy 43.16), who used the privilege available to the defendant of dispensing with the earlier accusations and pled his case at the Saepta. His fate was in doubt after the vote of the first class, but, on the plea of the leading senators and of his colleague, the elder Tiberius Gracchus, he was acquitted by a narrow margin (Chap. III) and the tribune announced his abandonment of the accusation he had expected to make against Gracchus.

In trials for *perduellio* the written ballot, used in centurial and tribal elections after 139 and in trials in the tribal assembly after 137, was not introduced until 107. The leading men were thus successful for some time in keeping the votes on *perduellio* under the supervision of *rogatores* appointed by the praetors who conducted the assemblies. In time the charge of *perduellio* was included in the charge of *maiestas* for which a special court with jurors was established in a law of 103 or 100. A permanent public court for *maiestas* with jury trial was a feature of the Sullan constitution.

After Sulla the only known trial for *perduellio* was held under Caesar's influence in the stormy year of Cicero's consulship, 63. It was preceded by a revival or an invention of an ancient form of condemnation for *perduellio* judged by two *duumviri,* an office to which Caesar and his cousin Lucius Caesar were appointed. The charge was against an aged senator C. Rabirius, accused of having murdered the tribune Saturninus thirty-seven years before. The judges condemned Rabirius to death, but the execution of the sentence was prevented by Cicero as consul (*Rab. perd.* 10). There followed a formal charge of *perduellio,* made by the tribune T. Labienus, a close associate of Caesar. According to the well-argued view that has recently met with favor, it is to this trial that Cicero's fragmentary speech for Rabirius belongs. There is an allusion to one of the earlier *contiones* of Labienus on the Rostra, at which he exhibited an image of Saturninus (25), to Rabirius' own defense, that of his counsel Hortensius, and also to the hearing of witnesses (18) which must have taken place at those *contiones.* Cicero's defense, limited by Labienus to a half hour, must have been given at the final *contio* in front of the Saepta, for there is a prayer that the gods would permit the day that had dawned to bring safety to Rabirius (5) and there is an exhortation to the voters (35). Labienus' *crudelis accusatio,* the text of which was apparently known to Quintilian (5.13.20), was probably delivered after Cicero spoke. The whole case was political in its purpose, designed to arouse opposition to the use of the senatorial decree of martial law under which Saturninus met his death. A similar use of the decree against Catiline was in prospect at the time. The centuriate assembly, because of the power of senators in its organization, might have voted in favor of Rabirius. But the praetor Metellus Celer who, as Caesar's agent, was, in my view, to conduct the assembly, avoided any such outcome by dashing to the Janiculum before the voting began and pulling down the red flag, an act that implied that the height had been occupied, as it used to be in the Kingship and the early Republic, by enemy forces. The act was in accord with the anachronistic character of the assembly. The attack on the authority of the senate had had effect on public opinion even without the vote.[43]

The only known law passed in the centuriate assembly in the years 70–49 is that proposed and passed by the consul Lentulus Spinther to recall Cicero from exile in 57. A vigorous effort had been made to have Cicero recalled, as the great Metellus Numidicus had been, by a tribunicial bill passed by the tribes, but there were tribunes ready to veto, and in the end the plan had to be abandoned. The decision was then to call the centuries, with a preliminary senatorial decree making threats against tribunes who might veto. The decision was explained by the claim, based on provisions in the Twelve Tables, that only the centuries were competent to pass on the life (or exile) of a citizen, and there was also the claim that Clodius' laws which led to the exile were invalid.[44] The consul in charge, with the authority of the senate, summoned all Italy to the *comitia,* and men came in such throngs that according to Clodius they caused a food shortage. The same centuries from all Italy that had elected him consul, Cicero declares, now restored him to citizenship.[45]

As I have pointed out elsewhere (*PP* 60–62), the details we have on this vote show the fundamental difference between the tribal and the centuriate assemblies. The former, especially for legislation scheduled at no special season, was mainly in the hands of the people who lived in Rome or who chanced to be there at the time. The latter, taking place at a stated period—July after Sulla—brought throngs to Rome, and the most important groups in the throngs were the landed gentry of the Italian towns, many of them *equites,*[46] men who had long traditions of association with the Roman nobility and were ready to listen to their pleas to vote for the candidates they preferred.

It is significant that Caesar used the *comitia centuriata* for some at least of the constitutional legislation of his dictatorship (Cic. *Phil.* 1.19). By that time he had no reason to fear the power of the nobles over the voters of Italy. But he did have a good deal of trouble with tribunes whose choice in part he left to the people. The stories of the tribune Pontius Aquila's refusal to rise at Caesar's triumph in 45 and of Flavus and Marullus who removed a diadem from Caesar's statue in 44 are too familiar to require repetition. One can see why Caesar preferred the vote in the centuriate assembly. He could hardly have agreed with Cicero (*Leg.* 3.45) that the decisions of the people were wiser when they were divided according to wealth and rank and age, but he surely recognized that they were easier for him to control.

The power of the presiding magistrate, referred to often in this discussion, can be most clearly seen in the abundant sources for the consular elections. The consul in charge could discourage individuals from seeking the office and could refuse to put them on the official list of candidates. Occasionally he might go as far as a consul did in blocking the candidacy of the "restorer" of the tribunes' powers, Palicanus, and declare that he would not announce the victory even if Palicanus won. He could, perhaps on religious grounds, postpone the date of election until voters supporting his candidates arrived in Rome and other voters he distrusted had gone home. After the *comitia* met, he could "hear thunder" as Pompey did when he saw Cato being elected or find an excuse, perhaps in the auspices or the procedure in the lot (there he needed the help of an augur) to dismiss the *comitia* before the vote was completed. He could take account of charges of irregularity or violence. He could assign to empty units voters he trusted and he could appoint his henchmen as *custodes,* important sources of power that have not been sufficiently considered. Although the influence of the presiding magistrate has been overestimated by some scholars, it was undeniably great.[47]

But the patrician and plebeian nobility, that is the men of consular families who controlled the senate, found means to prevent too great abuse of power on the part of the consuls who presided over *comitia,* and to insure the distribution of the highest offices mainly among members of their own group. The seemingly democratic reform of the centuriate assembly after 241 made little change in the men who won the consulship. Of the 355 consuls from 218 to 49, more than half came from seventeen *gentes,* about four-fifths from thirty *gentes.* The majority were plebeians, for, although the Cornelii in many branches were the predominant house, with more than a tenth of the consulships, the old patricians were dying out. In this period there were not more than a dozen men who rose without senatorial ancestry to the consulship and only one, Cicero, in the last forty-four years of the period. The nobility was a comparatively closed group of men who, in passing the consulship from hand to hand (Sallust, *Jug.* 63.6), succeeded in circumventing attempts, like the proposal to destroy the classes, to democratize the assembly. The nobles maintained relations with the upper income groups in the first and second classes in citizen communities and they kept their power by slowing down grants of citizenship in the second century and by interfering with the census and thus preventing the registration of citizens after the Social War. They were so strong that even Pompey, Crassus, and Caesar in league were not sure that they could obtain a consulship for 55 for Crassus and Pompey, and so managed through tribunes to delay the elections until winter when some of the voters had gone home and when Caesar, his summer campaign over, had sent down many of his legionary soldiers to vote.

But by this time the men elected to win immortality by giving their names to years were comparatively unimportant, for they no longer controlled the prizes of empire, the zones of military command, and the armies assigned to them. These prizes had been won through laws passed in the tribal assembly by tribunes of the plebs in the service of the great generals, the younger Scipio, Marius, Pompey, Crassus, and the final victor Caesar. The tribal assembly, conducted by a tribune sitting like a member of the populace on a low bench, had provided the means of negating the power of the archaic centuriate assembly, still controlled by an oligarchy. The road led inevitably to monarchy.

Julius Caesar planned to dignify the assemblies in the Campus Martius by giving them a permanent marble structure. But he showed his scorn for the voting populace, when as dictator he had a consul chosen for a single day, a man in whose consulship, Cicero says, nobody breakfasted. "All this seems amusing to you," Cicero writes to a friend (*Fam.* 7.30), "for you aren't here. If you were a witness, you couldn't keep from crying." Caesar's successor, the Princeps Augustus, made a show of reviving the assemblies, giving them splendid settings at the Rostra, at Divus Julius, at Castor, and in the great hall of the marble Saepta, first planned by Caesar. Later emperors manifested little or no interest in the tribal assemblies, but they continued for generations to call the centuries for the consular *comitia*. The gathering place was still the marble Saepta, kept outside the much enlarged sacred limits of the city. There the citizens, with abandonment, it would seem, of the old divisions into voting units, continued to go through the *longum carmen,* the long ritual of the *comitia centuriata.* There the henchmen designated by the emperors for office were acclaimed as consuls elected by a sovereign people.

VI

THE ASSEMBLIES IN THEIR SETTING
A SUMMARY

THIS investigation of the centuriate and tribal assemblies in their setting has been presented in the hope that the procedure will be clearer not only to students of Roman civilization but also to historians and archaeologists who often fail to speak a common language. The most important results concern the tribal legislative and judicial assemblies held in the Forum (where our information on setting is better than it is for Capitol and Circus Flaminius) and the tribal elections and centuriate assembly held in the Campus Martius at a temporary structure that preceded the Saepta Julia. The choice of different places for the elective and legislative assemblies has been clarified by Fraccaro's demonstration that the tribes voted successively in legislation and simultaneously in elections. On methods of voting and lot-casting the *Tabula Hebana* has contributed new evidence both for the tribes and for the centuries and has provided an amazing confirmation of Mommsen's theory of the method of counting votes in the reformed centuriate assembly. My discussion of procedure has, I hope, been made clearer by the illustrations from Republican coins of voting symbols, of a voting scene, and of the Rostra on which stands the bench of the tribune of the plebs, and by the plan of the Saepta.

The Comitium, site of the curiate assembly and, until the midsecond century, of the successive votes of the tribes, was an enclosed area with steps which led up to the Curia where the senate met. Earlier suggestions that the area was stepped are now strongly supported by the discovery of the Comitium and Curia of the Latin colony Cosa. The steps at Cosa seem designed for standing, not sitting, and there is abundant evidence that the Romans stood in their public meetings and assemblies. Cicero in a remarkable passage in the *Pro Flacco* stresses the rashness of assemblies in Greek cities where, without previous consideration and without dividing citizens into their units, a seated audience voted the worst possible measures. As Theodor Mommsen suggested, fear that the Romans might adopt the Greek custom of using theaters for their assemblies is the real, though not the declared, reason for the effective opposition to the erection of a permanent theater at Rome.

The original inaugurated speaker's platform, perhaps on steps leading down from Curia to the floor of the Comitium, was replaced in 338 by a new platform, also inaugurated, which was erected between the Comitium and the Forum. Known from its adornment as the Rostra, it was designed for speaking to the larger audiences which could gather for *contiones* in the Forum. The magistrate presiding over legislation, after facing the Forum for the preliminary *contio*, would then, as the tribes were called in one by one to vote, face the Comitium, whose curve seems still to be preserved in the rear of the Rostra on the site to which Caesar moved it. Here there were steps by which the men, after advancing over the *pontes* to give their votes to the *rogatores,* could descend.

Perhaps because the limited space of the Comitium was too small even for one tribe, a tribune of 145 led the people out from Comitium to Forum to cast their ballots. Since there were no steps leading to the Rostra on that side, there was, I suggest, a wooden attachment with steps which could be added to the Rostra for *comitia,* a structure which would explain the curious phrase in the prescript of laws, stating that the measure was passed *pro rostris,* properly "in front of the Rostra." This structure, in place for an assembly, provides, in my view, an explanation for the scene on Palicanus' coin, issued to celebrate his father's revival of tribunicial legislation.

Across the Forum at the Temple of Castor, where *comitia* were frequently held in the first century, there seems originally to have been a separated tribunal in front of the temple, whose position, as Professor Frank suggested, may explain the phrase *pro aede Castoris,* "in front of the Temple of Castor"; it may have been used primarily by the censors for the quadrennial census of the eighteen centuries of *equites.* When Metellus Delmaticus rebuilt the temple after his triumph of 117, the tribunal, perhaps adorned with beaks of captured ships, became an organic part of the structure. The tribunal was approached not by central steps but by lateral staircases on either side of the forecourt. These curious stairs, maintained in Tiberius' reconstruction of the temple, served, I believe, as the rear of the Rostra had once served, for the attachment of the *pontes* and for the descent of the voters. There is a somewhat similar plan in the Temple of Divus Julius, which certainly had a platform adorned with beaks, though here the steps are on either side of the temple façade.

For simultaneous voting, which surely prevailed in tribal elections of the first century, much more space was needed than for the legislative votes, tribe by tribe, for it was necessary to have thirty-five separate columns of voters. The only recorded tribal elections before the first century consist of one in the Campus Martius for 121 B.C. and two on the Capitol, in 194 and 133. Since the Area Capitolina had inadequate space for thirty-five columns, Fraccaro suggested that until the written ballot was instituted tribal elections were also carried out by successive voting, but I have questioned the evidence for the two elections on the Capitol, suggesting that one was a vote on *imperium* in the curiate assembly, not attended by the people, and arguing that the other, Tiberius Gracchus' last assembly, was not an election but a vote on a law to permit reelection to the tribunate. The tribal elections had, I believe, long been carried out with simultaneous voting in the Campus Martius.

The Saepta Julia, planned by Caesar and built by Lepidus and Agrippa, replaced a temporary wooden structure on approximately the same site and probably of similar plan. The Saepta Julia are known from the Marble Plan and from the wall of the west portico beside the Pantheon. The entrance to the Saepta, as the fragmentary plan and a statement of Frontinus show, was on the northern end. There were exits for the voters, one of which is indicated on the plan, on the southern ends of the east and west walls. The entrance could be closed after the voters had entered the thirty-five divisions which ran not, as usually believed, from east to west but from north to south. The same divisions could have been used by the centuriate assembly, for, between 241 and 218, probably in the former year, the centuries had become divisions of the tribes. The vote here was successive by classes, and I have tried to show how the eighty-two centuries of the large first class could have been accommodated in the Saepta, with thirty-five centuries of juniors voting together, then thirty-five of seniors, and finally twelve of *equites*. The Republican Saepta were the place of legislative votes in the centuries, rare in our period, and also of the judicial assemblies, not infrequent before Sulla in trials for *perduellio,* but the Saepta were never used for legislative or judicial votes of the tribes. For them Augustus constructed a new voting place at the Temple of Divus Julius, site of the only imperial law (of 9 B.C.) for which the place of the doubtless perfunctory voting is attested.

The Saepta, with divisions through which the voters walked to cast their ballots, could not have been used for the opening *contio,* an unsorted gathering from which the citizens were sent into their tribes to vote. The site of the *contio* was the open space at the northern side, described by Frontinus as the front of the Saepta. In that space there was a large tribunal, inaugurated as a *templum,* and on it sat the magistrate with his colleagues, accompanied, if he was a consul or praetor, by the tribunes of the plebs. On the tribunal for elections were also the candidates on foot, in a place where the voters could see them. For the legislative and judicial assemblies of the centuries there were always speeches at the *contiones,* but for the elections the *contio* was limited to the preliminary prayer and the directions to the voters, with the addition in the centuriate assembly of the casting of lots to select from the juniors of the first class the *centuria praerogativa* which cast the first vote.

The opening *contio* was not the only *contio* at the Saepta. There was another for the announcement of the total vote of the tribal elections, and at the centuriate assembly there was one for the announcement of the vote of the *centuria praerogativa* and of every class, with the inclusion of any lot-casting required for later classes. But before these *contiones* the citizens had to vote, a lengthy process for the thirty-five tribes, and then, if they wished to hear the announcement of results, had a long wait while the votes were counted. This waiting period when many citizens were in the Campus was a good time for candidates and their friends to seek support at subsequent electoral *comitia.* When all the votes were counted in the tribes, the citizens gathered again at the front of the Saepta, with the candidates again in evidence. The final *contio* for tribal announcements began with lot-casting to determine the order of announcement of the tribal vote, an order that might have some effect on the outcome, since the winners for two places for the aedileship, for instance, would have been the first two men announced to have carried a majority of the tribes, not necessarily the two men with the largest number of tribes to their credit. But since the votes of all the tribes had already been counted, the announcements would have no such effect on votes of tribes called later as we can see in the successive votes of the states in our nominating conventions. There is evidence of such effects in the successive legislative votes of the tribes, and also in the successive votes in the centuriate assembly, with announcement of the results in the *centuria praerogativa* and then in each class. The *centuria praerogativa,* chosen by lot and therefore thought to show the will of Heaven, had such effect on the outcome that when Hannibal was in Italy proceedings were interrupted by protests of the presiding officer against the choice of consuls whom he deemed unfit to command the citizen soldiers. This *contio* and those held for the announcement of successive classes were noisy, with expressions of approbation and disappointment and sometimes with active electioneering for candidates threatened with defeat. The excitement was great when a majority was reached. As soon as a candidate secured a majority, he took the oath and was declared elected. When a majority of the 193 centuries was announced for a law or judgment or for the full slate of officers to be filled, the *contio* was dismissed without calling the other centuries, and the successful candidates, accompanied by friends, made their way to the Capitol to give thanks to Jupiter Optimus Maximus, the god of the *comitia.*

For me, this investigation has brought a realization of the difference, previously not clear to many, between the unsorted *contio* which opened every assembly and the succeeding *comitia* for which the people had divided themselves into their units in order to vote. To the *contio* belonged the addresses to the people, both by the presiding magistrate and by the people whom he admitted to the platform, and also the presentation to the people of the question (*rogatio*) to be answered in the *comitia.* The only business of the *comitia* was to secure, by oral or written vote, a positive or negative answer on a law or judgment or a list of the names preferred by each voter in an election to office.

Failure to distinguish between *contio* and *comitia* has led most scholars, unmindful of the protests of Lange and Gilbert, to misinterpret the act of the tribune of 145 B.C., who in Cicero's version turned on the Rostra from Comitium to Forum. It was for the *comitia,* not the *contio,* which he would already have addressed to the people in the Forum, that this tribune turned. The lack of realization of the contrast between the unsorted *contio* and the divided *comitia* has led to the view that patricians of the late Republic were not debarred from the *concilium plebis.* The patricians believed to have been present were either at the *contio* or were going about the Forum seeking to influence

groups of citizens divided up by tribes. The idea that patricians attended the *concilium plebis* has resulted in the mistaken belief that
the distinction between the *comitia tributa* conducted by a regular
magistrate and the assembly the plebs conducted by a tribune had
practically disappeared in the late Republic. But no Roman, looking at
the tribune's bench, whose restoration to the Rostra is celebrated by
Palicanus, or seeing the presiding tribune clad in an undecorated toga
and unaccompanied by lictors, would have had any doubt that he was
attending a meeting of the *plebs,* representing a sort of antistate at
Rome.

The most striking example of confusion between *contio* and *comitia*
in my view is the general assumption that in trials for *perduellio* the
tribune borrowed the auspices from a praetor and actually conducted
the centuriate assembly. The tribune was in charge not of the *comitia*
but of the *anquisitio,* the preliminary investigation which took place
at four *contiones,* the last held at the Saepta immediately before the
comitia. Debarred from bringing capital charges to the *concilium
plebis,* the tribune had, before the middle of the third century, acquired
the right to demand that a praetor call the centuries to pass on the
charge which he had made at the last of three *contiones* in the Forum,
and of holding his last *contio,* the *quarta accusatio,* at the Saepta just
before the praetor in a separate *contio* presented the accusation prepared by the tribune and sent the citizens in to vote. If I am right in
my analysis of the trials for *perduellio,* the result is of significance for
the nature of the assemblies before the limited period of this investigation.

It is not my purpose to outline here all the points of procedure that
I have sought to establish. The most important, the evidence derived
from the *Tabula Hebana* for the counting of votes in the centuriate
assembly, has already been analyzed and interpreted by Tibiletti and
other scholars. But in the investigation of the lot both in tribes and in
centuries I hope that I have been able to make a new contribution. It
is significant that the lot in the assemblies was used not for the choice
of individuals except in tie votes in tribes, but for the selection of voting
units, on which the outcome depended at Rome. The method of lot
casting is illuminated by the Second Act of the *Casina,* in which I
have seen a conscious attempt on the part of Plautus to make his
audience think of the lot-taking they knew in the assemblies. Of
particular interest is the evidence of the role of the augurs in seeing

that the lot was fairly taken. That was, in my view, one of their functions at the assemblies where they were always on call.

The role of the ordinary citizen, who appears in the sources mainly as a supporter of men of the senatorial class, is not enhanced by what we know of the setting. In theory there was universal suffrage, but the provisions for voting were not adequate for the qualified voters. In the Forum there was probably room enough in front of the Rostra and the Temple of Castor for the tribes to vote one by one on legislation, for which few Italians came to Rome, but until Caesar moved the Rostra to a central position there was hardly space for the masses in the unsorted *contiones*. The Area Capitolina, where crowding is repeatedly stressed in the sources, provided much less space. Yet it was here that the tribunes from the Hannibalic War to the Gracchi seem most often to have held their legislative and judicial assemblies. One suspects that the tribunes may have had a hand in determining who gained access to the area in the final *contio* before the *comitia* were called. In the Campus, if I am right that the Saepta Julia were based on the plan of the Republican Saepta, we can, with new evidence, make a better estimate of capacity. My tentative conclusion is that if all the equal units were filled, each with approximately the same number of men, the Saepta would have held about 70,000 men. The size was probably adequate for the centuriate assembly, where men without property were practically disfranchised and where the registration in the classes had declined drastically. But the situation was different in the tribal elections. In the city of Rome alone there must have been many more than 70,000 male citizens. The great bulk of them were in the four urban tribes, with suffrage of so little value that it was not worth exercising, even if it was possible to get into the Saepta. But in the rural tribes too there was great disparity, partly from the size of the tribes and their distance from Rome, partly from the fact that large numbers came on occasion to vote for a native son. In those cases many probably did not succeed in entering the Saepta, although the noise they had made in the campaign may have been an asset to the candidate. There is no doubt that manipulation was a constant feature of the assemblies. The arch manipulator was Caesar who, while moving the Rostra to a place which could accommodate great throngs at the *contiones* and while continuing his plans for the great marble Saepta in the Campus, actually destroyed the power of both legislative and elective *comitia*.

Notes

1. On the *contio* see Mommsen, *StR* 1. 197–202; Botsford, *RA* 139–51. See Asconius 71 C (56 Stangl, whose text I cite): *Astat populus confusus ut semper alias, ita et in contione. Id ⟨eo ceteris⟩ peractis, cum id solum superest, ut populus sententiam ferat, iubet eum is qui fert legem discedere: quod verbum non hoc significat quod in communi consuetudine: eant de eo loco ubi lex feratur, sed in suam quisque tribum discedat in qua est suffragium laturus.* The form *conventio* appears in the *S.C. de Bacchanalibus* (*ILS* 18) of 186 B.C. and in Varro, *L.L.* 6.88, a quotation from the *commentarii consulares*. See Chap. V, n. 41.
2. See Walde-Hoffmann, *Lateinisches etymologisches Wörterbuch* (Heidelberg, 1, 1938; 2, 1954), s.v. "Suffragium" and the valuable article of M. Rothstein, *Beiträge zur alten Geschichte, Festschrift Otto Hirschfeld* (Berlin, 1903) 30–33; Botsford, *RA* 156 f.
3. On the three types of assemblies see Aulus Gellius' quotation (15.27) from an imperial jurist, Laelius Felix: *Cum ex generibus hominum suffragium feratur, 'curiata' comitia esse; cum ex censu et aetate, 'centuriata'; cum ex regionibus et locis, 'tributa'; centuriata autem comitia intra pomerium fieri nefas esse, quia exercitum extra urbem imperari oporteat, intra urbem imperari ius non sit. Propterea centuriata in campo Martio haberi exercitumque imperari praesidii causa solitum, quoniam populus esset in suffragiis ferendis occupatus.*
4. Ovid, *F.* 2.531, *stultaque pars populi quae sit sua curia nescit,* with Frazer's notes on lines 525, 527; Wissowa, *RK²* 158. On the *comitia curiata* see Botsford's excellent chapter, *RA* 168–200, and Staveley's review of recent discussions by Heuss and others, *Historia* 4 (1956) 84–90.
5. Cic. *Corn.* in Ascon. 77 C. Livy, 3.54.1, seems to place the election on the Aventine. Mommsen, *StR* 3.378 f., held, on the basis of Dio 41.43,

that the *comitia curiata* had to meet inside the *pomerium,* but noted that the Capitol was not strictly within the *pomerium.* The limitation was perhaps to the city and a radius within a mile of the *pomerium.* See also Livy 5.52.15–16.

6. See Botsford on the *comitia calata, RA* 152–67. There is some uncertainty about terminology. See Antistius Labeo, quoted by Gellius 15.27.1.

7. See n. 3 above. The usual description of the site of the assembly (see Castagnoli, *CM* 121–25) is simply *in campo;* on one occasion (Pliny, *N.H.* 16.37) the site named is *in Aesculeto,* now proved, from the discovery of a record of the *vicus Aesculetus* found on the Via Arenula (*CIL* 6.30957 = *ILS* 3615), to be in the Campus Martius. Another place mentioned twice for the assembly in Livy's records of the fourth century is the *lucus Petelinus extra portam Flumentanam* (6.20.11; 7.41.3; cf. Plut. *Camil.* 36), whose position depends on the controversial location of the Porta Flumentana. To this place the assembly was moved from the Campus Martius in 384 for the trial of Marcus Manlius, the savior of the Capitol during the occupation of the city by the Gauls. The reason for moving the assembly was to find a place where the Capitol could not be seen; perhaps, as von Gerkan (*Röm. Mitt.* 46 [1931] 166) suggested, the view was cut off by the grove. The site was certainly outside the *pomerium,* but, with the new position of the Circus Flaminius, one may doubt whether Castagnoli is right in holding that it also was in the region of the Campus Martius. There is an imperial instance of *improbae comitiae* on the Aventine (*CIL* 6.10213 = ILS 6044), an unusual instance described in unusual Latin in an inscription recording the election of Sejanus to the consulship in 31 A.D. See Syme, *Hermes* 84 (1956) 257–66. It is, however, to be noted that the Aventine at the time was still outside the *pomerium* in which the Emperor Claudius later included it. The Saepta, attested as the place of regular elections in the early part of the reign of Tiberius (see *Tabula Hebana* 35), remained outside the *pomerium* when it was extended by Claudius and Vespasian. For the *pomerium* stones see Lugli, *Fontes ad topographiam veteris urbis Romae* 1 (Rome, 1952) 128–31. On the relation of the *pomerium* to the newly established site of the Saepta, I quote from a letter of Professor Lugli of Sept. 28, 1965: "I Saepta col Diribitorium rimanevano certamente fuori, insieme col Divorum e la Porta Triumphalis." See also Castagnoli, *CM* 186 f.

8. For the auspices see Botsford's excellent chapter, *RA* 100–18, where the relation of the auspices to Jupiter (disregarded by K. Latte. *Röm. Religionsgesch.* Munich, 1960) is clearly brought out, as it is also in A. Magdelain's interesting paper, "Auspicia ad patres redeunt," *Collection Latomus* 70 (1964) 427–73. See also Mommsen, *StR* 1.76–116, and, for the late Republic, my *PP,* chap. iv.

9. See 6.14 on the power of the people and 15–17 on interlocking power of magistrates, senate, and people, with F. W. Walbank's valuable notes, *A Historical Commentary on Polybius* 1 (Oxford, 1957). It is note-

worthy that here the *equites* are included with the people (17.1, with Walbank's note).

10. See the arguments of Kurt von Fritz, *The Theory of the Mixed Constitution in Antiquity* (New York, 1954) 123–54; for other views see Walbank's notes on Polybius 6.11a (pp. 663 ff.).

11. Particularly striking are three passages where *comitia capitis* (*capiti*) are referred to, *Aul.* 700, *Truc.* 819, and *Pseud.* 1232. In the last case the *comitia centuriata,* which had jurisdiction over capital cases, is specifically mentioned. Of interest for the *contio* is the paper of J. P. Morel, "Pubes et contio d'après Plaute et Tite-Live," *REL* 42 (1964) 375–88.

12. On Dionysius see the series of articles now being published by Emilio Gabba in *Athenaeum* (for the most recent, vol. 42 [1964] 29–41).

13. Konrat Ziegler's comprehensive article on Plutarch in *RE* (publ. 1951) devotes about ten times as much space to the *Moralia* as to the *Lives;* the general discussion of Plutarch's life, his training, his friends, his style, and so forth is of great value.

14. For Appian see the bibliography cited by E. Gabba in his *Appiano e la storia delle guerre civili* (Florence, 1956), in his edition of Appian *B.C.* 1 (Florence, 1958), and in *Riv. Filol.* 92 (1964), 230–32.

15. Fergus Millar's excellent book, *A Study of Cassius Dio* (Oxford, 1964), stresses Dio's relation to his own times and his method of collecting his material and writing his history. Earlier investigations have dealt mainly with Dio's sources. For a favorable evaluation of Dio for the late Republic see Eduard Meyer, *Caesars Monarchie und das Principat des Pompeius,* 2nd ed. (the third is practically identical), Stuttgart and Berlin (1919) 610 f.

16. *CIL* 1.2².583, 585. For the entire set of Republican laws, collected from literary as well as inscriptional sources, see *FIRA* 1, pp. 23–156.

17. There is need of a comprehensive survey of investigations and interpretations of the Roman constitution before Mommsen; a discussion of the assemblies along that line would be revealing for modern developments.

18. See Alfred Heuss, *Theodor Mommsen und das 19. Jahrhundert* (Kiel, 1956), especially 44–57 on the *Staatsrecht.*

19. From the preface of the second edition, reprinted in the third, Vol. 1, p. xiii. Mommsen's earlier treatments of many of the problems are to be found in the two volumes of his *Römische Forschungen* (Berlin, 1864, 1879). See also, for earlier and later discussions, the seven volumes of Mommsen's *Gesammelte Schriften* (Berlin, 1905–13). For later interpretations of the judicial assemblies see his *Römisches Strafrecht,* published in Leipzig in 1899, four years before his death.

20. P. F. Girard's French translation, *Le Droit public romain* appeared in Paris in 1889–90.

21. W. Kunkel's summary of recent work on constitutional history, *Zeitsch. Sav. St.* 77 (1960) 345–82, pays more attention to the later Republic,

but limits the publications considered to volumes 2 and 3 of De Martino's work and J. Bleicken's *Volkstribunat.*
22. See Staveley's review, *CR* 12 (1962) 73–75. For significant recent work
    on the trials for *perduellio* in the *comitia centuriata,* see Chap. V, with
    notes 40–44.

CHAPTER II

1. Livy 43.16; *De vir. ill.* 73. Cf. Mommsen, *StR* 2.289, n. 1, and, for general
   treatment of the tribunate, 272–330. Recent bibliography is extensively
   cited in J. Bleicken's important *Volkstribunat.*
2. See the text of the *lex repetundarum* and the *lex agraria,* both of the last
   quarter of the second century. *CIL* 1.2².583, 585; *FIRA* 1, pp. 84 ff.,
   102 ff. For a recent English translation see *ARS,* nos. 45, 51.
3. See my *FG.* On the desertion of the Rostra see Cic. *Cluent.* 110. Mommsen's view was that Sulla permitted legislation by tribunes only with
   the authority of the senate, but his view was based on his dating of the
   Lex Antonia de Termessibus before 70. My dating of the law in 68
   (*CP* 36 [1941] 121, n. 32) has been accepted, with additional arguments,
   by Broughton (*MRR* 2. 130, n. 4 and 141, n. 8) and, more recently, by
   Syme (*JRS* 53 [1963] 55–60). Other evidence supports the view that
   Sulla removed all law making from the tribunes.
4. The general belief that *contiones* could not be held on *nundinae* (a belief
   in conflict with the clear evidence of Cicero, *Att.* 1.14.1) is based on
   Macrobius, *Sat.* 1.16.29, who quotes the augur Julius Caesar, evidently
   Lucius, *cos.* 64: *Iulius Caesar XVI auspiciorum libro negat nundinis
   contionem advocari posse, id est cum populo agi, ideoque nundinis
   Romanorum haberi comitia non posse.* But the phrase *agere cum
   populo* (Gell. 13.16, quoted at the beginning of Chap. I) definitely
   refers to *comitia;* as the end of the perhaps abbreviated passage from
   L. Caesar shows, the *contio* described here is the one that immediately
   preceded the *comitia.* See *StR* 1. 191 f. In Cic. *Att.* 4.3.4, *a.d. X. Kal.
   nundinae. contio biduo nulla,* the point is that the election of aediles was
   prevented by the *nundinae* and that incidentally the *contiones,* which
   Cicero had just mentioned, were discontinued.
5. Val. Max. 6.2.3. Cf. Vell. 2.4.4.; *De vir. ill.* 58. For the Circus Flaminius
   as the probable site of this interview, placed by Valerius Maximus on the
   Rostra, see n. 13 of this chapter.
6. For *privati* as speakers see Cic. *Leg.* 3.11; *Corn.* quoted in Ascon. 71 C.
   See Chap. IV, n. 37. Cf. Livy 45.21.6, *ne quis prius intercederet legi
   quam privatis suadendi dissuadendique legem potestas facta esset.* See
   also Livy 45.36.1; Dio 39.35.1; Dion. Hal. 5.11.2; Plut. *Publ.* 3.2. Botsford, *RA* 147, is mistaken, in my view, in accepting the statement of
   Dionysius (10.41.1) that the herald invited anyone who wished to
   speak against a law. Cf. Mommsen, *StR* 3.395, with n. 2.
7. The most important evidence is provided by Cic. *Dom.* 45. For discussion

and citation of other evidence see Mommsen, *StR* 3.356, n. 2; *Strafrecht* 168–70; A. H. J. Greenidge, *The Legal Procedure of Cicero's Time* (Oxford, 1901) 345–49. See Chap. V, with notes 40–43.

8. For citation of the evidence, see Wissowa, *RK*² 527 ff.; for interesting comments see K. Latte, *Röm. Religionsgesch.* (Munich, 1960) 42 f. For the Rostra as a *templum* see Livy 8.14.12; Cic. *De imp. Cn. Pomp.* 70; *Sest.* 75; *Vat.* 24.

9. For *comitia* on the Capitol see Chap. III, n. 38.

10. Auctor ad Heren. 4.68. See Fraccaro, *Studi sull'età dei Gracchi* (Città di Castello, 1914) 182.

11. *Capitolium* 35 (1960), no. 7, 3–12; see H. Bloch *JRS* 51 (1961) 143–52, with map prepared by Professor Gatti and his associates.

12. See Castagnoli, *CM* 113 ff.

13. The specific use of the Circus for a *contio* is attested before Cicero only in the case of M. Claudius Marcellus recorded below, but it was probably the site used by every proconsul who spoke to the people. Although Valerius Maximus has Scipio Aemilianus speak on the Rostra (see n. 5 above), if he was brought to a platform almost from the city gate, it must have been that at the Circus Flaminius, for Scipio surely had some time to wait before his triumph. For Pompey's *contio* there before his triumph see Cic. *Att.* 1.14.1–2; for Clodius' interrogation of the consuls Gabinius and Piso held there in order to insure Caesar's presence (Dio 38.17.1), see Cic. *Red. sen.* 17; *Sest.* 35. Augustus, refraining from entering the *pomerium* because he was just returning from a campaign, gave his funeral oration for the Elder Drusus there (Dio 55.2.2).

14. Livy 27.21.1; Plut. *Marc.* 27. The Claudian associates of Marcellus (*necessarii Claudii*) obtained permission, apparently from the senate, for his return and his presence when action was taken (Livy 27.20.12). For the bill for election of consuls to end the decemvirate, passed in the *prata Flaminia*, see Livy 3.54.15. It is possible but by no means certain that the tribuncial bill for the triumph of the consuls Valerius and Horatius was also passed here (Livy 3.63.7–11).

15. Varro, *L.L.* 5.155, *comitium ab eo quod coibant eo comitiis curiatis et litium causa.* When Suetonius says, *Aug.* 65, that Augustus adopted Tiberius by a *lex curiata, in foro*, he probably means *in comitio*.

16. *Ant.* 2.50.2; 6.67.2; 11.39.1. The Volcanal seems to be the site of *comitia* as well as *contio* in 7.17. No one else speaks of *contiones* here.

17. Livy 2.56.10 (471 B.C.), *occupant tribuni templum postero die;* 3.17.1 (460). *P. Valerius ... se ex curia proripit, inde in templum ad tribunos venit.* The usual belief is that these passages refer to the Volcanal, but it seems to me more likely that Dionysius is confused about the *templum*. The elevation of the Volcanal is probably the *collis* on which candidates stood to make themselves known to the people who came to the Comitium on market days. See Macrob. *Sat.* 1.16.35 (cf. Festus 290 L).

18. Livy 1.48.3; cf. Dion. 4.38.5, with E. Sjöqvist's comments, "Pnyx and Comitium," *Studies Presented to David Moore Robinson*, 1 (St. Louis,

1951) 400–411, esp. 405. For steps of the Comitium see also Livy 1.36.5, *statua Atti . . . in comitio in gradibus ipsis ad laevam curiae.*

19. "Cosa and Rome, Comitium and Curia," *Archaeology* 10 (1957) 49–55. Through the courtesy of the author I have seen his unpublished paper, "The Rostra and the Forum Romanum," delivered at the annual meeting of the Archaeological Institute of America, December 1962.

20. For detailed references see Sjöqvist, *op. cit.* and John Arthur Hanson, *Roman Theater Temples* (Princeton 1959) 37–39. See the Map facing p. 1 for indications of the circular floor of the Comitium. The curved rear of the Rostra in the position to which Caesar moved it probably shows the original curve of the steps of the Comitium.

21. Livy 8.14.12. *Naves Antiatium partim in navalia Romae subductae, partim incensae, rostrisque earum suggestum in foro exstructum adornari placuit, Rostraque id templum appellatum.* In his narrative before 338 Livy never uses Rostra of the speaker's platform, employing instead *templum* (see n. 17 above), *tribunal* (2.29.2), and *contio,* on the use of which for a platform see Verrius Flaccus in Gell. 18.7.5–8. For the phrase *in contionem escendere* see Livy 2.7.7; 2.28.6; 3.49.4; 5.50.8. Livy's *in foro* for the site of the Rostra is not significant, for in the early books he associates the Forum much oftener than the Comitium with the Curia. See 2.23.7–12; 2.29.6; 2.55.9; 3.38.9 and 52.5; 7.16.12; 8.28.6–7. Cf. Eugen Petersen, *Comitium, Rostra, Grab des Romulus* (Rome, 1904) 25, n. 27. For Livy's use of Comitium and for the assignment of voting to the Forum when he apparently means the Comitium, see Chap. III, n. 27.

22. *Ad Comitium prope iuncta curiae,* Asconius 42 C; in front of the Curia Hostilia, Varro, *L.L.* 5.155; Diod. 12.26; close to the Curia, Val. Max. 9.5.2. For the position between Comitium and Forum the best evidence is provided by C. Licinius Crassus' story. See also Cic. *Sest.* 76; Fronto p. 98, Naber (Loeb text 2, p. 42). Pliny, *N.H.* 7.212, could refer to the position of the Rostra vetera on the map if one assumes that the Graecostasis was in a parallel position in front of the Curia. For a different position of the Rostra favored by various scholars, see Lugli, *Roma antica; il centro monumentale* (Rome, 1946) 115 ff., with Tav. III, facing p. 80, where the Rostra are located opposite the Curia. The actual location of the Rostra depends on the position of the Curia, which was burned in 52 b.c., in relation to the Curia Julia, dedicated in 29. See Lugli, *op. cit.* 131 ff.

23. The most recent comprehensive discussions of the remains are those of E. Gjerstad, *Acta Inst. Sueciae* 5 (1941) 97–104, 108 f., 127 f., 138–58 and E. Sjöqvist, *op. cit.* in n. 18 above, 400–411. Giacomo Boni's excavations of this region, made at the beginning of this century, have lately been uncovered and reexamined. As a result of careful systematization, it is now possible to see important remains of early structures. Dr. Maria Squarciapino Floriani is preparing a publication of the new investigations. For recent bibliography and photographs see *PDAR* s.v. "Comi-

tium" and "Rostra." For the preparation of the Rostra for *comitia* see Chap. III, with notes 36–37.

24. *C. Gracch.* 5. καὶ τῶν πρὸ αὐτοῦ πάντων δημαγωγῶν πρὸς τὴν σύγκλητον ἀφορώντων καὶ τὸ καλούμενον κομίτιον, πρῶτος τότε στραφεὶς ἔξω πρὸς τὴν ἀγορὰν δημηγορῆσαι, καὶ τὸ λοιπὸν οὕτω ποιεῖν ἐξ ἐκείνου, μικρᾷ παρεγκλίσει καὶ μεταθέσει σχήματος μέγα πρᾶγμα κινήσας καὶ μετενεγκὼν τρόπον τινὰ τὴν πολιτείαν ἐκ τῆς ἀριστοκρατίας εἰς τὴν δημοκρατίαν, ὡς τῶν πολλῶν δέον, οὐ τῆς βουλῆς, στοχάζεσθαι τοὺς λέγοντας.

25. See Cic. *Leg. agr.* 2.13 for a description of a man, who, after he was elected tribune, began to go about in old clothes, unwashed and unshaved.

26. Cic. *Lael.* 96; Varro, *R.R.* 1.2.9 See Lange, *RAl* 2.472, 484 f., 718; O. Gilbert, *Geschichte und Topographie der Stadt Rom im Alterthum* (Leipzig 1883–90) 3.151, n. 1. De Ruggiero's view, *FR* 69, was that Crassus moved the voters to the tribunal of the Castor temple. For the interpretation of Varro I cite also the unpublished paper of Richardson (n. 19 above).

27. See *TLL* s.v. "Ago," col. 1393. Compare, with Gellius 13.16, Cic. *De imp. Cn. Pomp.* 1 (of the Rostra) *hic autem locus, ad agendum amplissimus, ad dicendum ornatissimus.* For the passage quoted, probably in abbreviated form, by Macrobius from the augur L. Julius Caesar, see n. 4 above. As Gilbert indicates, *op. cit.* 151, n. 4, Mommsen is inconsistent in accepting the Crassus story as a reference to a *contio* (*StR* 3.385 with n. 1), for he recognizes the application of the language of Cicero and Varro to *comitia*.

28. Allotments to citizens from land acquired by the state were often of seven *iugera*. I am attracted by the suggestion of Professor Frank Brown that the *septem iugera forensia* may be a direct quotation from a speech of Crassus, with a description of the center of the Forum as common property of the people.

29. See s.v. "Accipio," *TLL* 318 f. and Merguet's Cicero *Lexika* for examples in Cicero's orations and philosophical works not cited there.

30. See Preface and Chap. III, with n. 26.

31. Two laws of the Gracchan and slightly post-Gracchan period provide that men were to face the Forum while taking oaths: *Lex repet.* 36, of jurors' oaths (*CIL* 1.2².583, *FIRA* 1, p. 93): *Iudices, quei in eam rem erunt, omnes pro rostreis in forum [vorsus iouranto....]. Lex Bantia* (*CIL.* 1.2².582; *FIRA* 1, p. 83) of the magistrates who take oath to abide by the law: [.... *eis consistunto pro ae]de Castorus (sic) palam luci in forum vorsus.* It is possible that Gaius Gracchus' act, reflected in Plutarch, was the institution of the requirement that oaths should be taken by men facing the Forum. But it is more likely that he was using a Greek source which referred to Crassus, as the Greeks often did, simply by his *praenomen*, Gaius.

32. Tenney Frank, *MAAR* 5 (1925) 79–102, with Fig. VIII for Metellus' tribunal; O. Richter, *Jahrb. arch. Inst.* 13 (1898) 87–114. Richter as-

sumed the existence of a speaker's platform on the pre-Metellan temple. Frank's examination of the monument led him to believe that the earlier platform was a separate structure in front of the temple, and that its position explains the origin of the phrase *pro aede Castoris* (see n. 36 below). Mommsen (*StR* 2.398, n. 2) suggested that the censors had a tribunal in front of the temple. Scipio Aemilianus' speech *pro aede Castoris* is assigned to his censorship of 142 by Fraccaro and Malcovati (*Or. Rom. frag.*[2] 126). That is the only speech known there before the temple was rebuilt by Metellus. The Lex Bantia with the provision for an oath *pro ae]de Castorus* has been dated in 133–18 through acceptance of Mommsen's view that the *IIIviri a.d.a.* mentioned there were the commissioners under Tiberius Gracchus' land law, but Maschke, followed by Carcopino, Gelzer, Piganiol, and Tibiletti, have dated the law in 104–100, identifying the officials with later commissioners. See bibliography cited by G. Barbieri s.v. "Lex," *DE* (published 1956) 715–17. If, as seems to me likely, the later date of the Lex Bantia is to be accepted and if Aemilianus' speech is explained by the use of the Castor temple for the census of *equites,* the employment of a platform there for assemblies is not attested before Metellus' reconstruction of the temple.

33. On his campaign see Livy, *Per.* 62; Appian, *Illyr.* 11.33; Eutrop. 4.23.2; Cic. *Scaur.* 46 with Ascon. 28 C; Cic. *Verr.* II.1.154 (*ex L. Metelli manubiis*) with Pseudo Ascon. p. 254 St. Metellus' campaign, according to Appian, was occasioned by a desire for a triumph, and apparently roused no enmity among the people of Salonae, where he spent the winter under friendly treatment. Perhaps he had freed them from pirates.

34. See *Notitia* and *Curiosum* in Jordan, *Topographie der Stadt Rom im Altertum* (Berlin 1871) 2.551. See also Richter, *op. cit.* n. 32 above, 108; Lugli, *Roma Antica, Il Centro monumentale* (Rome, 1946) 182.

35. See Richter's restoration of the tribunal, *op. cit.* and *Topographie der Stadt Rom* (Munich, 1901) 86, from which Pl. IV is taken.

36. From the Lex Bantia, on whose date see n. 32 above. For the suggestion that the letters STOR in Festus' text, 256 L, line 2, should be restored *pro aede Ca]stor[is,* see Frank. *Riv. Filol.* 53 (1925) 105 f. The character of the note is indicated by Paulus' summary, *Pro significat in, ut pro rostris, pro aede, pro tribunali.* See Chap. III, n. 29.

37. Plut. *Cato min.* 27–29; Dio, 37.43. On the scene see my *PP* 127 f.

38. For Caesar's first agrarian law see Dio. 38.6.2; for Clodius' legislation, especially the bill that led to Cicero's exile, see Cic. *Dom.* 110; *Sest.* 34; *Pis.* 23. The *templum* of Cic. *De Or.* 2.197 and of *Sest.* 75, used for the scene set for an assembly, might be either the temple of Castor or the Rostra. For the temple of Castor as the site of a *contio* of Octavian, apparently unrelated to *comitia,* see Cic. *Phil.* 3.27.

39. Some response was normal from the Roman *contio* as an expression of

the will of the people. See *Sest.* 106. But Cicero holds that the *contiones* with hired claques were different.

40. Cic. *Sest.* 126. *At vero ille praetor, qui de me non patris, avi, proavi, maiorum denique suorum omnium, sed Graeculorum instituto contionem interrogare solebat, 'velletne me redire,' et cum erat reclamatum, semivivis mercennariorum vocibus, populum Romanum negare dicebat* . . . Such questions were not entirely unknown earlier. Cf. Cic. *De imp. Cn. Pomp.* 59. On the adoption of Clodius' methods by his opponents see Cic. *Qfr.* 2.3.2.

41. Cic. *Flacc.* 15–17. *O morem praeclarum disciplinamque quam a maioribus accepimus, si quidem teneremus! sed nescio quo pacto iam de manibus elabitur. Nullam enim illi nostri sapientissimi et sanctissimi viri vim contionis esse voluerunt; quae scisceret plebes aut quae populus iuberet, submota contione, distributis partibus, tributim et centuriatim discriptis ordinibus, classibus, aetatibus, auditis auctoribus, re multos dies promulgata et cognita iuberi vetarique voluerunt.* 16. *Graecorum autem totae res publicae sedentis contionis temeritate administrantur. Itaque ut hanc Graeciam quae iam diu suis consiliis perculsa et adflicta est omittam, illa vetus quae quondam opibus, imperio, gloria floruit hoc uno malo concidit, libertate immoderata ac licentia contionum. Cum in theatro imperiti homines rerum omnium rudes ignarique consederant, tum bella inutilia suscipiebant, tum seditiosos homines rei publicae praeficiebant, tum optime meritos civis e civitate eiciebant.* 17. *Quod si haec Athenis tum cum illae non solum in Graecia sed prope cunctis gentibus enitebant accidere sunt solita, quam moderationem putatis in Phrygia aut in Mysia contionum fuisse? Nostras contiones illarum nationum homines plerumque perturbant; quid, cum soli sint ipsi, tandem fieri putatis?* . . . *porrexerunt manus; psephisma natum est.*

42. On the use of theaters for Greek assemblies see K. Kourouniotes and H. A. Thompson, "The Pnyx at Athens," *Hesperia* I (1932) 90–217, esp. 135, 138; W. A. McDonald, *The Political Meeting Places of the Greeks* (Baltimore, 1942) 56 ff. Except for a brief statement on Athens, the evidence is omitted by Fensterbusch s.v. "Theatron," *RE* (publ. 1934) 1386. For Roman references to theaters as the place of Greek assemblies, see Cic. *R.P.* 3.48 (of Rhodes) *et in theatro et in curia res capitales et reliquas omnis iudicabant idem.* Cf. Val. Max. 2.2.5; Livy 33.28.4.

43. 3.396. (Die Bürgerschaft) "soll den Reden für und wider stehend und schweigend zuhören," with note 3 on "stehend": "Dies ist vermutlich die Ursache, wesshalb die Römer der Republik ein ständiges Theater nicht gestattet haben." (See also 3.1178.) Mommsen's references, all of which apply to *contiones,* are *Flacc.* 16; *Brut.* 289; *Leg. agr.* 2.13; *Acad. pr.* 2.144; *Tusc.* 3.48; *Orat.* 213. To these I can add *Red sen.* 26; Livy 5.11.15; Gell. 18.7.8 (definition of a *contio* as *populi adsistentis coetus*); also the following passages (perhaps ambiguous) for *contio* with a form

of *consistere:* Cic. *Leg. agr.* 1.25; *Sest.* 107, 127; Livy 2.56.10; 6.27.7.

44. The ancient Roman custom of having the people stand *ne si consideret theatro dies totos ignavia continuaret* (Tac. *Ann.* 14.20) is reflected at the Ludi Latini of the secular games which took place *in scaena quoi theatrum adiectum non fuit nullis positis sedilibus* (*ILS* 5050, line 100). The opposition to the theater of Pompey is mentioned by Tacitus, and, more significantly, by Tertullian, *De spect.* 10.5 where Pompey is said to have described the theater as a shrine of Venus beneath which steps were put for spectacles (*templum ... cui subiecimus ... gradus spectaculorum*). See M. Bieber, *The History of the Greek and Roman Theater* (Princeton, 1961) 167 ff.; J. A. Hanson, *op. cit.* in n. 20 above, 29 ff. But there was no lasting opposition to temporary seats for the spectacles and they were built year after year by the aediles at great expense.

The tradition on the opposition to a permanent theater centers on P. Cornelius Scipio Nasica Corculum, *cos.* 162, 155, *censor* 159, *pontifex maximus* 150–41. His objections were moral rather than, as is often stated, religious. A speech of his in the senate is mentioned by Orosius and Augustine, and other comments may be based on reports of what he said. The epitomator of Livy and Augustine associate Nasica's objection to the theater with his stand on Carthage. On that see Gelzer's well-known discussion (from *Philologus* 86, 261 ff.), now available in his *Kleine Schriften* 2 (Wiesbaden, 1963) 39–72 (not, to my mind, refuted by W. Hoffman, *Historia* 9 [1960] 309–44; cf. his comment on the theater, 338, n. 74).

The sources on Nasica's opposition are as follows: Livy, *Per.* 48 *Cum locatum a censoribus theatrum exstrueretur, P. Cornelio Nasica auctore tamquam inutile et nociturum publicis moribus ex senatus consulto destructum est, populusque aliquamdiu stans ludos spectavit.* Val. Max. 2.4.2. *Quae ⟨theatra⟩ incohata ... auctore P. Scipione Nasica omnem apparatum operis eorum subiectum hastae venire placuit, atque etiam senatus consulto cautum est ne quis in urbe propiusve passus mille subsellia posuisse sedensve ludos spectare vellet ut scilicet remissioni animorum †standi virilitas propria Romanae gentis nota esset.* Oros. 4.21.4. *Eodem tempore censores theatrum lapideum in urbe construi censuerunt. quod ne tunc fieret, Scipio Nasica gravissima oratione obstitit, dicens, inimicissimum hoc fore bellatori populo ad nutriendam desidiam lasciviamque commentum, adeoque movit senatum, ut non solum vendi omnia theatro comparata iusserit, sed etiam subsellia ludis poni prohibuerit.* Aug. *C.D.* 1.31. (from Varro?). *Avarus vero luxuriosusque populus secundis rebus effectus est, quas Nasica ille providentissime cavendas esse censebat.* After an allusion to Nasica's opposition to the destruction of Carthage, described in *C.D.* 1.30, and a statement that the senate voted him the best man of the state, a distinction that actually belonged to his grandfather, Augustine continues with Nasica as subject: *caveam theatri senatum construere molientem ab hac dis-*

positione et cupiditate compescuit persuasitque oratione gravissima, ne Graecam luxuriam virilibus patriae moribus paterentur obrepere et ad virtutem labefactandam enervandamque Romanam peregrinae consentire nequitiae, tantumque auctoritate valuit, ut verbis eius commota senatoria providentia etiam subsellia, quibus ad horam congestis in ludorum spectaculo iam uti civitas coeperat, deinceps prohiberet adponi. Velleius (1.15.3), who gives the location of the theater, begun by the censors of 154 *a Lupercale in Palatium versus,* attributes the opposition to the consul Scipio (Cepio in mss.), though the date of his second consulship was the previous year: *cui* (sc. *Cassio censori*) *in eo moliendo eximia civitatis severitas et consul Scipio restitere, quod ego inter clarissima publicae voluntatis argumenta numeraverim.* See E. T. Salmon, *Athenaeum* 41 (1963), 5 ff. Appian, *B.C.* 1.28.125, in which Scipio, whose name is again confused in mss. with that of Caepio, is mistakenly identified with Nasica's grandson, the consul of 111 (see Gabba's note in his edition of Appian, book 1, Florence, 1958): τῷ δ' αὐτῷ χρόνῳ Σκιπίων ὕπατος καθεῖλε τὸ θέατρον, οὗ Λεύκιος Κάσσιος ἦρκτο (καὶ ἤδη που τέλος ἐλάμβανεν), ὡς καὶ τόδε στάσεων ἆρξον ἑτέρων ἢ οὐ χρήσιμον ὅλως Ἑλληνικαῖς ἡδυπαθείαις Ῥωμαίους ἐθίζεσθαι.

45. See Sjöqvist, *op. cit.* in n. 18, 405 f.
46. *Op. cit.* in n. 19 of this chapter, 51 f.
47. *Handbuch der röm. Alterthümer,* 1st ed. (Leipzig, 1844) 2.1.361, with Mommsen's comment, *StR* 3.396, n. 3.
48. The fact that legislative *comitia* were normally held on the site of the last *contio* is in itself evidence that the Romans stood there as well as in the *contiones.* For the evidence of the *stans populus Romanus* in the *comitia* held in the Saepta see Serv. on Verg. *Buc.* 1.33, a passage cited by Mommsen (who does not discuss standing in the *comitia*) with the reading of the one manuscript which omits *stans.* See Chap. III, n. 44.

CHAPTER III

1. On the *rogatores* see Mommsen, *StR* 3.403 f.; on *puncta,* 3.407, n. 5. Note the choliambic of unknown authorship (Porphynio on Hor. *Ser.* 2.2 50–51) on a candidate who *suffragiorum puncta non tulit septem.* Except for Livy's statement (26.18.9) that not only all centuries but also all men voted to give Scipio the Spanish command in 210, this is the only information we have of a specific number of votes of individuals.
2. Cicero, *Leg.* 3.33–39, is the major source on oral and written voting. The four *leges tabellariae* were the Lex Gabinia of 139 for elections, the Lex Cassia of 137 for judicial decisions except for *perduellio,* the Lex Papiria of 130 (or 131) for legislation, and the Lex Coelia of 107 for *perduellio.* For the evidence see *MRR* and Niccolini, *I Fasti dei Tribuni della Plebe* (Milan, 1934) under the tribunes of these years.
3. See Busolt, *Griechische Staatskunde* 1 (Munich, 1920) 454.
4. See *Tabula Hebana* 19 and, for ballots in the extortion court, Cic. *Div. in*

Caec. 24. The *lex repetundarum* (*CIL* 1.2².583.50–54) provides for jury ballots of boxwood (*buxus*), which were surprisingly large, four digits, about seven and a half cm., wide, with a length that is lost in a lacuna. The ballots here are described as *Sorticulae*.

5. Cic. *Dom.* 112, with Mommsen's comments, *StR* 3.405, n. 5. See Chap. IV, n. 50.

6. On the question whether these votes were distributed already prepared, see Chap. IV, with n. 43.

7. *CP* 49 (1954) 10; cf. Scullard, *JRS* 50 (1960) 70.

8. Cic. *Leg.* 3.33: *de suffragiis quae iubeo nota esse optimatibus, populo libera ... ego in ista sum sententia ... nihil ut fuerit in suffragiis voce melius ... (39) habeat sane populus tabellam quasi vindicem libertatis, dummodo haec optimo cuique et gratissimo civi ostendatur ultroque offeratur.*

9. Note the use of *liber, libertas* throughout the discussion between Cicero and his brother from which citations are made in the previous note. See also Cic. *Leg. agr.* 2.4, *tabellam vindicem tacitae libertatis;* Cic. *Sest.* 103. *Tabellaria lex ab L. Cassio ferebatur; populus libertatem agi putabat suam; Schol Bob.* p. 135 St. *Hanc ⟨legem⟩ L. Cassius tulit ut non voce suffragium pronuntiarent sed tabellae inscriberent quasi securo et liberiore iudicio;* Cic. *Planc.* 16. *tabella ... dat ... eam libertatem ut quod velint faciant.* See the excellent discussion of Ch. Wirszubski, *Libertas as a Political Idea at Rome* (Cambridge, 1950) 50.

10. The conspirator (Cassius, no. 59, *RE*) may well have been the son of C. Cassius L. f. cos. 73, (58 *RE*) though there is no proof that he was. The consul of 73 was probably a grandson of L. Cassius Longinus Ravilla (72 *RE*), proposer of the Lex Cassia tabellaria of 137; his father may have been either L. Cassius L. f. cos. 107 (no. 62 *RE*) or L. Cassius, tr. pl. 104 (63 *RE*), famous for introducing laws to lessen the power of the nobility. See the coin of Longinus, n. 11 of this chapter. I suggest that the coins of the Cassii associated with ballot laws (of which Ravilla's was the second) were all issued by descendants honoring an ancestor. There are no such symbols on the coins of the conspirator, but for Libertas see his Asian issues, Sydenham pp. 204 f. For a family tree of the Cassii see Drumann-Groebe, *Geschichte Roms* 2 (1902) 93.

11. Sydenham 935; *CRRBM* 1.3929 f., dated usually in the late fifties. The name on the coin is simply Longin(us) IIIv(ir), usually identified with the conspirator's brother Lucius, *tr. pl.* 44, a Caesarian (*RE* 65). The symbol V for a favorable vote on a law refers perhaps to the Lex Peducaea which established Ravilla as judge of the Vestals under accusation in 113.

12. Sydenham 917–18; *CRRBM* 1.3871–3; dated usually about 57. The name is Q. Cassius. See n. 13.

13. Sydenham 502; *CRRBM* 1.1032, coin of late second century, inscribed C. Cassi. For interpretation see Alföldi, *Netherlands Year Book for*

History of Art, 1954, 162 f., with his Pl. II, 5–7 (to the significance of which Mrs. Jane Cody, who is studying the coins of the Cassii, called my attention). Alföldi identifies the object in the hand of the goddess in the *quadriga* not as a *pileus* but as a "wappenartiges Abzeichen" of the Cassian family. He interprets the receptacle on the reverse as a voting *cista* with cover and cites a similar representation on an uninscribed intaglio (see his Pl. II, 6) from the Arndt collection in Munich. I would suggest the possibility that the receptacle is a hydria for jurors' votes rather than a *cista* for *comitia.* See the coin above, with the letters A C (Pl. V no. 2).

14. Sydenham 891, dated ca. 62. The reverse has an image of Sol. For interpretation see Chap. IV, with n. 43.

15. Sydenham 960; see De Ruggiero, *FR* 352. The coin is usually dated ca. 47.

16. Appian, *B.C.* 1.121.560, with Gabba's note; Ps. Ascon. 189 St. As consul designate for 70, Pompey, brought into a *contio* by the tribune of 71, made his promise to restore the power of the tribunate. See Cic. *Verr.* I. 44–45, with Pseudo-Ascon. 220 St. On this Lollius see Sall. *Hist.* 4.43–47 M. The curule chair on another *denarius* of Palicanus (Sydenham 961) probably refers to the elder Palicanus' praetorship, an office he must have held, since he was a candidate for the consulship of 66 (Val. Max. 3.8.3). My identification of the younger Palicanus with the Παλλακεῖνος of the *senatus consultum* of 39 (see *VD* 226) should have been proposed tentatively, but it still seems to me more likely than the identification proposed by E. Badian, *Gnomon* 33 (1961) 496.

17. Sydenham 963. The urn on the obverse has no handles; the tablet on the reverse has a ring attached.

18. I refrain from discussing the coin of L. Hostilius Saserna, whose genuineness Professor Alföldi tells me he doubts. See *CRRBM* 1, p. 514, n. 1, and, for a photograph, Babelon. *Rev. num.* 6 (1902) 11, Pl. I. It is a supposedly Gallic issue with Gallia on the obverse and a crude representation on the reverse of three men advancing on an elevation, apparently with a balustrade.

19. Sydenham 548; *CRRBM* 2, pp. 274, 526. For the interpretation I follow in most details the view of Mommsen, *Röm. Münzwesen* (Berlin, 1860) 544; *StR* 3.400, n. 4.

20. Friedländer, *Zeitschr. für Num.* 2 (1875) 86. See Mommsen, *StR* 3, 400, n. 4.

21. Suet. *Iul.* 80.4 (of the conspirators) *qui primum cunctati utrumne in Campo per comitia tribus ad suffragia vocantem partibus divisis e ponte deicerent atque exceptum trucidarent.* For the *pontes* at the assemblies (not discussed in the article "Pons" in *RE*) see Mommsen, *StR* 3.401, n. 3 with 2.408, n. 2.

22. Auctor ad Heren. 1.21. Caepio, acting against Saturninus' grain law, *pontes disturbat, cistas deicit;* Cic. *Att.* 1.14.5. *operae Clodianae pontes occuparant.* The allusions to *pontes* in the sources refer in general to

legislative or judicial assemblies, but Festus, 452 L, quoted in Chapter V, n. 18, shows that they were also in use for elections. See n. 55 below.

23. Nothing certain is known of the identity of Nerva (see Muenzer, s.v. "Licinius" 136, *RE*, who argues rightly against his identification with the praetor of Sicily of 104; see *MRR*). Sydenham, no. 548, associates the coin with the institution, through the tribune of 107 (misdated in 106) C. Coelius Caldus, of the written ballot for *perduellio*, and proposes that the *P* on the coin (n. 20 above) stands for *perduellio*. (For another suggestion, *provoco*, see *CRRBM* 2. p. 275, n.) Mommsen's suggestion of a tribal initial is more likely; the connection of Nerva with Caldus' law, proposed to facilitate his prosecution of C. Popillius Laenas, is uncertain. But T. E. Carney's suggestion (*Numis. Chron.* 19 [1959] 87) that Nerva was an associate of Marius, whose tribunate he may have been celebrating, is not unlikely.

24. Dion. 7.59.1 (trial of Coriolanus, where the tribune calls the people to a tribal assembly): οἱ δὲ δήμαρχοι συνεκάλουν τὸ πλῆθος ἐπὶ τὴν φυλέτιν ἐκκλησίαν, χωρία τῆς ἀγορᾶς περισχοινίσαντες ἐν οἷς ἔμελλον αἱ φυλαὶ στήσεσθαι καθ' αὑτάς. The word χωρία suggests separated spots. Appian, *B.C.* 3.30.117–18. Antony had shut off approaches to the Forum. ἡ μὲν βουλὴ τὴν λοχῖτιν ἐνόμιζεν ἐκκλησίαν συλλεγήσεσθαι, οἳ δὲ νυκτὸς ἔτι τὴν ἀγορὰν περισχοινισάμενοι τὴν φυλέτιν ἐκάλουν, ἀπὸ συνθήματος ἐληλυθυῖαν.

25. On *consaeptum* see *TLL*. The distinction cannot be pressed too hard, for Cicero uses the word *saepire* for Antony's enclosure of the Forum for which Appian employs περισχοινίσματα (*Phil.* 1.25; 5.9). For *saepire* and *consaepta* of the Comitium and the Forum see Cic. *R.P.* 2.31; Quint. 12.2.23. The existence of Saepta in the Forum has been assumed from Cicero's comment on the use of *fragmenta saeptorum* and *fustes* as weapons when an assembly was about to be held, *Sest.* 79. But *saepta* could refer to any sort of material used for divisions or fences, and such divisions were occasionally used for the law courts. See, on the trial of Clodius for *incestus*, Seneca, *Epist.* 97.2

26. Mommsen's view, *StR* 3.396–415, of simultaneous voting in all assemblies of the tribes has been generally accepted until recently. (But see Herzog, *RSV* 1.1184.) Mommsen depended mainly on the method of electing local magistrates described in the Charter of Malaga 55, providing that the *duumvir* in charge was to call all the *curiae* at once (*uno vocatu*), and that members of each *curia* in separated *consaepta* should cast their ballots *per tabellam*. He noted that two accounts of elections of curule aediles (Cic. *Planc.* 49 and Varro in passages cited n. 58, this chapter) indicate that all votes were counted at once and that the vote was therefore, as at Malaga, simultaneous. But, as Fraccaro points out (*PVCTR*), this simultaneous vote belongs to elections.

Successive voting is, however, attested for legislative and judicial assemblies of the tribes, and the results for each tribe were known at once. The evidence cannot be explained by Mommsen's theory that the announcement and not the voting was successive. The passages demon-

strating successive voting (cited in Fraccaro's order) are as follows:
(1) Vote (legislative) on the triumph of L. Aemilius Paulus, Livy 45.
36.7 (Plut. *Aem.* 31), *intro vocatae primae tribus cum antiquarent.* (2)
Vote on the Licinian-Sextian laws, Livy 6.38.5, *cum ... 'uti rogas' primae
tribus dicerent.* (3) (judicial) Livy 40.42.10, *cum plures iam tribus
intro vocatae ... iuberent.* (4) (legislative) Livy 4.5.2, *ego tribunus
vocare tribus in suffragium coepero.* (5) (legislative, of Gabinius' bill to
revoke tribunate of Trebellius in 67) Ascon. p. 72 C (Dio 36.30). *Introvocare tribus Gabinius coepit ... sed postquam X et VII tribus roga-
tionem acceperunt et ... modo una supererat ⟨ut⟩ populi iussum con-
ficeret, remisit intercessionem Trebellius.* (6) Similar legislative procedure with Tiberius Gracchus' bill to remove his colleague Octavius from
office, except that in this case Octavius did not abandon his veto and the
18th tribe settled his dismissal. See Appian, *B.C.* 1.12.52 ff.; Plut. *Ti Gr.*
12. (7) Bill of 87 to annul Marius' exile, Plut. *Mar.* 43, statement that
before three or four tribes had voted Marius entered the city. (8) Trial
of Q. Flavius, Val. Max. 8.1.7, in 329 when there were only 29 tribes;
after 14 tribes had condemned Flavius, the prosecutor Valerius lost the
vote of the rest by an unrestrained declaration (*cum quattuordecim tri-
buum suffragiis damnatus esset ... Valerius ... reliquas tribus adver-
sario donavit*).

To these cases which show successive voting Fraccaro adds two
more in which the interpretation is problematical. The first is Appian
B.C. 1.49.214, a description of the new tribes to be created for new citizens under the Lex Julia of 90, tribes which were to vote after the old
tribes. Fraccaro would assign their vote to legislation (rightly, I think).
The other case, Polyb. 6.14.7 on φυλαί in jurisdiction, is uncertain because it is not clear whether the passage deals with the centuriate or
with the tribal assembly. The former (see Walbank's note) is more
likely. If my interpretation of the accounts of Appian and Plutarch of
the last assembly of Tiberius Gracchus is correct (n. 41), another case
is to be added. Both accounts of the assembly indicate that the vote was
successive, and I have argued (*TiGLA*) that it was legislative.

It is clear that in the cases dealing with legislation and judgments
the tribes were called in to vote successively; in passages 5, 6, and 8
(which Mommsen interpreted on the theory that tribes which had already voted simultaneously could change their vote during the period
when the vote was being announced) influences were exerted at the
moment when the tribes lacked only one vote of a majority. For successive voting there is another important testimony in the institution of
the *principium* (see Chap. IV), a tribe whose name was listed with that
of the man who cast the first vote in it (*primus scivit*) in the prescript
of laws (*FIRA Leges* 1, nos. 8, 10, 14 cf. 11; see Hall, *VPRA* 277, n. 36).
The vote of the first tribe is mentioned for (6) by Appian and for (1) by
Plut. *Aem.* 31 instead of Livy's *intro vocatae primae tribus.* This tribe
would have been chosen by lot to cast the first vote. See Chap. IV.

Against this evidence for successive votes of the tribes in legislation and judgments Fraccaro cites only one passage, Dionysius' account of the mythical trial of Coriolanus assigned to 492, two years after the institution of the tribunate, a time when the tribes can hardly have acquired legislative and judicial functions. Dionysius says (7.59.9) that the tribes were called μιᾷ κλήσει which Fraccaro takes to be equivalent to *uno vocatu* in the Spanish Charter. But here, as elsewhere in the passages dealing with the assemblies, κλῆσις seems to be an equivalent of the Latin *classis*, which Dionysius (4.18.2) agrees with modern etymologists in deriving from the same root as καλέω. The word is used in 4.20.5 for the first and fifth classes and in 7.59.9, immediately before the reference to μιᾷ κλήσει, for the first and last classes. Dionysius' emphasis is on the difference in voting between the centuriate assembly in five classes and the tribal assembly in one, and μιᾷ κλήσει means "in one class" with stress on the democratic character of the vote and without reference to successive or to simultaneous voting within the class.

Fraccaro's conclusion that successive voting belonged to the legislative and judicial assemblies and simultaneous voting to the elections is, in my view, established.

27. For the Comitium in relation to the senate see Livy 45.24.12, speech of Rhodians, *in comitio, in vestibulo curiae;* for other cases of Curia with Comitium, 5.7.9; 22.7.7; 22.60.1. There are allusions in Livy to statues, omens, floggings, seats of magistrates, burning of books in the Comitium; legates stand there, a *signifer* stops there. But there is not a reference either to a *contio* or to a voting assembly held there. In Livy 10.24.18 the reading *Fabius . . . comitio abiit,* an emendation found in corrections of two *codices* and in the Milanese edition of 1478, is adopted in the Teubner, Oxford, and Loeb texts. The mss. reading *comitia habuit* is, in my opinion, correct. For Livy's use of *in foro* when he means *in comitio* see Chap. II, n. 21. For assignment to the Forum of *comitia* which probably took place in the Comitium, see Livy 3.17.4, *comitia interim in foro sunt, senatus in curia est;* cf. 5.30. There are other cases in Livy and Dionysius.

28. This incident (Chap. II, with n. 28) in the account of Varro, *R.R.* 1.2.9 provides the only evidence we have for a tribal assembly in the Comitium, site of the *comitia curiata*. The sources often report the site simply as the Forum. See the speech of C. Titius, *Or. Rom. frg.*² 202 f. (with Malcovati's note on the date, probably the end of the second century). Here the meaning is Forum, not Comitium: *iubent puerum vocari ut comitium eat percunctatum quid in foro gestum sit, qui suaserint, qui dissuaserint, quot tribus iusserint, quot vetuerint.* The Rostra were the site of the vote on C. Flaminius' *lex agraria* of 232 (Val. Max. 5.4.; *templum* in Cic. *Inv.* 2.52); apparently of the comitial trial of P. Furius in 98 (Val. Max. 8.1, *damn.* 2); of a bill proposed by the tribune C. Cornelius in 67, but interrupted before the voting began (Ascon. 60 f. C); of the legislative assembly on a consular bill

of 61 (Cic. *Att.* 1.14.5; see Chap. IV, n. 43). The frequent use of the Rostra for *comitia* as well as for *contiones* is indicated by Cicero's description of the Rostra (*De imp. Cn. Pomp.* 1), *hic autem locus ad agendum amplissimus, ad dicendum ornatissimus.* Even more significant is the standard abbreviation in Valerius Probus' list headed *litterae singulares in iure civili de legibus et plebiscitis* (recognized as a genuine work of the great Neronian antiquarian): P.I.R.P.Q.I.S.I.F.-P.R.E.A.D.P., *populum iure rogavit populusque iure scivit* (mss. *suscepit*) *in foro pro rostris ex ante diem pridie.* See Mommsen's edition in Keil, *Grammatici Latini* 4 (Leipzig, 1864) 272 and Hanslik s.v. "Valerius" 315, *RE* 208 f. Cf. *StR* 3.383, n. 1. The abbreviation represents a standard prescript of a law presented to the *populus* by a consul or a praetor.

29. See Nash, *PDAR* 1, p. 210, no. 239. For the retaining wall limiting the pronaos before these stairs were built see the photograph (Pl. viii) of 1895; for the excavations carried out at Richter's suggestion see *NS.* 1896, 290 f. and Richter's discussion. *Jahrb. arch. Inst.* 13 (1898) 87–114, esp. 88 ff. For a recent study of the temple arguing for the Tiberian date of the monument as we have it, see D. E. Strong and J. B. Ward Perkins *PBSR* 30 (1962), 1–30.

30. Cic. *Pis.* 23, *sublato aditu, revolsis gradibus; Dom.* 54, *cum vero gradus Castoris convellisti ac removisti.*

31. Cic. *Att.* 1.14.5, *operae Clodianae pontes occuparant;* Auctor ad Heren. 1.21 (of interference with legislation) *pontes disturbat.*

32. On the reconstruction of Divus Julius see Richter, *Jahrb. arch. Inst.* 4 (1889) 137–51. On the law of 9 b.c. see *FIRA* 1, p. 152, from Frontin. *Aq.* 129.

33. There were two side staircases on the façades of the temples of Apollo Palatinus and of Apollo Sosianus, but neither seems to have been combined with a tribunal. For the latter see Colini, *Bull. com.* 68 (1940) 9–40, with plan p. 33. The temple was often the site of senate meetings, and the neighboring prata Flaminia were apparently used on at least one occasion for a plebeian assembly.

34. See the attempt of the late Gunther Fuchs to show how the so-called Comitium of Pompeii could have been used for elections, *Röm. Mitt.* 64 (1957) 154–64. Fuchs was familiar with Fraccaro's work on voting procedure. The election units of Pompeii were probably *curiae,* but we do not know how many there were. An examination of municipal temple architecture might be of interest here.

35. In the *lex repetundarum* of the Gracchan period (*CIL* 1.2².582.36) jurors are ordered to take oath *pro rostreis in forum* [*vorsus*]. *Pro rostris* is also used in the obviously Republican abbreviation quoted in n. 28. Besides Festus' use reflecting the Augustan Verrius Flaccus, the phrase *pro rostris aedis divi Iulii* is found in the prescript of the law of 9 b.c. cited n. 32 above. For the use of *pro aede Castoris* see Frank, *Riv. Fil.* 53 (1925) 105 f. Cf. Chap. II, n. 36.

36. Mommsen, *StR* 3.383, with n. 5, held that the Rostra had a higher and
    a lower level for speakers, and quoted a communication from Richter
    supporting his view. The presentation of Richter's view in a meeting
    of the German Archaeological Institute in Berlin in 1887 gave rise to
    objections which Mommsen answered in a footnote (*StR* 3,1, Inhalt, p.
    XII) suggesting that there could have been a temporary wooden
    structure in front of the Rostra. Richter, *Jahrb. arch. Inst.* 4 (1889)
    1–17, examined the structure of the Rostra in the position to which
    Caesar moved it, and concluded that there was no place for a lower
    level on the front of the Rostra. Richter also examined the use of the
    phrase *locus inferior* and concluded, with good evidence, that it could
    refer to ground level, and that in the context *inferior pars* in Livy 8.33.9
    could have the same meaning. Mommsen apparently did not return
    to the subject again, though there was opportunity in the *Römisches
    Strafrecht* published in 1899. Mommsen's chief argument for two levels
    was based on the provisions for levels in the tribunals of the public
    courts, also temporary wooden erections in the Forum; he thought that
    a judicial assembly would have similar arrangements. But, as he points
    out, the occasion on which Caesar refused Catulus access to the Rostra
    and forced him to speak from a lower level was the proposal of a bill,
    later abandoned (Suet. *Iul.* 15), by which the curatorship of the re-
    construction of the Capitoline temple was to be transferred from Catulus
    in alium. Cicero mentions Caesar's treatment of Catulus after Caesar
    had brought the informer Vettius to the Rostra to speak (*Att.* 2.24.3):
    *Caesar, is qui olim praetor cum esset Q. Catulum ex inferiore loco
    iusserat dicere, Vettium in rostra produxit eumque in eo loco constituit
    quo Bibulo consuli adspirare non liceret.* Catulus would have appeared
    as a *dissuasor* of the bill and I cannot believe that he would have been
    forced to speak from the level of the Forum where he could not have
    been heard.
37. The seeming curve of the Rostra itself would result from the limita-
    tion of space on the coin. If, as I believe, the temporary structure in
    front of the Rostra was in place on the day (Jan. 1, 62) of Caesar's
    proposal of a bill which was immediately abandoned, either the
    Rostra were already prepared for Comitia (perhaps for voting on the
    tribune Metellus Nepos' bill recalling Pompey) or the attachment
    would be put in place at *contiones* at which a number of men were
    asked to speak. The existence of such an attachment for the Rostra,
    with all the material for the tribunals of some seven public courts,
    would have been a heavy tax on storage space for the Forum. The
    whole subject of the upper and lower level in legislative and judicial
    assemblies and in public courts deserves further investigation.
38. For tribal legislative and judicial assemblies presided over by tribunes
    on the Capitol, see Livy 25.3.15 in 212 (tribunicial trial); Livy 33.25.7,
    in 196, tribunicial *rogatio* to ask people if they wanted peace; 34.1.4 in
    194, repeal of Lex Oppia proposed by tribunes; 43.16.9, in 169, tribun-

icial bill against contracts of censors; 45.36.6 (Plut. *Aem.* 31) in 167, tribunicial bill on *imperium* of L. Aemilius Paulus. This was perhaps the scene of all Tiberius Gracchus' legislation in 133, though it is specifically attested only for the vote to remove his colleague Octavius from office (Cic. *N.D.* 1.106) and for the last assembly which (see n. 41 below) I think was legislative. This was the place where the assembly of 121 was called to abrogate a law of C. Gracchus (Appian, *B.C.* 1.24.106; Plut. *C. Gracch.* 13). For the only *comitia* of regular magistrates on the Capitol see n. 40 below. For crowding on the Capitol see Livy 25.3.14; 34.1.4; 45.36.6.

39. For the election of tribunes of the plebs in the *comitia curiata,* conducted after the decemvirate by the *pontifex maximus,* see Chap. I with n. 5.

40. Livy 34.53.2. *Ea bina comitia Cn. Domiitus praetor urbanus in Capitolio habuit.* For a *lex curiata,* to be conducted by a praetor to confirm *imperium* for commissioners, see Cic. *Leg. agr.* 2.26–32. The vote of 194 is the only instance of choice of commissioners for which place of *comitia* or grant of *imperium* is recorded by Livy. For further discussion see my *TiGLA* 65 f.

41. The detailed accounts are Plutarch, *Ti. Gracch.* 16–19 and Appian, *B.C.* 1.14.58 to 16.70. Appian's statement in 1.2.4 that Tiberius perished νόμους ἐσφέρων provides conflicting evidence. See also Obsequens 27 a, *Tiberius Gracchus legibus ferendis occisus.* Other sources of importance are Cicero, *Cat.* 4.4; Livy, *Per.* 58; Oros. 5.9.1; *De vir. ill.* 64; Ampelius 26.1. See my *TiGLA.* D. C. Earl's objection to my interpretation of this assembly (see *Athenaeum* 43 [1965] 95–105) will be considered in a forthcoming paper in *Athenaeum.*

42. *C. Gracch.* 3.1. As I suggested in *TiGLA* 66 f., Livy's statement (9.46.11) that the distribution of *humiles* in all the tribes in 312 *forum et campum corrupit* is probably to be taken as a reference to legislation in the Forum and elections in the Campus. By metonymy *Campus* is often used as a term for elections.

43. See Servius' further comment on the line, with citation for *ovile* of Lucan 2.197 and Juvenal 6.528–29. See also Livy 26.22.11 of *ovile* at the centuriate assembly, a passage discussed in Chapter V. Cf. Mommsen, *StR* 3.399 f.

44. The word *stans* is found in all the eight mss. cited for this part of the *Bucolics* in the Thilo-Hagen edition (1902), except the 12th century Reginensis 1495. For the merits of this ms. see praef. to *Bucolics* VI ff. Mommsen, *StR* 3, 399, n. 4, cites the passage without *stans.*

45. See Ovid's description of *dies comitiales, Fasti* 1.53, *est quoque quo populum ius est includere saeptis.* See the Charter of Malaga 55 for the provision for individual *consaepta* and *custodes* for each *curia.*

46. *CM,* esp. 119–24, 148–51, 186–88. For Gatti's discovery, first published in 1937, see n. 47. The articles "Saepta" in Platner-Ashby, *Topographical Dictionary of Ancient Rome* and in *RE* (by Rosenberg) are

useful for sources, but are based on a mistaken identification of the Saepta.

46a. D. R. Shackleton Bailey in his *Cicero's Letters to Atticus* (Cambridge, 1965), which did not reach me until this book was ready for the printer, translates Saepta as "booths" and misinterprets the passage, partly because of unfamiliarity with the identification of the Saepta. See Vol. 2.113 f., 204 f. See my forthcoming review in CP.

47. G. Gatti, *L'Urbe* 2 (1937), no. 9.8–23; for summary see *Bull. com.* 66 (1938) 265 f.; on the Porticus Argonautarum see Gatti's paper in the *Atti del terzo Convegno nazionale di Storia dell'Architettura* (1940) 61–73. See *PM Testo,* pp. 97–101; Tav. XXXI, reproduced here, Pl. IX.

48. *Ibid.* Cozza's identification of the Diribitorium has led to some changes in the earlier suggestions of Gatti.

49. *Aq.* 22, *arcus Virginis finiuntur in Campo Martio secundum frontem Saeptorum.* See F. W. Shipley, *Agrippa's Building Activities in Rome, Washington University Studies,* Lang. and Lit. New Ser. no. 4, St. Louis 1933.

50. Cf. Cic. *Rab. perd.* 11, *in campo Martio comitiis centuriatis auspicato in loco; Cat.* 4.2. *campus consularibus auspiciis consecratus.* Cf. Livy 5.52. 16.

51. The impossibility of roofing the entire structure is pointed out by Gatti in the first article cited in n. 47. For the first use of awnings at Rome see Pliny, *N.H.* 19.23; the date is established by Livy, *Per.* 98 and Cassiodorus, *Chron.* under the year 69. See Lucretius 4.75–83; 6. 108–12, passages discussed in my paper "Lucretius on the Roman Theatre," *Studies in Honour of Gilbert Norwood* (Toronto, 1952) 147–55.

52. See Jordan-Huelsen, *Topographie der Stadt Rom* 1.3 (Berlin, 1907), 561, where Huelsen discusses possible remains of the divisions. Mommsen, *StR* 3.401, n. 2, found the remains ill-adapted for the Saepta. He would surely have liked the new identification better. Ernst Meyer, *RSSG²*, makes no reference to the discovery of Gatti, and Hall, *VPRA* 281, cites the *Staatsrecht* and Platner Ashby for the Saepta.

53. See his signed comment, *PM, Testo* 100.

54. See on Tiberius' return to Rome in 9 A.D. Suetonius, *Tib.* 17: *positumque in Saeptis tribunal senatu astante conscendit ac medius inter duos consules cum Augusto simul sedit.* This seems to have been a specially constructed tribunal. See Dio 56.1.1.

55. I interpret the *pons* from which the conspirators thought originally of hurling Caesar as the magistrate's tribunal (Suet. *Iul.* 80.4, quoted n. 21 above). I have considered the possibility that there might have been broad central stairs which all citizens would have ascended to reach the *cistae* on a single *pons,* with the magistrates seated in the rear. But the stories of hurling old men down from the *pons* (Chap. V, n. 18), which, even if apocryphal, give the setting of the elective as-

semblies, indicate that each voter crossed a *pons* to ballot. Separate *pontes* leading to the tribunal from each division therefore seem more probable, and they have been indicated in the drawing on Pl. XI. The ballots would have been handed down to citizens below in the manner shown on the Nerva coin, which appears to represent a legislative vote.

56. Cic. *Sest.* 114; *Dom.* 49. In that time of violence Milo's henchmen may have kept the Clodians from entering the Saepta.

57. *StR* 3.405–8. See on *loculi* Varro, *R.R.* 3.5.18. *Narrat ad tabulam, cum diriberent, quendam deprensum tesserulas conicientem in loculum, eum ad consulem tractum a fautoribus competitorum;* Ausonius, *Grat. act. ad Gratian.* 3. Ausonius is thanking Gratian for the consulship of 379 A.D. and emphasizing the contrast with Republican elections, *non passus saepta neque campum, non suffragia, non puncta, non loculos; Corp. gloss.* 4.57.23 (omitted by Mommsen, but see Liebenam s.v. "Diribitores," *RE*): *divisores et diribitores dicebantur qui suffragia populi divisa in locos tributim separabant.* Each *custos* had a *tabula* on which he put *puncta* (see n. 1 above) for the votes of candidates in the tribe he guarded, and agreement among the *custodes* had to be reached for the final count. The ballots were perhaps placed in *loculi* in groups according to the slate elected. See Cic. *Planc.* 53 for two candidates said to have received the same number of *puncta* in certain tribes.

58. For the setting in the *comitia aedilicia* see in Book Three 2.1–2; for disturbances in the Campus see 5.18, cited in n. 57 above; for the summoning of the augur and his return see 7.1 and 12.1; for the completion of the count and the announcement of results, 17.1 and 10, all discussed in Chapter IV. The dramatic date of the dialogue, completed in 37 B.C., is probably within the two decades before 50 when Appius Claudius Pulcher, *cos.* 54, was an augur. The accepted dating of the scene in 54 or 53 is unlikely, for in 54, when Appius was consul, there were no regular elections and Appius seems to have departed for his province Cilicia before the elections of 53. The basis of the dating is Cicero's allusions in 54 (*Att.* 4.15.5; *Scaur.* 27) to the difficulties between Interamna and Reate created by the flooding of the Nar (cf. *R.R.* 3.2.3). But those difficulties existed from the days of M'. Curius Dentatus until modern times. See *VD* 63, n. 63. In the writing of his dialogues Varro was less careful than Cicero. I note that the impossibility of placing the scene of Varro *R.R.* 3 in 54 is pointed out by D. R. Shackleton Bailey, *op. cit.,* in n. 46a above, 2. 209 f.

59. For the Villa Publica (omitted s.v. "Villa" *RE,* publ. 1958) see most recently Castagnoli, *CM* 116–21, with a plan putting the Villa tentatively between the Saepta and the Via Lata. See *PM, Testo,* 100, n. 17, where Cozza is disposed to accept the view of Castagnoli that the Villa no longer existed when the Marble Plan was produced. The fragment of the plan once assigned to the Villa is now shown to belong to the enigmatic structure marked DE]LTA. For a coin of P.

Fonteius Capito with a representation of a building in the Villa, see
Sydenham 901.

60. Cic. *Att.* 1.1.1. Similarly Scipio Aemilianus went down to the consular
comitia for 134 to canvass for his nephew, who was seeking the
quaestorship at elections to be held soon afterwards. See Val. Max. 8.15.
4, as interpreted by Mommsen, *StR* 3.382, n. 3. The incident is related
because it was the occasion of Aemilianus' election to a second consulship.

61. This interpretation, not accepted by Kent, Loeb text, is surely correct.
See Mommsen, *StR* 3.399, n. 3. The meaning of *licium,* girdle or apron,
is known from the phrase, going back to the Twelve Tables, *lance et
licio quaerere.* See A. Berger, *Encyclopedic Dictionary of Roman Law,*
Philadelphia, 1953, s.v. "Lance et licio." On *licium* in the meaning girdle,
cord, or thread, see L. A. Holland, *Janus and the Bridge* (Rome, 1961)
338, n. 28. For Varro's interpretation of *in licium* as a place where the
people could see and hear the magistrate summoning them to a *contio,*
see Chap. V, n. 41.

62. L. Lange, *RAl* 2.522, is specific in saying that the *contiones* before the
centuriate assembly took place "auf dem freien Raume" in front of
the Saepta. Mommsen, describing procedure in tribal and centuriate
assemblies together, is less specific, but notes (*StR* 3.389, n. 6) that
the use of *introvocare* (cf. 399, n .1) shows that the voters were outside.
In his comments on the magistrates on the platform (1.479, n. 1; 3.
399–401), he does not distinguish, as I try to do, between the tribunals
inside and outside the Saepta.

63. For a centuriate judicial assembly the presence of praetors and tribunes
is specified by Varro, *L.L.* 6.91 (cf. 6.87 for the census). The same
officers are present at the assembly of the *Tabula Hebana* (18).

64. Val. Max. 4.5.3. *Ut vidit ⟨Cicereius⟩ omnibus se centuriis Scipioni
anteferri, templo descendit abiectaque candida toga competitoris sui
suffragatorem agere coepit.* See *StR* 1.479, n. 1. For *templum* see also
Varro, *L.L.* 6.86,87,91. The other details we have on the position of
candidates all come from Africanus and his Aemilian associates,
some of the incidents directly and indirectly from Polybius. See 10.5.2,
where Polybius is mistaken in dating Africanus' curule aedileship
(213) with that of his brother. The two brothers are represented as
standing together in the appointed place: προελθόντος εἰς τὸν ἀποδεδειγ-
μένον τόπον καὶ στάντος παρὰ τὸν ἀδελφόν, οὐ μόνον τῷ Ποπλίῳ περιέθεσαν
οἱ πολλοὶ τὴν ἀρχήν, ἀλλὰ καὶ τἀδελφῷ δι' ἐκεῖνον. With a different
account, Livy (25.2.6–8) indicates a similar setting. Then there are
the stories, evidently based on Polybius, of Africanus' election to the
command in Spain in 210. A more reliable account (Mommsen,
StR 2³. 659, n. 4; De Sanctis, *StorRom* 3.2.453 ff.) is that in Livy
26.2.5, according to which the tribunes asked the plebs *quem cum
imperio mitti placeret in Hispaniam,* but Livy follows Polybius in
another version in 26.18–19; cf. Appian, *Hisp.* 18 and Dio frg. 57.38–

40 (Zonaras 9.7). In this version the election is placed in the centuriate assembly. Livy says that, when no one offered himself for the command, the young Scipio (26.18.7) *professus se petere, in superiore unde conspici posset loco constitit.* The scene is evidently outside the voting place, as is clear from section 9. *Iussi deinde inire suffragium, ad unum omnes non centuriae modo sed etiam homines P. Scipioni imperium esse in Hispania iusserunt.* Similarly Plutarch (*Aem.* 10) has L. Aemilius Paullus suddenly appear among the candidates for the consulship of 168, to which he was immediately elected. In the consular election for 192 Africanus was conspicuous when he led to the *comitia* before the voting his cousin, P. Scipio Nasica, who was not elected until the next year (Livy 35.10.9). The appearance was evidently outside the Saepta, as was the announcement in the election for 190 of the victory of Africanus' brother Lucius, when everyone looked at Africanus (Livy 36.45.9, *Africanum intuentibus cunctis*). On the announcement outside the Saepta of the vote of the *centuria praerogativa,* see Chap. V, with notes 20, 21.

65. Livy 31.6–8.1. See 7.1, *Consul in campo Martio comitiis, priusquam centurias in suffragium mitteret, contione advocata* . . . and 8.1, *ab hac oratione in suffragium missi uti rogaret bellum iusserunt.* On the reading see A. H. McDonald's Oxford text (1965).

66. Cic. *Sest.* 108 (of Clodius), *illius inimici mei de me eodem ad verum populum in campo Martio contionem.* The speech is mentioned immediately after speeches of the consul Lentulus, of Pompey, and of other prominent men (*Sest.* 107–8), which were probably made in the Campus. There had been earlier *contiones,* presumably in the Forum, but the statement that Pompey spoke *apud universum populum* (Cic. *Red. sen.* 29), like the *verus populus* in *Sest.* 108, seems to refer to the citizens, mainly men of property, who gathered for the *comitia centuriata* rather than to the city crowds in the Forum, men repeatedly described by Cicero as Clodius' rabble. For the view that all the speeches were in the Campus see Gelzer s.v. "Tullius," 29, *RE* 925. Clodius' speech, clearly assigned to the Campus, as Lange, *RAl* 3.314, realized, is an example of debate before the vote there of which Mommsen, who accepted the view of Drumann, could find no example (*StR* 3. 395).

67. See Chap. V, with notes 40–43, on the importance of the final *contio* before trials for *perduellio* in the centuriate assembly, where the tribunes acted as prosecutors in the *contio.*

CHAPTER IV

1. For rejection of this tradition and a different reconstruction of early tribal development see the last volume of the Jerome Lectures, A. Alföldi, *Early Rome and the Latins* (Ann Arbor, 1965) 304–18.

2. This outline of the development of two types of tribal assembly is based

in general on Mommsen's discussion, presented first, with acknowledgment to a suggestion of Rubino, in *Röm. Forsch.* 1 (Berlin, 1864) 151–217, and later in revised form in *StR* 3.146–60, 321–25. Subsequent discussions are reviewed fully, regrettably in Dutch, by A. G. Roos, *Mededeelingen nederland. Akad. Wettenschappen,* N.R. 3 (1940) 251–94, and more briefly by E. S. Staveley, *Athenaeum* 33 (1955) 1–31. Both of these scholars and the majority of others in the abundant works on the constitution are much more interested in developments before 287 than in those in what we may term the historical period. By far the most comprehensive study is that of Botsford, *RA* 119–38. It is extensively used by Roos, and is, of course, known to Staveley as to British scholars in general.

3. The distinction between *lex* and *plebiscitum* is maintained in the prescript of two laws, the Lex Antonia de Termessibus (*CIL* 1.2².589, probably to be dated 68; cf. Chap. II, n. 3): *tr(ibunei) pl(ebei) de s(enatus) s(ententia) plebem [rogaverunt...] preimus scivit,* and Lex Quinctia de aquaeductibus of 9 B.C. (*FIRA* 1 p. 152), *consul populum iure rogavit populusque iure scivit.* The distinction was not maintained within the text of tribunicial laws where we find phrases like *ex h(ac) l(ege)* of the *lex repetundarum* or the references to Lex Sempronia in the *lex agraria* (*CIL* 1.2².583 and 585). There are instances of a bureaucratic effort to be exact in the phrase *ex hace lege plebive scito* of the Lex Bantia (*ibid.* 582) and in the Lex de Gallia Cisalpina (592), *ex lege Rubria seive id pl(ebei)ve sc(itum) est;* cf. also the *Fragmentum Atestinum* referring to the same Lex Rubria, *CIL* 1.2².600, *ante legem seive id pl. sc. est [quod L. Roscius a.d. V] eid. Mart. populum plebemve rogavit.* On *plebiscita* see Siber, s.v. *RE* (publ. 1951).

4. In general the word *comitia* alone refers to the elections. See Cicero's *campus pro comitiis, De or.* 3.167. For legislation the *comitia centuriata* is specified in various cases. For meetings of the tribes there is often no name for the gathering, the emphasis being on summoning to vote *populus* or *plebs.*

5. For *concilium* as a description of plebeian gatherings the essential evidence, not cited by Botsford, is to be found in the *Staatsrecht,* 3.149 f. In Cicero there are ten examples of *concilium* for the plebeian assembly, only one of which, *Inv.* 2.52, specifies *concilium plebis.* The examples of *concilium* alone are *Red. sen.* 11; *Dom.* 79; *Sest.* 65 and 75; *Vat.* 5, 15 and 18; *Leg.* 2.31 and 3.42. Eight of these surely refer to legislative assemblies, most of them held by Clodius in his tribunate of 58, and a ninth, *Red. sen.* 11, should, I believe, be added to this list (*FG* 22). I would also interpret similarly the tenth example, *Leg.* 2.31 (on the power of the augurs): *posse a summis imperiis et summis potestatibus comitiatus et concilia vel instituta dimittere vel habita rescindere.* There is perhaps a reflection of Cicero's use of *concilium* in the *Pro Cornelio* in Ascon. 50 C. Livy frequently uses *concilium*

alone as well as *concilium plebis* for plebeian legislative assemblies; the cases are not completely cited by Gudeman in *TLL* who reports twenty-five examples of *concilium plebis* and more than twenty-five of *concilium* alone, some of which surely do not refer to the *plebs*. *Comitia* is used by Cicero for plebeian legislative assemblies in *Sest.* 109 (*comitia sive magistratuum . . . sive legum*) and *Leg.* 3,45, a reference to the vote on Clodius' bill that led to Cicero's exile, described as taken at *comitia tributa* which had no right to pass on the *caput* of a citizen. For the use of *comitia* for plebeian elective assemblies, there is, as Botsford shows (126 f.), more evidence than Mommsen cites: *Att.* 1.1.1, *comitiis tribuniciis; Fam.* 8.4.3, *aedilium plebis comitiis;* for *comitia* alone where the reference is to plebeian elections, see *Att.* 2. 23.3; *Qfr.* 2.15 (14) 4. Although Cicero does not use *concilium* of plebeian elective assemblies, Livy, who often employs the Republican language of his sources, does in two cases—2.60.5, with *comitia* also in the same sentence, and 3.60.8. In the text of Republican laws (see index of *CIL* 1, second edition) both *concilium* and *comitia* are used for municipal assemblies. See also *comitia conciliumve* in the Lex Bantia of the end of the second century (on date see Chap. II, n. 32), *CIL* 1.2².582, line 5. As Botsford has shown, citing expressions like *concilium populi*, Laelius Felix's distinction (Gell. 15.27.4, quoted n. 7 below) between *concilium* for part of the people and *comitia* for all the people does not hold. But it is valid between *comitia* and *concilium plebis,* and Gellius may have omitted *plebis* from the quotation.

6. For the prescripts of laws see n. 3. Cicero sometimes distinguishes the action of *populus* and *plebs* (Mommsen, *StR* 3.150, n. 2): *Att.* 4.2.3, *neque populi iussu neque plebis scitu; Flacc.* 15, *quae scisceret plebs aut quae populus iuberet; Balb.* 42, *scita ac iussa nostra.* But, as Mommsen points out, *sciscere* is sometimes used of *populus* and *iubere* of *plebs.*

7. For the exclusion of patricians see Festus 372 L and Zonaras 7. 17 (Boissevain's edition of Dio 1, 60 f.). The major source is Laelius Felix, a jurist, probably of Hadrianic date, quoted by Gell. 15.27.4: *Is qui non universum populum, sed partem aliquam adesse iubet, non 'comitia,' sed 'concilium' edicere debet. Tribuni autem neque advocant patricios neque ad eos referre ulla de re possunt. Ita ne 'leges' quidem proprie, sed 'plebisscita' appellantur, quae tribunis plebis ferentibus accepta sunt, quibus rogationibus ante patricii non tenebantur, donec Q. Hortensius dictator legem tulit, ut eo iure, quod plebs statuisset, omnes Quirites tenerentur.* For the provision of the Lex Hortensia that plebiscites were to bind *universus populus* or *omnes Quirites* (that is patricians as well as plebeians), see also Gaius 1.3 (*FIRA* 2, p. 9); Pomponius in *Dig.* 1.2.2.8; *Pliny N.H.* 16.37. The evidence is discussed by Siber, *op. cit.* (n. 3). Livy's stories of the removal of patricians from early plebeian assemblies (n. 9) are also significant here.

8. See Staveley, *op. cit.* (in n. 2), with his list, p. 4, n. 4, of scholars, in-

cluding Lange, Herzog, De Sanctis, H. Stuart Jones, who have agreed with Mommsen. (To them may be added the scholars, listed in Chap. V, n. 40, who have discussed the judicial assemblies of the centuries, and De Martino, *Stor. Costituzione rom.* 2 [Naples, 1960], 154 ff.) In opposing their views Staveley is convinced by the arguments of Roos, *op. cit.* (in n. 2), cited also by Ernst Meyer. See Meyer's statement, RSSG² 199 "Sicherlich ist in historischer Zeit kein Patrizier von einer Plebsversammlung ausgeschlossen worden, wenn er hatte kommen wollen." Cf. also R. M. Ogilvie, *A Commentary on Livy Books 1–5* (Oxford, 1965) 385 f.

9. On the Clodius question in 60 Cicero (*Att.* 1.18.4) says that a tribune was proposing a bill *ut universus populus in campo Martio suffragium de re Clodi ferat.* The site indicates a bill to be proposed to the centuries. See Cic. *Att.* 1.18.5 and 2.1.4–5, with the fuller account in Dio 37.51.1: Κλώδιος δὲ ἐπεθύμησε μὲν διὰ . . . . . . τοὺς δυνατοὺς ἐπὶ τῇ δίκῃ δημαρχῆσαι, καί τινας τῶν δημαρχούντων προκαθῆκεν ἐσηγήσασθαι τὸ καὶ τοῖς εὐπατρίδαις τῆς ἀρχῆς μεταδίδοσθαι, ὡς δ' οὐκ ἔπεισε, τήν τε εὐγένειαν ἐξωμόσατο καὶ πρὸς τὰ τοῦ πλήθους δικαιώματα, ἐς αὑτόν σφων τὸν σύλλογον ἐσελθών, μετέστη. Clodius had forsworn his patrician status, probably at the proper place for an oath, a *contio*, the one, I think, which immediately preceded the tribunicial election, and then entered the *comitia* as a candidate. On questions about the validity of his claim see the statement in Dio which follows and 38.12.2, the account of Caesar's *lex curiata* of 59 which legalized the transfer. For bibliography on the subject, with comment on Mommsen's alteration of his view, see Kübler s.v. "Sacrorum detestatio," *RE.* The point of interest here is that attendance at the plebeian assembly, as well as the assertion of the right to hold the tribunate, was apparently in question.

For the not always successful attempt to remove the patricians in order to convene the *plebs*, see Livy 2.56.10; 2.60.5; 3.11.4. In each of these passages Livy uses the verb *submovere*, often employed for the removal of obstructive persons, for instance by the consul's lictor. Without referring specifically to patricians, Cicero and Livy both use *submovere* of the act of clearing out the *contio* in preparation for the *comitia* (see Mommsen, *StR* 3.390, n. 1). The Cicero passage with the phrase *summota contione,* comes from the contrast between the Roman and the Greek assemblies in the *Pro Flacco* 15, quoted above, Chap. II, n. 41. Livy, describing a plebeian assembly of 212, says of the moment when voting is about to begin (25.3.16) *tribuni populum submoverunt,* and later (18) adds that the *publicani* moved in a wedge *per vacuum summoto locum. Populus* means the entire people, including the patricians, who would have left vacant a favorable position now occupied by the *publicani.* Livy's descriptions of removing patricians in the early Republic were based on no good source, but he was describing the scenes in terms of customs known from later times when the patricians were a far less numerous and less important group.

10. For the Caesar incident see Plut. *Cato min.* 26–28; Dio 37.43. The

examples cited by Botsford, *RA* 302, n. 1, are clearly *contiones,* namely Livy 27.21.1–4 (preliminary *contio* before the vote on revoking Marcellus' command) and 43.16.8 (preliminary *contio* before a vote which did not take place). There is no doubt that patricians could take part in the *contio* before the *comitia* opened, but Botsford confuses *contio* and *comitia* which he elsewhere distinguishes. An earlier case cited by Botsford for the presence of patricians in plebeian gatherings concerns the first proposal in 377 of the Licinian-Sextian laws (6.35.7–8): *Qui* (referring to the tribunes who had agreed to veto the bills) *ubi tribus ad suffragium ineundum citari a Licinio Sextioque viderunt, stipati patrum praesidiis nec recitari rogationes nec sollemne quicquam aliud ad sciscendum plebi fieri passi sunt. Iamque frustra saepe concilio advocato. . . .* The last words show clearly that the voting assembly had not yet begun and that the narrative belongs to the *contio.* The tribunes were using a familiar form of the veto. See n. 37. In 6.38 Camillus is represented as using his dictatorial power to break up the *concilium plebis* after the first tribes had voted, and then resigning the dictatorship for reasons variously reported in the sources. Livy is at a loss to explain the situation.

11. See Mommsen, *StR* 3.364 ff. Tribunes of the plebs abdicated *vitio creati* in 292 (Livy 10.47.1) and aediles of the plebs for the same reason in 202 (Livy 30.39.8). There had perhaps been thunder at the elections, a sure sign of Jupiter's displeasure at *comitia* (Cic. *Div.* 2.42–43), and plebeian officers, although they were not subservient to the augurs at the *comitia,* would have hesitated to remain in office when Jupiter had shown his opposition. On the Lex Aelia and Lex Fufia, which I date ca. 150, see my *FG* 22–24. G. V. Sumner, *AJP* 84 (1963) 337–58, makes not improbable distinctions between the two laws. For an interesting estimate of the Ciceronian evidence on these laws, see A. E. Astin, *Latomus* 23 (1964) 421–45. I do not agree with Astin (430, n. 3) that "the conditions for *spectio* and *obnuntiatio* must have been broadly the same for legislative and electoral assemblies." Otherwise we should find postponements because of *obnuntiationes* of plebeian elections like those known for elections of regular magistrates.

12. On the schedule of elections see Mommsen, *StR* 1.580–88. Before 153, when the beginning of the consular year was transferred from March 15 to January 1, the tribunes, who entered office on December 10, were elected before the regular magistrates, but no such custom is established for the late Republic. In 91 the date of tribunicial elections was late September or perhaps early October (Cic. *De or.* 3.1–6). In the Ciceronian period the established date for both types of magistrates was the latter half of July, though the election of regular magistrates was often postponed. See my *TiGLA* 61, n. 19, with comments on Ch. Meier's article, *Historia* 10 (1961) 68–98.

13. See Chap. III, n. 63 for the presence of magistrates at the centuriate assembly.

14. Livy's account of the plebeian gathering of 212 (25.3, see n. 9) shows

the tribune whom the publicans wished to persuade to veto seated in the wings of the tribunal on the Capitol (§ 17–18, *forte primus in cornu sedebat*). The coin of Palicanus shows only one *subsellium,* obviously that of the presiding tribune, in the center of the Rostra, but the sides are not shown (Chap. III, with n. 37). Caesar as praetor is represented by Plutarch seated with the tribune Metellus on the tribunal of the temple of Castor in 62 (*Cato min.* 27), but the incident occurred before the beginning of the voting, at which Caesar as a patrician could not have been present.

15. Q. Cicero, *Comm. pet.* 30. I am still convinced that the document is genuine. But see M. I. Henderson, *JRS* 40 (1950) 8–21 and R. G. M. Nisbet, *JRS* 51 (1961) 84–87. On the inconclusiveness of their arguments see J. P. V. D. Balsdon, *CQ* 56 (1963) 242–50, with additional bibliography cited there.

16. The failure of the country people to come to Tiberius Gracchus' last assembly is given as a reason for his difficulty with the vote, but I have argued (see Chap. III, n. 41) that the assembly was legislative and that the voters would therefore have come mainly from men resident in Rome.

17. On this trial see my paper, *Athenaeum* 42 (1964) 12–28.

18. See J. A. O. Larsen, *Representative Government in Greek and Roman History* (Berkeley, 1955) 159 ff., and my comments, *VD,* 15 f., 293 f., with Larsen's review of *VD, CP* 57 (1962) 35 f.

19. An excellent general discussion of lot and ballot, to which my colleague Professor Caroline Robbins called my attention, is that of C. Seymour and D. P. Frary, *How the World Votes* (Springfield, Mass., 1918), Chaps. I and II. The subject merits a detailed study, but I have been unable to find one. For Greece and particularly for Athens the evidence has been thoroughly collected and analyzed. See recently C. Hignett, *A History of the Athenian Constitution to the End of the Fifth Century* B.C. (Oxford, 1952), index s.v. "Sortition." For the ancient evidence in general see Lécrivain s.v. "Sortitio," *DS* and Ehrenberg s.v. "Losung," *RE.* As Ehrenberg notes, there is no general treatment of the lot at Rome. For the method of lot-casting in the assemblies the excellent article of Eduard Wunder is of fundamental importance, "Dissertatio de discrimine verborum cistae et sitellae," *Variae Lectiones* (Leipzig, 1827) clviii–clxvii. The essential evidence for the assemblies is cited in convenient form by Pease in his great edition of Cicero's *De Natura Deorum* on 1.106 (Cambridge, 1955).

20. The lot was used to settle tie votes in a tribe; it was also employed apparently in the choice of *interreges* and of *duumviri perduellionis* in 63.

21. *HSCP* 50 (1939) 1–34. For illustration and brief description see Mabel Lang, *The Athenian Citizen,* Agora Picture Book, No. 4, Princeton, 1960.

22. On the forms and the use, for instance for storing ballots, see Poittier

s.v. "Hydria," *DS*. H. B. Walters, *History of Ancient Pottery* 2 (London, 1905) 464, suggests that such vessels were made of metal.

23. SHA (Flavius Vopiscus), *Probus* 8.6 (on lots taken among his soldiers for the possession of a horse). When the name Probus came out (*emergere*), and there was contest among the four soldiers of that name, *iussit iterum agitari urnam, sed et iterum Probi nomen emersit; cumque tertio et quarto fecisset, quarto Probi nomen effusum est.*

24. *Urna extractum,* Val. Max. 6.3.4. For the use of the hand in drawing numbers (of athletes for the Olympic games) see Lucian, *Hermot.* 40 and 57. A Cupid drawing a lot by hand is shown in a relief, Fig. 6521, s.v. "Sortitio," *DS*. For *ducere* of lots see *TLL* s.v., 2147, lines 84 ff.

25. 5.394, of the sham election of consuls for 48. The scholiast says that the lots were mixed by hand: *urna est vas, quod et orca dicitur, in quo antiqui sortes mittebant, et manibus conversantes movebant.* See *urnam agitari* in the passage from SHA quoted in n. 23. For the scholiast's explanation of the use of the lot in this case see Chap. V, n. 34.

26. Ascon. 39 C (on the *pro Milone*), *quarta die adesse omnes iuberentur ac coram accusatore ac reo pilae in quibus nomina iudicum inscripta essent aequarentur.* Propertius 4.11.19–20:

> aut si quis posita iudex sedet Aeacus urna,
> in mea sortita vindicet ossa pila.

27. Cic. *Verr.* II.2.126–27. *Syracusis lex est de religione, quae in annos singulos Iovis sacerdotem sortito capi iubeat ... cum suffragiis tres ex tribus generibus creati sunt, res revocatur ad sortem ... ut, quot essent renuntiati, tot in hydriam sortes conicerentur; cuium nomen exisset, ut is haberet id sacerdotium.*

28. The story appears in variant versions in Apollodorus, *Bibl.* 2.8.4–5 (see Frazer's note, Loeb text); Pausanias 4.3.4–5; Polyaenus, *Strateg.* 1.6. Why water should have been used in these cases is puzzling, for stones and oven-baked clay would not rise to the surface of the water, though Pausanias' ἀνέλθῃ might suggest that they could. Drawing by hand is indicated by Apollodorus' ἑλκυσθείσης. On the story, see also Sophocles, *Ajax* 1283–85, with the scholiast, and Plautus, *Casina* 307, 398 f.

29. *Planc.* 35. Cicero continues, *Si sortis, nullum crimen est in casu; si consulis ... hunc a summo viro principem esse ordinis iudicatum.* See also, on the sort of lot-taking that Cicero attributes to the tribune Rullus, *Leg. agr.* 2.21: *Sortietur tribus idem Rullus. Homo felix educet quas volet tribus,* with a further comment in section 22 that Rullus could call the tribes he desired, *nullo custode sortitus.* Evidently *custodes* were expected to watch over the lot.

30. There are many references to the gods and their favor in the scene from the *Casina.* See 346–49, 382–83, 389–90, 402, 410, 417–18. Cicero's descriptions of the *praerogativa* as the *omen comitiorum* (*Div.* 1.103; 2.83) are found in the discussions of *divinatio* placed in the mouth of Cicero and his brother Quintus, with allusions to the customary appeal

to the gods, *quod bonum faustum felix fortunatumque esset,* or *favete linguis.* Cicero is specific also in the *Pro Murena* 38, *si tanta illis comitiis religio est ut adhuc semper omen valuerit comitiorum.* I can see no basis for Ehrenberg's insistence (s.v. "Losung," *RE* 1465) on separation between the political and the religious meaning of the lot.

31. Livy 41.18.7–8 (of consuls of 176, Valerius and Petilius): *divisis copiis ⟨prius⟩ quam digrederentur, communiter ambo exercitus lustraverunt, tum sortiti, quia non ab eadem utrumque parte adgredi hostem placebat, regiones quas peterent. Valerium auspicato sortitum constabat, quod in templo fuisset; in Petilio id vitii factum postea augures responderunt, quod extra templum sortem in sitellam † in templum latam foris ipse oporteret.* Petilius was slain, and it was learned afterwards that the omen *ex pullario* was bad. Ehrenberg doubts this evidence because it is unique.

32. See my paper, "Symbols of the Augurate on Coins of the Caecilii Metelli," *AJA* 48 (1944) 352–56. As I pointed out there, the vase is an ordinary water pitcher, not a *praefericulum* as Babelon called it, for that vase had no handle, nor yet a *capis,* the name given to it by Grueber and Sydenham, for that vase belonged not to the augur, the priest with the *lituus,* but to the pontifex. The pitcher appears with the more common *lituus* on coins of the following men known to have been augurs (see Sydenham's index s.v. "Lituus" p. 296): Sulla, Pompey, the younger Lentulus Spinther, Mark Antony, A. Hirtius, and Octavian. The only men not known to have been augurs on whose coins the two symbols appear are Q. Cassius, probably *tr. pl.* 49 (Sydenham 916) and the two Caecilii Metelli discussed in my paper, Metellus Pius and Metellus Scipio, both of whom were *pontifices* (Sydenham 751, 1049). I interpreted their use of the symbols as evidence that their ancestor, Metellus Numidicus, was an augur. I now interpret the symbols on Q. Cassius' coins as an indication that he was a descendant of Q. Cassius Longinus Ravilla, and that this ancestor also was an augur. See Chap. III, with notes 10–13 for the suggestion that the other Cassii whose coins refer to ballot laws were also descendants of Ravilla. As far as I know, there has been no explanation of the appearance of the water jug on coins recording augurates.

33. Discussions of procedure usually consider together tribal and centuriate assemblies. See Mommsen, *StR* 3.369–419; Botsford, *RA* 462–72; Ernst Meyer, *RSSG*[2] 182–202.

34. For curule and plebeian aediles as presidents of judicial assemblies see Botsford, *RA* 325–27. Cf. Cicero's threat to take action as plebeian aedile against Verres, *Verr.* II.2.5.173. See my *PP,* Chap. V.

35. On this interval known as a *trinum nundinum* see Mommsen, *StR* 3.375–77, and, for diminution of the interval in judgments, *Strafrecht* 169 f. The interval was confirmed for legislation by the Lex Caecilia Didia of 98, but it seems to have been customary earlier for judicial and perhaps also for legislative assemblies. In elections the interval may have

been established by the early second century. See A. E. Astin, *Historia* 11 (1962) 252–55. Recently A. W. Lintott, unaware of the fact that he was reviving the view of Lange (*RAl* 2. 469–71), has argued that the *trinum nundinum* was an interval of varying length, including three *nundinae,* the market days in the Roman eight-day week. See *CQ.* 15 (1965) 281–85.

36. Every case of *discedite* that I have found belongs to a legislative or a judicial assembly. The word perhaps reflects the separated groups of tribes called to vote one by one. For elective assemblies see n. 47. For the use of *mittere, inire, vocare* in legislative and elective assemblies, see Mommsen, *StR* 3.400, n. 1.

37. See Cic. *Leg.* 3.11: *lex recitata est; discedere et tabellam iubebo dari;* Cic. *Corn.* in Ascon. 71 C, 56 St., cited with restorations of Mommsen and Buecheler in Stangl's text. Cicero, according to Asconius, is explaining *cum lex feratur, quot loca intercessionis sint.* The right to veto existed, according to Cicero, as long as the men who had the right to vote were being transferred (that is into their tribes).

38. See Plutarch, *Cato min.* 28; Dio 37.43.2. It was actually forbidden by law in the late Republic for the tribune himself to read the law. See Cic. *Corn.* in Ascon. 71 C. 57 St., with Mommsen, *StR* 3.391, n. 4. For Octavius' interference with Ti. Gracchus see Appian, *B.C.* 1.12.48–49; cf. also Livy 6.35.7–8, quoted in n. 10.

39. On the bringing of the *sitella* as a sign that voting was at hand, see Livy 25.3.16: *testibus datis tribuni populum submoverunt sitellaque lata est ut sortirentur ubi Latini suffragium ferrent;* Auctor ad Heren. 1.12.21 (of Saturninus' *lex frumentaria* of 100), *Saturninus ferre coepit. Collegae intercedere, ille nihilominus sitellam detulit;* Cic. *N.D.* 1.106: *Ut Ti. Gracchum cum videor contionantem in Capitolio videre de M. Octavio deferentem sitellam.*

40. The *principium* also existed in the *comitia curiata* (Livy 9.38.15), and that is one of the indications that the procedure in the tribes was based on the *curiae.* For references to the *principium* in laws of the second and first centuries see *FIRA* 1, pp. 103, 132, 152. Mommsen, who held that all tribes voted at once in legislation, interpreted the *principium* as the first tribe to have its vote announced. Lange, *RAl* 2.483 f., Herzog, *RSV* 1.1184, and Botsford, *RA* 466, differed from Mommsen, and Herzog suggested the possibility of successive voting, now proved by Fraccaro to have been regular policy (Chap. III, n. 26). Lange, Herzog, Botsford, and Fraccaro, with their view of the meaning of the *principium,* all insist, in opposition to Mommsen, that the *sitella* served for the choice of the *principium* as well as for the selection of the tribe where the Latins were to vote. References to a separate vote of the first tribe are found in the sources only in Plut. *Aem.* 31.1 and in Appian, *B.C.* 1.12.52, but there are allusions in Cicero (see *Planc.* 35) to the man who *primus scivit.*

41. Cic. *Sest.* 109. *Omitto eas ⟨leges⟩ quae feruntur ita vix ut quini et ei*

ex aliena tribu qui suffragium ferant reperiantur. This type of substitution was the basis of Cicero's charge that the men who voted for the law which led to his exile were slaves and brigands. See *PP* 60 f. For the filling of empty tribes see *Tabula Hebana* 33–34.

42. *Leg.* 3.38, on laws passed to strengthen the *leges tabellariae,* laws *quae postea latae sunt, quae tegunt omni ratione suffragium, ne quis inspiciat tabellam, ne roget, ne appellet; pontes etiam lex Maria fecit angustos.* Marius' law is thus associated definitely with the protection of the secret ballot. See Chap. III, n. 23.

43. Cic. *Att.* 1.14.5 (Sjögren's text, following the mss., without the usual insertion of *in* before *rostra* or the emendation of *commulcium* to *convicium*): *Piso autem consul, lator rogationis, idem erat dissuasor. operae Clodianae pontes occuparant; tabellae ministrabantur ita, ut nulla daretur VTI ROGAS. hic tibi rostra Cato advolat, commulcium Pisoni consuli mirificum facit, si id est commulcium, vox plena gravitatis, plena auctoritatis, plena denique salutis. accedit eodem etiam noster Hortensius, multi praeterea boni; insignis vero opera Favoni fuit. hoc concursu optimatium comitia dimittuntur; senatus vocatur.* The suggestion has been made that, as in the law courts at Athens (Lang, *op. cit.* in n. 21, figs. 21, 22), each voter took two symbols, one for a positive, one for a negative vote, and, with careful concealment, placed one in the discard. But aside from the fact that concealment would not have been easy with wax tablets, the story of the big *stili* prepared by Gaius Gracchus' followers and the scene on the Nerva coin where a ballot is handed to a man below the *pons* indicate that the voter was expected to do something to the ballot. Both the A and C for the law courts on the tablet of Pl. V, no. 2 and the L and D for an assembly on Pl. V, no. 5 (Chap. III with notes 12 and 14) are on the same side of the *tabella,* but in the Gracchan jury law (Chap. III, n. 4) provision is made for placing the letters on opposite sides. Variations in such details were evidently features of the directions for procedure in laws.

44. See the fragment of C. Titius' speech *Or. Rom. Frag.*[2] 202 f. (with Malcovati's discussion of date): *iubent puerum vocari ut comitium eat percontatum quid in foro gestum sit, qui suaserint, qui dissuaserint, quot tribus iusserint, quot vetuerint.* For details from the sources on specific votes see Fraccaro, *PVCTR* 250.

45. We do not actually know who presided at the election of plebeian aediles. Since, at least from the Second Punic War and particularly in the Sullan period, they ranked above the tribunes, it is possible that a plebeian aedile presided. That might explain why in one instance a curule aedile is erroneously represented as conducting the election for his successors (Gell. 7.9.2–3). The consul was regularly the presiding officer for choice of curule aediles and quaestors.

46. There is no actual evidence that the Latins voted at tribal elections as we know they did at tribal legislative assemblies, but Mommsen's view that they did is probably to be accepted. It is based on the provision in

the Lex Malacitana 53 for the choice by lot of the *curia* in which the *incolae* who were Roman citizens or Latins should vote for magistrates at Malaga. See *Gesamm. Schr.* 1 (1905) 318.

47. This seems to have been the usual command in the Campus. For *discedite* in legislative assemblies see n. 36. *Suffragium inire* is used for all types of assemblies. See Mommsen, *StR* 3.400, n. 2. In describing an election of curule aediles Livy (25.2.7) says *in tribus discursum est.*

48. For the tribal assemblies there is no evidence for any magistrate besides the president on the major *pons,* but for the centuriate assembly see Chap. III, n. 63. The candidates perhaps remained outside during the voting.

49. The official order of the tribes, whose existence is known from Cic. *Leg. agr.* 2.79, is discussed in *VD,* 69–78. The urban tribes came first in the order given with numbered regions in Varro, *L.L.* 5.45, Suburana, Esquilina, Collina, Palatina. I have tried to show that the order of the rural tribes was based on counterclockwise orientation from the center of Rome. The first of the rural tribes was the Romilia, named by Varro, *L.L.* 5.56 as the fifth tribe, and the last was the Arnensis (Cic. *l. c.*). See the drawing of the Saepta, Pl. XI. The names of the first five tribes and the thirty-fifth have been placed at the entrance to the tribal divisions of the structure in the official order, with a similar counterclockwise order from the center of the city. The exact order of the other rural tribes is not known.

50. Cic. *Dom.* 112 (of Appius Claudius Pulcher, *pr.* 57, *cos.* 54, who became praetor without holding the aedileship): *Is postea quam intellexit posse se interversa aedilitate a L. Pisone consule praetorem renuntiari, si modo eadem prima littera competitorem habuisset aliquem....* See Mommsen, *StR* 3. 405, n. 5.

51. For the date and the interpretation of this election, see my paper, *Athenaeum* 42 (1964) 12–28. The election, identified as that for curule aediles held by Pompey in 55 for that year and dismissed because of violence, is interesting because a majority of the tribes had already been announced as favorable to Plancius before the *comitia* were dissolved.

52. In the centuriate assembly a member of each century, apparently in reply to a question from the herald, read out the results of his century. See Chap. V, n. 31.

53. The method followed in counting the votes of each *curia* is described in the Malaga Charter 56 and, except in certain provisions for deciding tie votes which were based on Augustan marital laws, the method would apply to the tribes at Rome, where we know that the lot was used. Chapter 56 provides for the reports of results of each *curia,* to be made to the *duumvir* in charge of the election. Chapter 57 concerns the announcement of the final result, with the *curiae* called in an order determined by lot. Mommsen (*Gesamm. Schr.* 1. 319 ff.; *StR* 3. 411 ff.), whose results are tentatively accepted by Fraccaro, *PVCTR*

236 ff., held that there were two announcements made by the presiding
officer. Against this view see the convincing arguments of Arthur
Rosenberg, *URZV* (Berlin, 1911) 66–71 and De Sanctis, *StorRom* 3.
1.363–68. The views of Rosenberg and De Sanctis are accepted by
Hall, *VPRA* 294.

54. Plut. *C. Gracch.* 12.4. καὶ τὴν τρίτην ἔδοξε δημαρχίαν ἀφῃρῆσθαι, ψήφων
μὲν αὐτῷ πλείστων γενομένων, ἀδίκως δὲ καὶ κακούργως τῶν συναρχόντων
ποιησαμένων τὴν ἀναγόρευσιν καὶ ἀνάδειξιν. ἀλλὰ ταῦτα μὲν ἀμφισβήτησιν
εἶχεν. ἀναγόρευσις seems to be *renuntiatio,* ἀναδείξις *designatio.* See Hall,
VPRA 298.

55. *R.R.* 3.17.10 of curule aediles; for censors, elected by the centuries, see
Livy 40.46.15.

56. On this assembly see Mommsen, *StR* 2.27–32. The major source is
Cicero, *Leg. agr.* 2.16–22, a discussion of a tribune's extraordinary
proposal to assign to this assembly the choice of land commissioners.
Cicero's comments are revealing for an election created by a majority
(nine tribes) of a body which was a minority of the people.

CHAPTER V

1. The chief ancient sources on the "Servian" centuriate assembly are Livy
1.42.4 to 43.13; Dionysius, *Ant.* 4.16–21, with further details in 7.59.2–8;
Cic. *R.P.* 2.39–40. Livy and Dionysius give in detail the census rating
and the armor for each class, with secondary emphasis in Livy and
in Dionysius' first account on voting; Cicero's major interest is the
voting. For analysis of the evidence see Mommsen, *StR* 3.240–99; Botsford, *RA* 66–99, 201–61; for analysis of the recent bibliography see
Staveley, *Historia* 5 (1956) 75–84.

2. Livy and Dionysius agree on the number of centuries of *equites* and of
those of infantry in each of the five classes, but disagree on the rela-
tively unimportant unarmed centuries and on the classes in which
they were to vote. Livy's six unarmed centuries bring his total to 194
centuries instead of the 193 mentioned several times by Dionysius;
Cicero's figures on the vote also add up to 193. The text of Livy has
suffered from emendations. In 1.43.7 the mss. reading is: *Quinta classis
aucta; centuriae triginta factae; fundas lapidesque missiles hi secum
gerebant; in his accensi cornicines tubicinesque in tres centurias dis-
tributi.* Sigonius, to make Livy's numbers accord with Dionysius' (he
did not know the Cicero), changed *tres* to *duas,* and Perizonius
bracketed the *in* before *his.* The emendations have been retained in
practically every text of Livy (including Teubner, Oxford, and Loeb,
where Foster translates *his accensi* "rated with these"). Constitutional
specialists have been aware of the original text (see Botsford, *RA* 66).
See Fraccaro's illuminating discussion of *accensi, Opusc.* 2.315–25, with
convincing revision of Mommsen's view (accepted by Ogilvie, *op. cit.*
in Chap. IV, n. 8). The century of the *proletarii* is described by Cicero,

R.P. 2.40, as one in which *plures censebantur quam paene in prima classe tota.* Cicero's list of the unarmed centuries are the *fabri* in the first class (here Livy apparently makes a mistake with his two centuries of *fabri*), *accensi velati, liticines, cornicines* (the *cornicines* added by the corrector of the codex), *proletarii.* The variation in names of the five unarmed centuries and in their assignment to the classes may reflect changes in an organization which was not static. To the unarmed centuries some scholars would add the *ni quis scivit centuria* of Festus 184 L, an antiquarian invention, unnoticed in the detailed enumeration of the centuries by Livy, Dionysius, and Cicero. See Mommsen, *StR* 3.286, n. 3.

3. Variation in the size of centuries is indicated by the equal number of centuries of *iuniores* and *seniores,* though the number of men in the former should have been about three times that in the latter (cf. Botsford, *RA* 81, n. 7). It was the view of Mommsen that the first class of 80 centuries which included all *pedites* with a rating of 40,000 sesterces or more (representing, it is estimated, at least 20 *iugera* of land) contained approximately four times as many men as each of the 2nd, 3rd and 4th classes, with 20 centuries apiece. But if the property of the four lower classes, with a minimum running from 30,000 sesterces down to 11,000, consisted respectively of 15, 10, 5, and 2 or 2½ *iugera,* Mommsen's view is unlikely. (On Huschke's estimates of the holdings, based proportionately on the ratings, see Botsford, *RA* 86.) The citizen body of the early Republic was made up largely of small landholders; the minimum *heredium* was two *iugera,* and perhaps the most common assignment of land was seven *iugera,* which would have put men in the fourth class. Rosenberg, *URZV* 23–31, has shown strong reason to believe that the first class centuries, the *classici* proper (the other *pedites* were *infra classem*), were much smaller than those of the lower classes. See his figures on small landholders in several countries of Northern Europe.

4. Dion 4.21.3. He goes on to say that he knows the form from having been present often at the assemblies. Mommsen's argument that Dionysius is referring to the third century reform of the *comitia centuriata* has been disputed by Fraccaro, Tibiletti, and others, who believe that he is speaking of a change under Augustus. See recently, in favor of Mommsen's view, Nicholls, *AJP* 77 (1956) 252 f. and P. A. Brunt, *JRS* 51 (1961) 82 f.

5. The essential feature of the later organization was that after the institution of the last two tribes the centuries were coordinated with the tribes. There was always some relation with the tribes since they were the units in which the census was taken for the classes. See Hugh Last, *JRS* 35 (1945) 30–48, esp. 38 ff. For my reasons for suggesting that before the reorganization the centuries, like the military units in the legions, were mixed from all the tribes, see my *ComCent* 338 ff. A statement of Livy, 1.43.12–13, often cited to prove that in the

"Servian" assembly centuries and tribes were unrelated, actually refers (see Nicholls, *op. cit.* 241 ff.) to the four urban tribes. Livy's statement is, however, of some importance for the reform because his words *post expletas quinque et triginta tribus, duplicato earum numero centuriis iuniorum seniorumque* are a description at least of the first class in the later centuriate assembly.

6. See particularly De Sanctis, *StorRom* 3.1.353–81.
7. De Sanctis, *ibid.;* Herzog, RSV 1119 ff.; Klebs, *Zeitschr. Sav. Stift. Rom. Abt.* 12 (1892) 181–244; Frank, *CAH* 7. 801 f.; Botsford, *RA* 220 ff. Ernst Meyer, *RSSG,* accepted this number in the first edition, 83 ff., 434 ff.; for a revision of his view in the 2nd ed. see 89 ff.; 492 ff.
8. Rosenberg, *URZV* 73; Cavaignac, *Journal des Savants* 9 (1912) 247 ff. and *Rev. Ph.* 8 (1934) 72–82; Niccolini, *Atti Soc. Ligust. Sc. Lett.* 4 (1925) 38–96: Fraccaro, *Opusc.* 2.171–90 (publ. 1929); Arangio-Ruiz, *Scritti C. Arnò* (Modena, 1928) 3 ff. See also my *PP* 203, n. 35.
9. *Studia et documenta historiae et iuris* 4 (1938) 509 ff.
10. One of the troublesome features of the evidence was still Cicero's apparent attribution to Servius of the count of votes existing in the reformed centuriate assembly. G. V. Sumner, *AJP* 81 (1960) 136–56 and *Athenaeum* 40 (1962) 37–84, attempted to solve the problem, as several scholars had a century earlier, by rejecting the corrector of the codex and rewriting the passage, though Mommsen, De Sanctis, and Fraccaro had been fully aware of the reliability of the corrector. See my papers, *AJP* 82 (1961) 337–45 and 84 (1963) 66 f. On the meaning of Cicero's text illumination has been provided by Staveley, *Historia* 11 (1962) 299–314 and, with cogent brevity, by Nicholls, *CP* 59 (1964) 102–5. Cicero was engaged, Nicholls holds, not in giving a history of the assembly but in showing its timocratic character, its emphasis on property that was in accord with Servius' supposed design to keep power out of the hands of the masses; that design was accomplished by the later as well as by the earlier assembly; hence Cicero did not trouble his audience with all the counting of centuries in classes that has obsessed modern scholars.
11. *Reden und Aufsätze* (Berlin, 1905) 11. See Hugh Last, *Gnomon* 22 (1950) 363; Tibiletti, *FCC* 231.
12. See Staveley's review of discussions, *Historia* 5 (1956) 112–19, with emphasis on his own objections (*AJP* 74 [1953] 1–33) and those of Schönbauer; cf. also F. De Martino, *Storia della costituzione romana* 2 (Naples, 1960), who holds, 145 f., that the sole value of the *Tabula Hebana* is the demonstration that voting centuries were transformed at the time of voting into election districts.
13. *ComCent* 344, n. 19, where I suggest that combinations in classes two to four could have been made in groups of three and four. For recent discussion with bibliography supplementing that given by Staveley, see F. Cassola, *GPR* 96–102, 110–16. His treatment is excellent on the

opinions of scholars, but he fails to give adequate consideration to the *centuria praerogativa*.

14. Festus 290 L. *Praerogativae centuriae dicuntur, ut docet Varro rerum humanarum lib. VI, quo rustici Romani, qui ignorarent petitores, facilius eos animadvertere possent. Verrius probabilius indicat esse, ut cum essent designati a praerogativis, in sermonem res veniret populi de dignis, indignisve, et fierent caeteri diligentiores ad suffragia de his ferenda.* The plural *praerogativae* here, as in Livy 10.22.1 (296 B.C.), refers presumably to the centuries of *equites* who originally voted first (cf. Mommsen, *StR* 3. 290, n. 3). The distinction between *erststimmende* and *vorstimmende* units made by Chr. Meier, s.v. "Praerogativae centuriae," *RE,* Suppl. 8 (1956) 567–98, is not convincing in my opinion. Meier's detailed discussion lays great emphasis on the uncertainties in our information. The essential evidence is given by Mommsen, *StR* 3.290–94, 397 f., and I still (cf. *PP* 56 f.) accept his conclusions. The date of the change in the *praerogativa* was after 296 when the *equites* seem still to have functioned. It is possible that a century of the first class began to be used before the last two tribes were added in the censorship of 241–40, but a date after the tribes in the first class had become established as centuries seems more likely. See n. 15.

15. The date of the reduction of the *pedites* in the first class to seventy centuries, thirty-five of juniors and thirty-five of seniors from each tribe, is not earlier than the census of 241–40, and might belong to any census between 241 and that of C. Flaminius in 220. I argued, *ComCent* 351 (against Mommsen's final dating, 220), that the year was 241. The reorganization, which apparently put an end to the formation of new tribes, probably took place before 232 when, under C. Flaminius' agrarian law, citizens, settled in Picenum and on neighboring land taken from the Gauls, were enrolled in extensions or new districts of old tribes. I therefore doubt Cassola's date for the reorganization, 232, censorship of Fabius the Cunctator (*GPR* 268–75, 289–92, with an interesting reconstruction of the *elogium* of Brundisium which he agrees with me in assigning to Fabius and not to a local magistrate). There were later changes in registration of citizens in the assembly. On the temporary registration of freedmen see n. 38. There was also the exclusion in the Gracchan period of senators from the *equites equo publico* (Cic. *R.P.* 4.2.) and there was an abortive attempt by Sulla as consul in 88 to restore the old Servian assembly (Appian, *B.C.* 1.59.266). But changes like these do not, in my opinion, amount to reorganization of the assembly such as G. V. Sumner has proposed. See *Athenaeum* 40 (1962) 37–84 and *Historia* 12 (1963) 125–28. For arguments for changes in the assembly after the Second Punic War see M. I. Henderson, *JRS* 53 (1963) 71 f.

16. Cic. *Planc.* 49. *Una centuria praerogativa tantum habet auctoritatis ut*

*nemo umquam prior eam tulerit quin renuntiatus sit aut eis ipsis
comitiis consul aut certe in illum annum.* The puzzling *illum annum*
may refer to an assembly dissolved before the consular election was
completed, and to a subsequent choice of the man in the first place
at a later assembly that same year.

17. See Klotz s.v. "Sexagenarii," *RE,* where, however, all the evidence is
    not cited. Cf. Frazer, *The Fasti of Ovid* (London, 1929), 4.81 ff.,
    109 f.

18. Verrius Flaccus, as quoted by Festus 452 L, prefers this explanation:
    *Sed exploratissimum illud est causae, quo tempore primum per pontem
    coeperunt comitiis suffragium ferre, iuniores conclamaverunt, ut de
    ponte deicerentur sexagenarii, qui iam nullo publico munere funge-
    rentur, ut ipsi potius sibi quam illi deligerent imperatorem; cuius
    sententia⟨e⟩ est etiam Sinnius Capito.* Ovid (*F.* 5. 633 f.) attributes
    the same explanation to some authorities:

    > pars putat, ut ferrent iuvenes suffragia soli,
    >   pontibus infirmos praecipitasse senes.

    Varro, *De vita p. R.,* as quoted by Nonius, p. 523, line 23, appears to
    doubt this explanation. It is accepted by Lange, *RAl* 1. 475 f. and is
    preferred by Mommsen, *StR* 2. 408, n. 2; 3. 401, n. 3. The explanation,
    Mommsen points out, means not that men over sixty were disfran-
    chised, but that their right to vote was challenged.

19. See my paper, "The Four Urban Tribes and the Four Regions of
    Ancient Rome," *Rend. Pont. Accad. Arch.* 27 (1952–54) 225–38 and
    VD 11 f., 71, 148 f., 278. Patrician members of the Aemilii, Claudii,
    Cornelii, and probably Manlii were in the Palatina and two or perhaps
    three senatorial names are known in the Collina (see T. P. Wiseman
    CQ 14 [1964] 125 for a name not in my list). No Republican names
    are known from the Esquilina and only one from the Suburana (a
    senator or a knight, *VD* 147 f., 277 f.). The *Tabula Hebana* (32–33)
    indicates that the law of 5 A.D., on which the law of 19 was based,
    had made provision for the vote of any senators or knights who might
    belong to these tribes.
        Of significance here, as I have recently realized from reading the
    footnotes of the *Staatsrecht* (3. 272, n. 2; 293, n. 5), is a passage in
    Ausonius' letter to the Emperor Gratian expressing thanks for the
    consulship conferred for the year 379 A.D. (*Grat. act. ad Gratian.* 9):
    *Valete modo classes populi et urbanarum tribuum praerogativae et
    centuriae iure vocatae.* The letter shows familiarity with Republican
    contests for the consulship, and the reference to *praerogativae* of urban
    tribes may not be confused, as Mommsen thought it was. The first
    class of these tribes may have been particularly advantageous to the
    nobles. The first class of the Palatina and the Collina would have been
    composed mainly of senators and knights, while that of the Suburana
    and the Esquilina would probably have been empty except for men

appointed to vote there in the assembly (*ComCent* 349–51). Protests against such an advantage would explain why these two latter tribes were excluded from the *praerogativa*.

20. The fact that in both these cases T. Otacilius was a rejected candidate has led to the suggestion that there is a duplication in the stories. See De Sanctis, *StorRom* 3.2.256, n. 111; Cassola, *GPR* 318 f. I see no reason why there could not have been repeated objections to Otacilius.

21. For similar interruptions in the time of the great Samnite War see Livy 10.15.7 and 10.22. In both cases the interruption was created in the interest of Q. Fabius Maximus Rullianus, who was holding the *comitia* on the first occasion. In the second case the consul holding the *comitia* is reported to have insisted at a preliminary *contio* on the election of Fabius (10.21.13–15).

22. According to the *Tabula Hebana* 35, the sealed votes from the *comitia* of senators and knights (whose site is unknown) were to be brought to the Saepta. See Ausonius, *Grat. act. ad Gratian.* 3 (on consular elections), *non passus Saepta neque campum.*

23. See Cicero on his conduct of the consular elections for 62, *Mur.* 1: *Quae precatus a dis immortalibus sum, iudices, more institutoque maiorum illo die quo auspicato comitiis centuriatis L. Murenam consulem renuntiavi....* For the *rogationis carmen* see (on the *tribunus plebis*) Livy 3.64.10 and Mommsen's reconstruction of the form for the consulship, *StR* 3.391, n. 1.

24. See Varro's citation from the *commentarii consulares, L.L.* 6.88, where, after the opening *contio* had been called, the consul *eloquitur ad exercitum 'Impero qua convenit ad comitia centuriata.'*

25. See n. 19 and also n. 38, with my *ComCent* 349 ff.

26. For the provision of one *custos* for each candidate in each unit see the Charter of Malaga 55. But Cicero tells us (*Pis.* 11) that Piso in the consular elections for 58 gave him *primam comitiis ... tabulam praerogativae.* That must mean that Cicero was serving as *custos* for Piso (an extraordinary detail of his course at that time). Evidently each *custos* was given a *tabula* on which he put dots (*puncta*) for the count, and since Cicero got the first *tabula,* it would appear that the candidate had more than one *custos* for the *praerogativa.* See also Q. Cicero, *Comm. pet.* 2.8.

27. Plut. *Cato min.* 42.3–4; *Pomp.* 52.2. Pompey was augur as well as consul and could thus claim authority for his action.

28. Cic. *Phil.* 2.82–83. There is no reason to follow A. C. Clark in his Oxford text in omitting the second *renuntiatur.* In this case the election was over speedily (*quae omnia sunt facta citius quam dixi*) after the vote of the second class (*confecto negotio*), but Antony, who as consul was conducting the assembly, proceeded to dissolve it, acting, as Pompey had, both as consul and as consulting augur.

29. Separate voting of seniors and juniors is also suggested by Cic. *Verr.* II.5.38 (of Verres' election to the praetorship): *praeconis voce ... te*

totiens seniorum iuniorumque centuriis illo honore adfici pronuntiavit. For perhaps erroneous indication of successive voting of individuals in the early third century, see Livy 10.13.11, with Hall's comments, *VPRA* 278–83, esp. 281. The individual senators and knights voted successively in the assembly of the *Tabula Hebana* (28 ff.), but that was a managed vote on consuls and praetors together, with a slate probably fixed in advance, and a limited group of voters. Successive voting for entire classes would have been too time-consuming.

30. Livy 43.16.14 (trial of the censor C. Claudius Pulcher in 169): *cum ex duodecim centuriis equitum octo censorem condemnassent multaeque aliae primae classis....* The inclusion of the twelve later centuries of knights in the first class and the separate vote of the *suffragia,* that is of the six original centuries of knights (see n. 33), show that the eighteen centuries of knights did not vote together.

31. Cic. *De or.* 2.260. *Ex eodem hoc vetus illud est, quod aiunt Maluginensem illum* [M.] *Scipionem, cum ex centuria sua renuntiaret Acidinum consulem praecoque dixisset 'dic de L. Manlio': 'virum bonum'* inquit *'egregiumque civem esse arbitror.'* From this story, told in Julius Caesar Strabo's discussion of wit, we may conclude with Mommsen (*StR* 3. 409, n. 4) that the herald asked the spokesman for each century about each candidate on the list and that Maluginensis, instead of making the expected reply giving the number of votes Acidinus had received, responded by conventional praise of the candidate. See A. E. Astin, *Historia* 11 (1962) 252–55, who concludes that a *professio* of candidates was necessary at this time, 179 B.C. The passage gives the identity of the spokesman, a senator of the patrician Cornelii who had not yet reached the praetorship. The *praeco* seems to have repeated the reports of the votes, using the archaic form *olla* for *illa centuria* (Varro, *L.L.* 7.42).

32. See Val. Max. 4.5.3 (Chap. III, n. 64). The candidate Cicereius took action *ut vidit omnibus se centuriis Scipioni anteferri.* A majority would not have been reached at the announcement of the vote of the first class, and it was probably then that Cicereius eliminated himself.

33. See Staveley, *AJP* 74 (1953) 32, whose view I questioned in *ComCent* 351, n. 57. These six centuries were made up originally of patricians and probably later of senators and senators' sons. The senators were forced in the Gracchan period to give up their public horse (Cic. *R.P.* 4.2; cf. *StR* 3.505, n. 2) and after that voted in the first class or, if they were *custodes,* in the tribe to which they were assigned.

34. Lucan's description of a sham election held by Caesar (5.394), *decantatque tribus et vana versat in urna,* is interpreted by the scholiast as a reference to the *praerogativa,* but the plural *tribus* suggests lots for a number of tribes, and the passage may refer to a lot for divisions of the second class. (Caesar's *comitia* would not have had to vote below that point.) Cicero's *extrema tribus suffragiorum* (*Leg. agr.* 2.4) is perhaps to be explained similarly.

35. If the vote was unanimous, the results would have been decisive as soon as eight of the centuries of the second class had had their vote reported. One can imagine congratulations to successful candidates at this point, but the announcement of the presiding consul would probably have been delayed until the whole second class had voted.

36. Ascon. 94 C. There is reason to believe that the century of *proletarii* was called last of all (Dion. 4.20.5; Cic. *R.P.* 2.40, where the *proletarii* are named at the end). The chance of a tied vote which would require this century to be summoned was slight, and the masses of men in it would probably not have attended the *comitia*. The century was not needed in the election for 63. An example of a vote carried through to the end in the centuriate assembly is the trial of the censor C. Claudius Pulcher in 169 (Livy 43.16), the result of which was *ut octo centuriae ad damnationem defuerint.*

37. In the late Republic there are other cases like the election for 63 in which not more than three candidates seem to have been in the running at the end. Candidates who won little support in their canvassing seem to have withdrawn in order to avoid the humiliation of a defeat. Cf. Horace, *C.* 3.2.17, *Virtus repulsae nescia sordidae;* Caes. *B.C.* 1.4, *dolor repulsae.* But for six candidates in the election of censors for 189 see Livy 37.57–58.

38. The freedmen, in the view of Rosenberg, *URZV* 89 ff., were in the classes of the centuriate assembly. But freedmen did not serve in the legions and the classes probably continued to be made up of men who had served or might serve in the legions. See my *ComCent* 349 f. Censors shortly before 169, probably in 179 (*VD* 138 ff.), had enrolled in rural tribes freedmen with sons more than five years old or with landed property of 30,000 sesterces or over. This was, as Mommsen noted, *StR* 3.249, n. 2, 437 f., the amount required for the second class, and the provision may mean that already at that time the enrollment in that class was inadequate. The enrollment probably made the freedmen eligible for legionary service as well as for a vote that would count. The bulk of the freedmen, and all of them after the censors of 169 ended the favorable registration of additional freedmen, were presumably in the five unarmed centuries.

39. *Har. resp.* 60. The mss. read *descripta,* which here, as often, should be emended (see Oxford text on Livy 1.42.5). Cicero notes a number of other signs of decay—*aerarium nullum est, vectigalibus non fruuntur qui redemerunt, auctoritas principum cecidit, consensus ordinum est divulsus, iudicia perierunt, suffragia discripta tenentur a paucis.* In comments on the decline of registration for the *comitia centuriata* this passage is not cited by Last, *op. cit.* n. 11 above, by Tibiletti, *SDHI* 25 (1959) 94–127, or by me, *VD* 120. On the role of the censors in the *discriptio* essential for the centuriate assembly, see Cic. *Leg.* 3.7: *censores populi . . . partes in tribus discribunto, exin pecunias, aevitates, ordines partiunto;* cf. Mommsen's discussion, *StR* 3.253, n. 1.

40. The subject calls for discussion that goes far beyond the scope of this book and the capabilities of the writer. In finding my way through the intricacies of the papers I have examined I am grateful for help from P. A. Brunt's review of Kunkel, *URKV, Rev. d'hist. du droit* 32 (1964) 440–49. The most important are Christoph Brecht, *Perduellio* (Munich, 1938) and s.v. "Perduellio" *RE;* also his paper, *Zum röm. Komitialverfahren, Zeitschr. Sav. St.* 59 (1939) 261–314, with later articles in the same journal by A. Heuss, 64 (1944) 57–133 and (on *provocatio*) by J. Bleicken, 76 (1959), 324–77, with his article "Provocatio" in *RE* 23.2.2444–63; see also his earlier *Volkstribunat.* Of importance also are H. v. Siber's studies, the substance of which is to be found in his *Röm. Verfassungsrecht* (Lahr, 1952). My references are mainly to Kunkel, who has given full credit to the contributions of Brecht, Heuss, Siber, and Bleicken. It appears to be established that tribunicial accusations for *perduellio* were politically inspired, and not in general concerned with criminal law; that the tribunicial trials were not *provocationes,* but were the result of appeals to tribunes of the plebs; the *comitia* were called to act upon the charge fixed by the tribune, to whom appeals had been made by opponents of the men prosecuted. The trial of Rabirius (see this chapter) was not an appeal from the judgment of the *duumviri,* from which there was no appeal (Cic. *Rab. perd.* 12), but a comitial trial in the centuriate assembly.

41. Varro, *L.L.* 6.86–95, especially 90–92. After a lacuna following a discussion of verbs of action, speaking, seeing etc., Varro quotes and comments on three excerpts from documents, the first from the tablets of the census, the second from the *commentarii consulares,* and the third from a *commentarius anquisitionis,* with details from directions for prosecution for a capital offense brought by the quaestor M. Sergius M.' f., the last to be dated after 243, perhaps early second century (Kunkel, *URKV* 34–36). The subject of all three documents is not voting but the summoning of the people to the Campus Martius, first for the censorship, with a preliminary *contio,* second for a meeting of the *comitia centuriata* held by a consul, and third for a prosecution. There is repeated use of the words *vocare* and *contio,* which in the first two documents appears in the unsyncopated form *conventio.* In those documents the phrase *in licium* is used, and the meaning of the phrase and of the verb *inlicere* (see the Goetz-Schoell text, Leipzig, 1910, p. xli) is a major concern of Varro; the words occur eleven times in his discussion. Varro has no such succinct definition as Paulus quotes from Festus (100 L), *in licium vocare antiqui dicebant ad contionem vocare* (see Chap. III, with n. 61). According to Varro (94) *in licium* is not the *contio* but a place in sight of the magistrate and within hearing of his voice as he calls men to a *contio.* In the commentary Varro says that only for this purpose, that is a capital prosecution, can a quaestor call together the *exercitus urbanus* (93). The statement here,

ad comitiatum vocatur populus, echoes the command in the document that the quaestor should ask his colleague *ut comitia edicat de rostris.* I take *comitiatus* and *comitia* to refer to the combination of the *quarta accusatio* and the voting *comitia.*

For the interpretation of the passage on the auspices I quote the first excerpt from the *commentarius anquisitionis* as it appears in the Goetz-Schoell text, based on the eleventh century Laurentian ms. F, from Monte Cassino, the sole independent basis of the text: 90. *circum muros mitti solitus quo modo inliceret populum in eum ⟨locum⟩, unde vocare posset ad contionem, non solum ad consules et censores, sed etiam qu⟨a⟩estores, commentarium indicat vetus anquisitionis M. Sergii, Mani filii, qu⟨a⟩estoris, qui capitis accusavit ⟨T⟩rogum; in [a]quo sic est:* 91. *'auspicio †orande sed in templo auspiciis. dum aut ad praetorem aut ad consulem mittas auspicium petitum, †commeatum praetores vocet ad te, et eum de muris vocet praeco; id imperare ⟨o⟩portet. cornic⟨in⟩em ad privati ianuam et in arcem mittas, ubi can[n]at. collegam roges ut comitia edicat de rostris et argentarii tabe⟨r⟩nas occludant. patres censeant exqu⟨a⟩eras et adesse iubeas; magistratus censea⟨n⟩t ex⟨qua⟩era⟨s⟩, consules praetores tribunosque plebis collegasque ⟨t⟩uos [et] in templo adesse iubeas [h]om[i]nes; ac cum mittas, contionem a⟨d⟩voces.'* For the first words of the *commentarius* Mommsen, using his own and Bergk's emendations, reads (*StR* 1.93, n. 3): *auspicio operam des et in templo auspices* (a reading which, with emendation of the succeeding *dum* to *tum,* is adopted by Kent, Loeb text). I have no restoration of the corrupt text. I take the message to the praetor or consul to be a request or a demand that he take the *auspicia* on the day he is to set for the *comitia centuriata.* Except in Varro, where either consul or praetor is to be asked, the request in the sources is made only by a tribune to a praetor. See Livy 26.3.9 (211 B.C.), where the tribune *perduellionis se iudicare Cn. Fulvio dixit diemque comitiis ab C. Calpurnio praetore urbano petit;* Val. Antias in Gell. 6.9.9 (204): *Licinius tribunus plebi perduellionis ei diem dixit et comitiis diem a M. Marcio praetore poposcit;* Livy 43.16. 11 (169, trial of censors), where a tribune *utrique censori perduellionem se iudicare pronuntiavit diemque comitiis a C. Sulpicio praetore urbano petit.* See also Cic. *Har. resp.* 7. The request to the praetor to set the day, and, I believe, to preside at the *comitia* is not unlike the bill of a tribune of 60 calling for the presentation of a matter to the centuriate assembly (Cic. *Att.* 1.18.4, discussed in Chap. IV, n. 9). For the role of Metellus Celer, praetor (probably urban praetor) in 63, see Dio 37.27.3.

42. The loaning of auspices to a tribune has troubled other scholars besides Mommsen. Bleicken, *Volkstribunat* 111-20, holds that it represents a long development after the Licinian Sextian laws. U. v. Lübtow, *Das römische Volk* (Frankfurt, 1955) 269 ff., assigns it to the third century. The significant rights which I believe the tribunes acquired

may date from the period of the Lex Hortensia of 287; they must be assigned to a period before the trial of P. Claudius Pulcher for *perduellio* in 249 (Cir. *N.D.* 2.7; *Schol. Bob.* on Cic. *In Clod. et Cur.* 91 St; see Bleicken, *Volkstribunat* 120).

43. On the trial of Rabirius see Dio 37.27; Suet. *Iul.* 12. The manuscript title of Cicero's speech, *Pro. C. Rabirio perduellionis reo,* is supported by Cic. *Pis.* 4. On the view, accepted by Lange, Mommsen, and Gelzer, that the oration was delivered at a subsequent trial in the *concilium plebis,* see Gelzer, s.v. "Tullius," no. 29, *RE* 870–72. On the *duumviri perduellionis* see Bleicken, *Zeitschr. Sav. Stift.* 76, 337–41; Kunkel, *URKV* 21–23 and 34 f.; Brunt, *op. cit.* 440 f. Suetonius appears not to agree with Dio that Rabirius would have been convicted if the trial had taken place.

44. Cic. *Leg.* 3.44–45, where the Twelve Tables are quoted for prohibition of *privilegia* and action *de capite civis* except in the *maximus comitiatus.* Cicero goes on: *discriptus enim populus censu ordinibus aetatibus plus adhibet ad suffragium consilii quam fuse in tribus convocatus.*

45. Evidence on procedure in the legislative centuriate assemblies is scant, but I think it likely that the *praerogativa* functioned as it did in the elections. The stress on the *principium* in legislative votes of the tribes shows that a first vote was considered important on laws. But Meier doubts this (*RE,* Suppl. 8, 573 f.).

46. On landholding as the primary source of wealth of the *equites* see M. Gelzer, *Kl. Schr.* 1 (Wiesbaden, 1962) 225 f. and P. A. Brunt's important paper, "The Equites of the Late Republic," *Acta, Second International Conference of Economic History* (Aix-en-Provence, 1962) 117–49, with comment by T. R. S. Broughton 150–62.

47. On the power of the presiding magistrate, Cassola, *GPR* 13–23, protests against the extensive use made by Münzer, Scullard, and others of successive names in the consular *Fasti* in the determination of political relationships. I agree with him on that point, but I think he tends to undervalue the power of the consul who presided.

Appendix

THE TABULA HEBANA
AND
THE CHARTER OF MALAGA

I. The Tabula Hebana

This bronze tablet, discovered in July 1947 at Magliano, the ancient Colonia Heba south of Vetulonia, was first published in *Notizie degli Scavi* 1947 (which appeared early in 1949) 49–68, with an account of the find by P. Raveggi, a text prepared by A. Minto, and a commentary by U. Coli. The excellence and the speed of the publication have been widely recognized. Two additional fragments of the tablet were acquired later. The portion of the text reprinted here is taken, with permission of authors and editor, from the edition of J. H. Oliver and R.E.A. Palmer, *American Journal of Philology* 75 (1954) 225–49. The tablet, the second of two (the first is lost), records the honors voted in 19 A.D. to Germanicus after his death. Among these honors was the naming for Germanicus of five centuries in a special assembly of senators and knights to vote on the *destinatio,* a type of nomination, of consuls and praetors. Of the sixty-two lines of the tablet, all preserved in whole or in part, lines 5–50 quoted deal with these centuries.

[Utiq(ue) ad x̄]

6 centur(ias) Caesarum, quae de co(n)s(ulibus) pr(aetoribus) desti-
   nandis suffragium ferre solent, adiciantur v̄. centuri[ae; et, cum]

7 primae x̄ citabuntur C. et L. Caesar(um), adpellentur insequen-
   ⟨t⟩es v̄ Germanici Caesaris inq(ue) i(i)s omnib[us centuri(i)s]

8   senatores et equites omnium decuriarum, quae iudicior(um) publi-
    cor(um) caussa constitutae sunt erun[t, suffragium]

9   ferant; quiq(ue)cumq(ue) magistratu(u)m destinationis facien-
    dae caussa sena⟨t⟩ores quibusq(ue) in [sena]tu sen[tentiam]

10 dicere licebit, itemq(ue) eq(uites), in consaeptum ex lege quam L.
    Valerius Messalla Volesus Cn. Corn[el]ius Cin[na Magnus]

11 co(n)s(ules) tulerunt, suffragi ferendi caussa convocabit is, uti sena-
    tores, itemq(ue) equites omnium decuria[rum, quae iudi]-

12 [ciorum publi]çorum *vvvvvvv* gratia constitutae sunt erunt, suffra-
    gium ferant quod eius r[--- $\frac{\pm\ 12}{}$ -- in]

13 [$\overline{xv}$ centur(ias) curet; qu]amq(ue) ex ea lege nongentor(um), sive
    ii custodes adpellantur, sortitionem ad $\overline{x}$ centu[rias fieri cau]-

14 [tum est perscr]iptumvest uti fiat, eam is quem ex ea lege exve hac
    rogatione{m} nongentorum, siv[e ii custodes]

15 adpella[ntur, sort]itionem facere oportebit, in $\overline{xv}$ centur(ias) faciat
    proinde ac si in ea lege in $\overline{xv}$ centuria[s nongentor(um)]

16 sive ⟨c⟩ustodum sortitionem fieri haberive oportebit *vv* Utiq(ue) co
    die, in quem ex lege quam L. Valerius M[essalla Vole]-

17 sus Cn. Cornelius Cinna Magnus co(n)s(ules) tulerunt exve h(ac)
    r(ogatione), senaṭores et eq(uites) suffragi ferendi caussa adess[e
    debebunt, is]

18 adsidentibus pr(aetoribus) e⟨t⟩ tr(ibunis) pl(ebis) cistas $\overline{xv}$ vi-
    mineas grandes poni iubeat ante tribunal suum in quas tabeḷ[lae
    suffra]-

19 giorum demittantur, itemq(ue) tabellas ceratas secundum cistas
    poni iubeat tam multas quam [opus esse ei]

20 videbitur, item tabulas dealbatas in quib(us) nomina candidatorum
    scripta sint, quo loco commo[dissime legi]

21 possint, ponendas curet; deinde in conspectu omnium magistratuum
    et eorum, qui suffragi[um laturi]

22 erunt, seḍentium in subselli(i)s, sicuti cum in x centurias Cae-
    sarum suffragium ferebatur seḍ[ebant, is]

23 trium et $\overline{xxx}$ trib(uum), excepta Suc(cusana) et Esq(uilina), pilas
    quam maxime aequatas in urnam versatilem coici eṭ [sortitio]-

24 nem pronuntiari iubeat ⟨et⟩ sortiri qui senatores et eq(uites) in
    quamq(ue) cistam suffragium ferre debeat, du[m in centur(ias)]

25 primas, quae C. et L. Caesar(um) adpellantur, sortitio fiat ita, u[t]i
    in primam, ĪI, ĪII, ĪIII cistas sortiatur bi̦[nas trib(us), in]

26 V̄ cistam tres, in V̄I, V̄II, V̄III, V̄IIII binas, in X̄ tres, in eas, quae Ger-
    manici Caesaris adpellantur, so[rtitio fiat ita],

27 ut in X̄I, X̄II, X̄III, X̄IIII cistas sortiatur binas trib(us), in X̄V tres
    trib(us); ita ut, cum tribum unam cuiu̦s[cumq(ue) sors e]-

28 xierit citaverit, senatores quibusq(ue) in senatu sententiam dicere
    licebit, qui ex ea trib(u) erunt [vocet - - ∓ ¹⁰ - -]

29 et ad primam cistam accedere et suffragium ferre iubeat; deinde,
    cum ita ț[uleri]n̦t suffra[gium et ad subsellia]

30 redierint, ex eadem tribu vocet equites e[osq(ue) in] e̦a̦ndem cis-
    tam suffragium fer[re iu]beat; de[inde alteram et]

31 alteram tribum sortiatur et singularum̦ [omnium trib]u(u)m sena-
    tores, deinde eq(uites), iț[a vocet ut in quam cistam suffra]-

32 gium ferre debebunt suffragium fer[ant, dummodo quod] a̦d
    eorum suffragium perti[nebit, si qui ex Suc(cusana) tribu]

33 Esq(uilina)ve erunt, item si qua [in] tribu senator [ne]m̦o er̦[it,
    a]u̦t si nemo eq(ues) erit, et senatore̦[s equitesq(ue) si minus
    quam V̄]

34 erunt, item quod ad cista[s suff]ragi(i)s latis signandas et pr(aeto-
    ribus) qui aer(ario) praesunt praerint tr[adendas ut cum suf-
    fragi(i)s]

35 destinationis in saepț[a d]e̦ferantur, deq(ue) signis cognoscendis
    suffragi(i)s diribend[is, omnia quae - - - ∓ ¹² - -]

36 [- -]rii caussa in ea lege quam̦ Cinna et Volesus co(n)s(ules) de X̄
    centuri(i)s Caesar(um) tuler(unt) scripta c[omprehensave sunt,
    ser]-

37 [vet] eademq(ue) omnia in ⟨X̄⟩V̄ centur(ias) agat faciat, agenda
    facienda curet, uti eum ex ea l(ege) qu̦[am Cinna et Volesus
    co(n)s(ules)]

38 [tuler]u̦n̦t [in X̄] c̦e̦n̦t[ur(ias) Caes]ar(um) agere facere oporteret,
    quaeq(ue) ita acta erunt, ea iusta r[ataq(ue) sint; deinde diri]-

39 [bitis co(n)s(ulum) pr(aetorum) destinationi]s suffragi(i)s ex x̄v̄
centuri(i)s C. et L. Caesar(um) et Germanici Cae[s(aris) ad-
ductaq(ue) tabella centur(iae)]

40 [quaecumq(ue) ducta eri]ṭ, is qui eam destinationem habebit eam
tabellam ita [recitet uti eum, ex ea lege]

41 [quam L. Valerius Messall]ạ Volesus Cn. Cornelius Cinna Magnus
co(n)s(ules) tuler(unt) x̄ centur(iarum) [Caesar(um), eam
tabellam quae ex]

42 [i(i)s centuri(i)s sorte duct]ạ esset recitare oporteret, dum quae
tabula centuriae C. [et L. Caesar(um) cuiusq(ue) sorte ex]-

43 [ierit, eam sub nomin]ẹ C. et L. Caesarum recitandam, quiq(ue)
ea centur(ia) candidati desṭ[inati sint, unumquemq(ue) sub
illo]-

44 [rum nomine pronunti]ạndum curet; quae tabula ex i(i)s cen-
tur(i)s quae Germanici Caẹ[saris ex h(ac) r(ogatione) adpellantur sorte]

45 [exierit, eam s]ụb nomine Germanici Caesar(is) recitandam, qui-
q(ue) ea centuria candid[ati destinati sint, unumquemq(ue)]

46 [item quoq(ue) pr]ọnuntiandum curet; isq(ue) numerus centuri-
arum, qui h(ac) r(ogatione) adicitur in nu[merum centuri-
ar(um) C. et L. Caesar(um)],

47 pẹṛịnde cedat atq(ue) eum numerum, qui x̄ centuriar(um) est,
cedere ex lege quam Cinna eṭ [Volesus co(n)s(ules) tulerunt
cautum]

48 comprehensumve est uti cedat; itaq(ue) qui co(n)s(ulum) pr(aetorum) creandorum caussa, destinatione ạ[cta, comitia habebit,
uti eorum]

49 ratio habeatur itaq(ue) suffragium feratur, curet; cetera quae no-
minatim h(ac) r(ogatione) scripṭ[a non sint, ea omnia perinde
atq(ue)]

50 ex ea lege quam Cinna et Volesus co(n)s(ules) tuler(unt) agantur
fiant serventur

The naming of five centuries for Germanicus, as we know only
from this text, followed the creation in 5 A.D. of ten centuries named
for Gaius and Lucius, the grandsons and adopted sons of Augustus,

after their death. (Five additional centuries seem to have been established in 23 A.D. for Tiberius' son Drusus after his death; see Oliver and Palmer, *op. cit.* 248 f. for the fragmentary inscription, long known from Elche in Spain.) The ten centuries named for Gaius and Lucius were provided for in the Lex Valeria Cornelia referred to repeatedly in the document. For the vast bibliography on the inscription see, besides Oliver and Palmer, Tibiletti s.v. "Lex," *DE* (published 1957) 740–48. Among more recent articles I cite particularly P. A. Brunt, "The Lex Valeria Cornelia," *JRS* 51 (1961) 71–79. For an English translation see *ARS* pp. 131–35.

The major subject of the discussions has been the significance of the document for continuance of elections in the Empire, a subject first explored fully by Tibiletti in his monograph, *Principe e magistrati re-pubblicani* (Rome, 1953). My interest here is not in the new evidence for the meaningless imperial *comitia* but in the bearing of the document on Republican institutions, first discussed in detail by Tibiletti, *FCC*. As Coli had already suggested and as Tibiletti demonstrated there, the fifteen centuries voting before the regular *comitia* in 19 A.D. replaced the *centuria praerogativa* of the last two hundred years of the Republic. The great significance for the Republican *comitia centuriata* is the method adopted in counting votes.

For general comments see above pp. viii, 11, 108; for counting in the centuriate assembly 89 ff.; for the lot 70, 79; for the *praerogativa* 92, 99; for translation of lines 23–31, 89 f. On specific passages see: *T.H.*(16) 40; (18–19) 35, 39, 125 n. 4, 136 n. 63; (20) 71; (23 and 32 f.) 92.

II. The Charter of Malaga (Malaca) in Spain
(known as the Lex Malacitana)

Bronze tablets discovered near Malaga in 1851 contain portions of the
charters of the Spanish towns Malaca and Salpensa, issued by Domitian
in 82–84 A.D. to implement the Latin rights accorded to the towns by
Vespasian. For the documents see the first volume of Mommsen's
Gesammelte Schriften 267–382 (Berlin, 1905), edited by B. Kübler and
O. Hirschfeld. In his commentary Mommsen demonstrated the dependence of the procedure in local elections on that of the Roman assemblies, particularly of the tribes; he also showed the value of many of
the details for an understanding of procedure in Rome, and made full
use of them in his treatment of procedure thirty years later, *StR* 3.369–
419.

The text of the *Lex Malacitana,* preserved practically intact for the
chapters numbered LI to (the beginning of) LXIX, is also published in
CIL 2. 1964; *ILS* 6089; *FIRA* 1. pp. 208–19; the successive editions of
C. G. Bruns, *Fontes iuris Romani antiqui;* A. d'Ors, *Epigrafia juridica
de la España romana* (Madrid, 1953) 311–41. For a useful translation
and commentary see E. G. Hardy, *Three Spanish Charters* (Oxford,
1912); for a translation see also *ARS* no. 192, pp. 155–59. My text of
chapters LI to LIX follows that of Mommsen as edited by Kübler and
Hirschfeld.

[Rubrica. De nominatione candidatorum.]

[LI]. [Si ad quem diem professio] fieri oportebit, nullius nomine
aut | pauciorum, quam tot quod creari opor|tebit, professio
facta eri[t]; sive ex his, | quorum nomine professio facta erit, |
pauciores erunt, quorum h(ac) l(ege) comitiis ra|tionem habere
oporteat, quam tot [quot] cre|ari oportebit: tum is qui comitia
ha|bere debebit proscribito ita u(t) d(e) p(lano) r(ecte) l(egi)
p(ossint) | tot nomina eorum, quibus per h(anc) l(egem) |
eum honorem petere licebit, quod de|runt ad eum numerum,
ad quem crea|ri ex h(ac) l(ege) oportebit. Qui ita proscripti |
erunt, ii, si volent, aput eum, qui ea co|mitia habiturus erit,
singuli singu|los eiiusdem condicion[i]s nominato | ique item,
qui tum ab is nominati erunt, si | volent, singuli singulos aput

eun|dem e[a]demque condicione nomina|to; isque, aput quem
ea nominatio fac|ta erit, eorum omnium nomina pro|ponito ita
[ut] d(e) p(lano) r(ecte) l(egi) p(ossint), deque is om|nibus
item comitia habeto, perinde | ac si eorum quoque nomine ex
h(ac) l(ege) de | petendo honore professio facta esset|intra
praestitutum diem petereque | eum honorem sua sponte c[o]-
epissent ne|que eo proposito destitissent. |

R(ubrica). De comitiis habendis. |

LII. Ex IIviris, qui nunc sunt, item ex is, qui | deinceps in eo muni-
cipio IIviri erunt, | uter maior natu erit, aut, si ei causa qu|ae
inciderit q(uo) m(inus) comitia habere pos|sit, tum alter ex his,
comitia IIvir(is), item | aedilibus, item quaestoribus rogandis |
subrogandis h(ac) l(ege) habeto, utique ea dis|tributione curi-
arum, de qua supra con|prehensum est, suffragia ferri debe|bunt,
ita per tabellam ferantur facito. | Quique ita creati erunt, ii
annum unum | aut, si in alterius locum creati erunt, | reliqua
parte eiius anni in eo honore | sunto, quem suffragis erunt con-
secuti. |

R(ubrica). In qua curia incolae suffragia | ferant. |

LIII. Quicumque in eo municipio comitia IIviris|, item aedilibus,
item quaestoribus rogan|dis habebit, ex curiis sorte ducito unam,
| in qua incolae, qui cives R(omani) Latinive cives | erunt,
suffragi[um] ferant, eisque in ea cu|ria suffragi latio esto. |

R(ubrica). Quorum comitis rationem habe|ri oporteat. |

LIIII. Qui comitia habere debebit, is primum IIvir(os) | qui iure
dicundo praesit ex eo genere in|genuorum hominum, de quo
h(ac) l(ege) cau|tum conprehensumque est, deinde proxi|mo
quoque tempore aediles, item quaesto|res ex eo genere ingenu-
orum hominum, | de quo h(ac) l(ege) cautum conprehensum-
que est, | creando[s] curato; dum ne cuiius comi|tis rationem
habeat, qui IIviratum pe|t[et], qui minor annorum XXV erit
qui|ve intra quinquennium in eo honore | fuerint; item qui
aedilitatem quaesturam|ve petet, qui minor quam annor(um)
XXV erit, | quive in earum qua causa erit, propter || quam, si

c(ivis) R(omanus) esset, in numero decurio|num conscrip-
torumve eum esse non lice|ret.

R(ubrica). De suffragio ferendo. |

LV. Qui comitia ex h(ac) l(ege) habebit, is municipes cu|riatim ad
suffragium ferendum voca|to ita, ut uno vocatu omnes curias
in | suffragium vocet, eaeque singulae in | singulis consaeptis
suffragium per ta|bellam ferant. Itemque curato, ut ad cis|tam
cuiiusque curiae ex municipibus | eiius municipi terni sint, qui
eiius cu|riae non sint, qui suffragia custodiant | diribeant, et uti
ante quam id faciant qu|isque eorum iurent, se rationem suf-
fra|giorum fide bona habiturum relaturum|que. Neve pro-
hibito q(uo) m(inus) et qui hono|rem petent singulos custodes
ad singu|las cistas ponant. Iique custodes ab eo | qui comitia
habebit, item ab his positi | qui honorem petent, in ea curia
quis|que eorum suffragi[um] ferto, ad cuiius cu|riae cistam
custos positus erit, e[o]rum|que suffragia perinde iusta rataque
sun|to ac si in sua quisque curia suffragium | tulisset.

R (ubrica). Quid de his fieri oporteat, qui | suffragiorum nu-
mero pares erunt. |

LVI. Is qui ea comitia habebit, uti quisque curiae | cuiius plura quam
alii suffragia habue|rit, ita priorem ceteris eum pro ea curia |
factum creatumque esse renuntiat[o]|, donec is numerus, ad
quem creari opor|tebit, expletus sit. Qu[a] in curia totidem |
suffragia duo pluresve habuerint, ma|ritum quive maritorum
numero erit | caelibi liberos non habenti, qui mari|torum nu-
mero non erit; habentem libe|ros non habenti; plures liberos
haben|tem pau[c]iores habenti praeferto priorem|que nuntiato
ita, ut bini liberi post no|men inpositum aut singuli puberes
amis|si v[i]rivepotentes amissae pro singulis | sospitibus nu-
merentur. Si duo pluresve to|tidem suffragia habebunt et eiius-
dem | condicionis erunt, nomina eorum in | sortem coicito, et
uti [c]uiiusque nomen sor|ti ductum erit, ita eum priorem alis
renunti|at[o].

R(ubrica). De sortitione curiarum et is, qui cu|riarum numero
par[e]s erunt. |

LVII. Qui comitia h(ac) l(ege) habebit, is relatis omnium | curiarum tabulis nomina curiarum in sor|tem coicito singularumque curiarum no|mina sorte ducito et ut cuiiusque curiae | nomen sorte exierit, quos ea curia fecerit, | pronuntiari iubeto; et uti quisque prior | maiorem partem numeri curiarum con|fecerit, eum, cum h(ac) l(ege) iuraverit caverit|que de pecunia communi, factum crea|tumque renuntiato, donec tot magistra|tus sint quod h(ac) l(ege) creari oportebit. Si toti|dem curias duo pluresve habebunt, | uti supra conprehensum est de is qui | suffragiorum numero pares essent, ita | de is qui totidem curias habebunt fa|cito. eademque ratione priorem quem|que creatum esse renuntiato. |

R(ubrica). Ne quit fiat, quo minus comitia ha|beantur. |

LVIII. Ne quis intercedito neve quit aliut fa|cito, quo minus in eo mun[i]cipio h(ac) l(ege) | comitia habeantur perficiantur. | Qui aliter adversus ea fecerit sciens || d(olo) m(alo), is in res singulas (sestertium X milia) mu|nicipibus munic[i]pii Flavi Malacitani | d(are) d(amnas) e(sto) eiiusque pecuniae deque ea pecun(ia) | municipi eius municipii, qui volet cuique | per h(anc) l(egem) licebit, actio petitio persecutio esto. |

R(ubrica). De iure iurando eorum, qui maiorem | partem numeri curiarum expleverit. |

LIX. Qui ea comitia habebit, uti quisque eorum, | qui IIviratum aedilitatem quaesturam|ve petet, maiiorem partem numeri curia |rum expleverit, priusquam eum factum | creatumque renuntiet, iusiurandum adi|gito in contionem palam per Iovem et di|vom Augustum et divom Claudium et divom | Vespasianum Aug(ustum) et divom Titum Aug(ustum) | et genium imp(eratoris) Caesaris *Domitiani* Aug(usti) | deosque Penates, se e[a] qu[a]e ex h(ac) l(ege) facere | oportebit facturum neque adversus | h(anc) l(egem) fecisse aut facturum esse scientem | d(olo) m(alo).

On the Charter, see pp. 11 f., 78; on the lot 70.

LI. The lack of candidates for municipal offices became increasingly common in the Empire, but is almost unknown in Roman Republican assemblies.

LII. The provision that the elder *duumvir* should hold the *comitia* seems not to have followed Roman traditions; before Sulla when the consuls were often away from the city the decision was made by the senate, by lot, or by arrangement between the two consuls.

LIII. See 146 n. 46.

LIV. The provisions for age here apply to municipalities.

LV. For *curiae* and tribes see 11; for *uno vocatu* 40; 128–30; for the vote *in singulis consaeptis* 94; for *custodes* 79, 153 n. 26.

LVI. The provision that the victors in each of the *curiae* were the men, to the number of the officers to be elected, who had the highest vote is probably based on Roman traditions; it is likely that tie votes in the Roman units were decided by lot. The other provisions here for the preference of candidates depend on Augustan marital laws.

LVII. For the *renuntiatio* and the relation between this chapter and chap. LVI see 147 n. 53 and, for fuller discussion, a forthcoming paper in *Athenaeum*.

LIX. The form of the oath and the requirement that the candidate swear to observe this particular law both depend on imperial developments. The names of Jupiter Optimus Maximus and the dei Penates go back to the Republican oath, on which see Steinwenter s.v. "Ius iurandum," *RE*. For the oath in elections see Plin, min. *Paneg.* 64; for legislation see Lex Bantia, *CIL* 1.2².582.3. Cf. Mommsen, *Gesam. Schr.* 1.320 f. See 56, 81.

Index

The notes on passages cited in the text are in general indexed separately only when they introduce new material. Dates, regularly in italics, are all B.C. For index of the *Tabula Hebana* and the *Charter* of Malaga see pp. 163, 167 f.

Abbreviations: (a) for magistrates, aed.—aedile (with cur. or pl. for curule or plebeian aedile), cos.—consul, dict.—dictator, pr.—praetor, tr. pl.—tribune of the plebs; (b) for assemblies, *cc.—comitia centuriata, c. cur.—comitia curiata, ctr.—comitia tributa, conpl.—concilium plebis.* In accordance with Latin usage the word *comitia* alone often refers in analysis to assemblies of all types.

absolvo 35

accensi 86

Adoption of Clodius 4, 61, of Augustus 4

Aediles, as presiding officers 144 n. 34, 146 n. 45; election of cur. aed. 55

Aemilius, *see* Lepidus, Paullus

aequatio 72

Aesculetum 116 n. 7

agere cum populo 2, 23 f., 121 n. 27

Agrippa, M. Vipsanius, and Saepta Julia 47, 49, 55

amnis Petronia 7

Aniensis iuniorum 93

Announcements, *see renuntiatio*

anquisitio 19, 101, 112

antiquo 35

M. Antonius, triumvir, candidacy in *50* 67, and Caesar 33

Appian 3; as source 11

Area Capitolina, *contiones* there 20, and crowding 133 n.; *comitia* there 45 f., 109, 132 n. 38; and tribunes 46; elections there questioned 46

Arnensis, last in order of tribes 147 n. 49

Artisans 86, 96

Asconius, as source 11

Assemblies, Greek vs. Roman 3, 29 f., 34; and lot 70 f. *See* Athens, Sparta

————, Roman, functions 1 ff.; places of meeting 40–58; preceded by *contio* 2,

15 ff.; vetoes 75; other interferences 75, 77, 82; common features 82 f. *See Comitia centuriata, curiata, tributa,* and *Concilium plebis;* chart facing p. 5

Athens, assemblies 29 f.; lot 70 f.

Augurs 4, 7 f., 77, 112; and lot 73 f., Pl. VI no. 6; in Varro, *R.R.* III 55; the Cassii and augurate 144 n. 32; Pompey and Mark Antony as aug. and cos. 96, 153 n. 28

Augustus (Octavian), adoption 4; preparation of sites for *contiones* and *comitia* 33, 58, 106; speech at Circus Flam. 119 n. 13; election as *pont. max.* 82

aureus of Caesar, and augurate 74, Pl. VI no. 6

Auspices 6, 7, 62 f.; loan of? 101 f.

Aventine, and *comitia* 115 n. 5, 116 n. 7

Awnings, use of 49

Ballots, *see tabellae,* Voting

Caecilius, *see* Metellus

M. Caelius Rufus, tr. pl. *52,* 68

Caesar, C. Julius, cos. *59* etc., dict. *49–45,* elected *pont. max.* 82; at *contio* before *conpl.* 62; and Catulus 44; and transfer of Clodius to plebs 61; and candidacy of Mark Antony 67; and assemblies 104 ff.; legislation in tribes 122 n. 38, in *cc.* 104;